# COUNSELING VICTIMS OF VIOLENCE

○   ○   ○

## About the Author

Sandra L. Brown, M.A., holds a Master's degree in Counseling. She was the founder and previous director of Bridgework Counseling Center, which provided outpatient clinical counseling to victims of violent crime for more than ten years. She was also the founder and director of The Sanctuary Residential Treatment Program, which provided long-term live-in counseling for women with chronic and extensive trauma-related disorders.

She has provided counseling services for psychopathology patients in a wide range of venues, including day-treatment programs, outpatient counseling centers, in-patient hospitals, domestic-violence shelters, and churches, and she still provides consultations on psychopathology for agencies.

She is a frequent speaker, consultant, and workshop leader on the topics of counseling, victimization, and pathological behavior. She is the author of the *How to Spot a Dangerous Man* book and workbook (Hunter House 2005), *Counseling Victims of Violence*, first edition (American Counseling Association 1991), and *The Moody Pews* (Tsaba House 2005). She is the current director of The Dangerous Relationship Institute (www.saferelationships.com), which provides books, workbooks, workshops, phone consulting, e-zine newsletters, and columns on the issue of dangerousness. She has been on more than twenty-five TV shows, including CNN, and thirty radio shows. Her books have been featured in such newspapers as *The Rocky Mountain News, The St. Petersburg Times, The Seattle Post-Intelligencer, The Tampa Tribune, The Dallas Morning News,* and *The Miami-Herald,* and in such national magazines as *Women's Health, The Examiner,* and *Today's Black Woman.* The author can be reached at sandrabrownma@yahoo.com.

**Ordering**

Trade bookstores in the U.S. and Canada, please contact
Publishers Group West
1700 Fourth Street, Berkeley  CA 94710
Phone: (800) 788-3123     Fax: (800) 351-5073

For bulk orders please contact
Special Sales
Hunter House Inc., PO Box 2914, Alameda CA 94501-0914
Phone: (510) 899-5041     Fax: (510) 865-4295
E-mail: sales@hunterhouse.com

Individuals can order our books by calling (800) 266-5592
or from our website at www.hunterhouse.com

# COUNSELING VICTIMS
# OF VIOLENCE

A Handbook for
Helping Professionals

SECOND EDITION

SANDRA L. BROWN, M.A.

Hunter House Inc., Publishers
PO Box 2914
Alameda CA 94501-0914

LIBRARY OF CONGRESS CATALOGING-IN-PUBLICATION DATA
Brown, Sandra L., 1957-
Counseling victims of violence : a handbook for helping professionals / Sandra L. Brown. — 2nd ed.
p. cm.
Includes bibliographical references and index.
ISBN-13: 978-1-63026-719-3

1. Victims of crimes—Counseling of—United States. 2. Violence—United States—Psychological aspects. 3. Post-traumatic stress disorder—Treatment—United States. 4. Crisis intervention (Mental health services)—United States. I. Title.
HV6250.3.U5B76 2007
362.88—dc22                                                          2006030559

## Project Credits

| | |
|---|---|
| Cover Design | Brian Dittmar Graphic Design |
| Book Production | John McKercher |
| Developmental and Copy Editor | Jude Berman |
| Proofreader | John David Marion |
| Indexer | Candace Hyatt |
| Acquisitions Editor | Jeanne Brondino |
| Editor | Alexandra Mummery |
| Senior Marketing Associate | Reina Santana |
| Customer Service Manager | Christina Sverdrup |
| Order Fulfillment | Washul Lakdhon |
| Administrator | Theresa Nelson |
| Computer Support | Peter Eichelberger |
| Publisher | Kiran S. Rana |

Manufactured in the United States of America

9  8  7  6  5  4  3  2      Second Edition      13  14  15  16  17

# Contents

# Foreword

Nobody *chooses* to be a victim of violent crime. The painful reality is that crime takes from its victims not only their choices, but too often their voices.

Historians agree that since the inception of the crime victims' field in the early 1970s, the driving force behind the many successes in expanding crime victims' rights and improving services for victims and survivors is "the power of the personal story." Crime statistics offer an important overall view of the devastation that violence wreaks, but it is the individual experiences of crime victims to which people can truly relate. It is the father of a murdered child who starts a support group for other survivors, or an adult survivor of incest who speaks out so that others may learn. It is the battered woman who is finally able to leave a horrific environment, or the stalking victim who offers painful images of a life in which every aspect of privacy is violated. It is average people whose lives are irrevocably altered because of violence, and who choose words as their weapons in the war on crime and tell their stories as part of an effort to better serve victims and survivors.

Over the past thirty-five years the power of victims' personal stories has resulted in amazing victories, large and small, in the campaign to improve how we as a society deal with the consequences of crime. Today there are more than thirty-two thousand laws that define and protect victims' rights, including constitutional amendments in thirty-two states. Over ten thousand community- and system-based organizations and agencies provide crisis intervention, support, and vital services to help victims cope with the aftermath of violence. Services for victims are specialized not only by the type of crime, but also by one's geography, gender, and culture. And perhaps most important, there are countless crime victims and survivors who help each other, drive political action, guide public discussion, and help people understand the short- and long-term impact of crime on individuals, families, and communities.

The power of Sandra Brown's personal story, following the murder in 1983 of her father, Frankie Brown, has helped create a strong foundation for understanding victimization and the need for appropriate responses. Through her writing and her longtime work as a dynamic victim advocate, she has shed new light on topics that thirty years ago were considered taboo. Sandra has made it *okay* to be a survivor of violent crime, without the stigma that was historically attached to victimization. She has paved a re-markable path of awareness—for victims and for those who seek to help them—through her examination of effective responses to victims' mental-health needs.

When I began my career as a victim advocate nearly a quarter century ago, we knew little about the impact of crime on victims' mental health. We were busy changing laws to provide victims with a role in criminal and juvenile justice processes that was more meaningful than simply that of witness. We spent our lives helping to create grassroots programs that would identify and address victims' most important needs. We tried to gen-erate public awareness that went beyond the scary crime statistics to the heart of the matter—the crime victims and survivors.

As we did so, the mental-health impact of crime became crystal clear. The laws we changed to protect victims and increase their participation in justice processes began to be based not only on "doing the right thing," but also on the fact that many victims perceived their participation in the jus-tice system as a "secondary victimization," one that was highly stressful and often exacerbated the initial psychological effects of the crime. The pro-grams that emerged (and continue to emerge today) focused on the need to be "victim-centered," and recognized that the degree of social support a survivor has is directly related to his or her ability to cope with the effects of the crime. The public awareness that still today remains a stalwart of our field put names and faces to statistics and humanized the very real psycho-logical, physical, financial, and spiritual consequences of victimization. The growth of our field reflected the growing awareness of the emotional impact of crime, and we began to address this issue through the develop-ment of public policy, programs, and public awareness.

Yet then, and to a lesser degree today, many mental-health profession-als lacked specific education and experience in victimology and the impact of crime on victims. Victim advocates are taught basic crisis-intervention skills but could benefit from a greater understanding of the dynamics of trauma and effective responses that help victims without the risk of hurting them. And while the countless victims who continue to drive our nation's "victims' rights movement" know and feel the psychological impact of crime, they may not fully understand the feelings they experience, and they may be unaware that effective counseling and support can greatly benefit them.

It is these people that the second edition of *Counseling Victims of Violence* is for.

Sandra Brown examines the mental-health impact of crime through case studies and extensive victimology research, and she takes an in-depth look at the effect of public policy, protocols, and public awareness on crime victim issues. Each chapter offers extensive background information specific to its topic while also providing concise checklists and recommended readings to augment the reader's journey. Readers will finish this book with a greatly improved understanding of the psychological consequences of crime and of recommended response strategies. They will also gain awareness of the simple fact that everyone with whom victims come into contact can help or hinder their recovery. *Everyone* has the power to either help or hurt a survivor of violent crime.

This new edition of *Counseling Victims of Violence* will undoubtedly increase our individual and collective ability both to help victims and to mitigate responses that are potentially hurtful. This book should be required reading for mental-health professionals, justice officials, victim service providers, and crime victims and survivors. It is a gift from a wonderful victim advocate, author, and friend whose painful personal experience as a survivor of homicide propelled her into a life's path she did not initially choose, but one in which she has truly become a pioneer.

— Anne Seymour
Washington, D.C.

*Anne Seymour acted as director of public affairs for MADD (Mothers Against Drunk Driving) from 1984 to 1986. She was cofounder of the National Victim Center (now National Center for Victims of Crime), where she served as Director of Communications and Resource Development from 1986 to 1992. She has worked as a victims' rights consultant, and in 2001 she cofounded Justice Solutions, a national organization dedicated to enhancing governmental and societal responses to crime and its consequences, where she currently serves as senior advisor.*

# Acknowledgments

A career in psychotherapy, speaking, and writing is not without sacrifices—made mostly by those closest to you. Those people in my case would be my husband, Ken, and my girls, Lindsay and Lauren, who gave up a lot of evening contact so I could be in the counseling chair, at the lectern, or at the computer. And my mother, Joyce, who ran my practice for years.

Many were teachers and mentors to me when I was a new, emerging counselor, filled with much hope and ambition, but less knowledge. Thank you to all who invested in my growth and learning—all the counselors, doctors, and countless victims who taught me through their strength and experiences.

Relationships that have spanned the years—with Dr. Kathie Erwin, Margaret Langes, Toni Roop, Randy Evans, and Phil and Sue Engelman—have been an ongoing source of support. And also more recent friendships have provided meaning and joy—Scotta Orr; and my unofficial brother, Bill Grimes, and his wife, Jan.

Many thanks to the whole Hunter House staff that is awesome to work with and filled with insight and support. It is a delight to work with you!

And to the new angels in my life, Aliyah and Bryce—the light of the world.

# Introduction

SINCE THE VICTIM'S RIGHTS MOVEMENT began in the 1970s, victims of violent crime have received increased attention—in the media, in research, and in the counseling office. Considering the number of people who become victims each day, counselors need to be prepared with the skills to treat the effects of a wide variety of crimes. In fact, counselors can expect victims to comprise a large percentage of those who seek treatment from them. This book exists to help you as a mental-health professional understand the counseling needs of victims of violence.

Just how large is the problem of violence? National statistics from the U.S. Department of Justice indicate that 11,849,006 criminal offenses were reported in 2001, and $24.2 million dollars was spent that year on the compensation and treatment of violent victimization.

How do these statistics break down to show us the specific kinds of victims violence produces, information especially pertinent to counselors? According to the National Center for Victims of Crime website, the following were reported in 2001:

- 248,000 people were raped.
- 61 percent of rape victims are raped before the age of 18.
- Only 1 in 50 female rapes are reported.
- 20 percent of crimes against women were committed by intimate partners.
- 20 percent of all women were sexually abused as children.

- Approximately 879,000 children were abused.
- One fifth of all sexually abused children will develop long-term psychological problems.
- 46 percent of sexually abused children are raped by family members.
- 1.8 million teens were victims of violence.
- 83,000 teens were sexually assaulted.
- On average, 1.7 million violent crimes are committed annually against persons at their place of work.
- 10,412,395 property crimes occurred.
- 15,980 people were murdered.
- 9,726 hate crimes were reported.
- More than 105,000 elderly persons were victims of violent crime.
- 1 out of 12 women and 1 out of 45 men will be stalked during their lifetime.
- 5,046 incidents of gay domestic violence occurred.

Although these statistics may seem alarming, they represent only the surface of the national problem of victimization. Many professionals who work with victims indicate that only a small portion of all violence and crime is reported. Although we do not really know the depth and breadth of victimization in the United States, we can feel the effects as counselors when our practices increase due to the number of victims coming through our doors.

Some categories of violence grow faster than do others. For instance, some years ago, rape on campus was the fastest growing classification of crime. The current decade may reveal the increasing threat of a different category of violence—perhaps cyberstalking, terrorism, or societal trauma. To this end, the mental-health field must respond not only to the increase in violence and crime, but also to the changing categories of victimization. Continuing education for practitioners is critical if we are to stay abreast of developments and know how to best serve clients who have been victimized.

This means that our knowledge of victimization needs to be as broad as the crime base itself. As new categories of victimization emerge, we must be trained to understand their impact on victims. This needs to occur in a timely manner because victims rely largely on the mental-health community for their recovery. One study indicated that about 1 in 8 victims of crime seeks professional mental-health assistance within the first few months after the incident. This estimate expands to 1 in 6 victims in the entire first year after victimization.

The mental-health industry did not begin to understand and train counselors in the field of victimization until the 1980s. Before that, in the absence of trained mental-health professionals, victims sought solace from peers and victim self-help support groups. These groups continue to be instrumental in assisting grieving and recovering victims. Additional assistance now comes through state and local victim advocacy programs and even through clergy. Nevertheless, as crime continues, we will continue to need counselors trained in the field of victimology, a field in which there never seem to be enough counselors.

One reason relatively few counselors are trained in victimology is that it is a subspecialty field within counseling. Many counselors specialize in other areas of psychology, or if they do work with victims, they are only familiar with one or two areas of victimization. For instance, some counselors focus on domestic violence and child violence, whereas other counselors treat only sexual traumas such as incest and rape. Other areas within victimology are less well covered by trained counselors.

This book, *Counseling Victims of Violence,* was written to address the lack of counselors trained in victimology. The first edition, printed in 1991, presented a unique overview approach to treatment issues in various categories of victimization. It also examined the growing field of victim services. Many of the theories now embraced by victimology came from this period (1980s) of clinical counseling history. For this reason, much of the foundational research from the first edition has been carried over into this edition. Newer research has been added to update the knowledge base. Thus, this volume gives not only a historical view of victimization, but a comprehensive one, as well.

Like its predecessor, the second edition of this book is designed as a handbook about victim issues. Unfortunately, since 1991, new categories of victimization have been recognized. Therefore, the wide range of topics has been expanded to include stalking, cyberstalking, terrorism, and more. The Internet came of age since the first edition, and so websites of national resources have been included, as well as other newly created agencies and resources. The most recent research on specific types of victimization and treatments is also included.

The book attempts to broaden the counselor's ability to treat clients across a spectrum of victim categories. If you are trained in only a few areas of victimization, this book will assist you in understanding issues victims face within a multitude of crimes and violent experiences. In this way, you can assess your own clinical training and compare it with what these clients will require during recovery.

## How to Use This Book

This is a resource book intended to be helpful for counselors, social workers, therapists, psychologists, psychiatrists, case managers, school guidance counselors, R.N.s and medical staff, victim advocates and legal personnel, members of the clergy, religious counselors, lay/peer counselors, those engaged in support or 12-step programs, and any others who desire to work with the population of victims of violence.

The book was designed to provide you with the maximum assistance for a minimal amount of reading. Therefore, we have tried to lay out the book in a fashion that is easy to use and thumb through. The book is divided into two parts.

Part I, which is comprised of Chapters 1 through 4, introduces you to clinical information you need to know about treating trauma, such as

- ○ the psychobiology of trauma
- ○ posttraumatic stress disorder (the most commonly seen disorder resulting from trauma)
- ○ information about the grief process
- ○ assessment

The chapter on assessment helps you not only to understand the reasons for and importance of testing, but also how to design treatment approaches based on the outcomes of testing. Various potentially helpful assessment tools are described, along with information about how to acquire them.

Part II features chapters on the specific victimization categories. Categories from cyberstalking to homicide are covered. Each chapter includes the following elements:

- Background information on the victimization and trauma-specific information
- Crisis-intervention issues
- Short-term and long-term counseling issues
- Client concerns
- Secondary victimizations
- Social and legal services
- National resources, websites, phone numbers, recommended reading, and bibliography
- An overview chart

A very useful aspect of each victimization chapter is the overview chart, found on the last page. You can see at a glance what the issues are for that category in terms of crisis intervention, short-term counseling, and long-term counseling. For instance, if you have a client whose problem is related to a recent homicide, you can turn to the overview chart in the homicide chapter and see the potential issues for crisis intervention. You can decide if you have the skill level to provide this care. If you decide to move forward, you can turn to the front of the chapter and read the background information and section on crisis intervention and note the possible client concerns and secondary victimizations. Having read this material, you can listen for these specific concerns during counseling sessions. In addition, a quick glance will alert you to any social or legal services for which the client may need a referral.

Next, you can scan the short-term and long-term counseling issues to see if you have the skill level necessary to proceed beyond crisis intervention. If you determine that you do not, after you have stabilized the initial crisis, you can refer the victim to another counselor. Or, you may feel you can pick up the necessary skills by going to a workshop, by doing some extra reading, or through clinical supervision. The resources at the end of each victimization section include websites and other resources you can use for further study.

*Counseling Victims of Violence* is designed to be your desktop quick reference book for reviewing what to focus on when counseling a victim.

## Thank You for Your Willingness

In closing, I came into the field of victim services through my own history of victimization. My father was murdered in 1983. Since that time, my life's work has been in the field of victimology. Although my work began not through any choice of my own, it has grown to be the passion that drives my outreach to victims of all types. Although victimology is a challenging field within psychology, helping victims in their recovery from crime and trauma is immensely satisfying work. As counselors, we are often witness to life's complicated dichotomy of pain working hand-in-hand with the triumph of the human spirit.

It is my hope, both as a survivor and as a mental-health counselor, that this book will be used as a stepping stone for you to bring help and healing to those touched by violence. I thank you—and the victims thank you—for your willingness to be part of the healing process in their lives.

# PART I

*Clinical
Trauma Treatment
Information*

# CHAPTER 1

# A Victim's Story

THIS VICTIM'S STORY, as well as the many stories you have or will undoubtedly hear as a counselor, help us to see the complexity of victimization. Interwoven into victims' lives—whether male or female—are personal histories of trauma, mental-health challenges, financial obstacles, relationship problems, community services shortages, missed intervention opportunities, and an array of other mitigating circumstances that make their treatment complicated. Victims bring to our offices their plethora of tangled problems, which we must try to unravel with them.

As you read Ladonna' story, begin to imagine what your intervention strategies might be. What kinds of treatment issues do you think might arise in her case? What kinds of social and public services might a case like hers require? How could you as a counselor be most effective in a complex situation such as this? Although Ladonna's life situation *is* complex, so are those of many victims.

| **VICTIM'S STORY** | *LADONNA* |
|---|---|

*Ladonna was one of what she referred to as "too many children" in her family. She was raised in abject poverty and her father was in and out of employment while she was growing up. A grandmother lived with the family and helped with all the children and the chaos. Alcohol and poverty went hand-in-hand in this family, and both the adults and young adults had drinking problems.*

*When Ladonna was a young girl, her grandmother began sexually abusing her. The grandmother was a matriarchal figure and highly re-*

spected in the family. Hints Ladonna gave to other adults about the abuse were ignored, and she was spanked for alleging that it had occurred. She continued to endure sexual abuse by her grandmother for years. In addition, at puberty, a male cousin began to rape her.

Ladonna's school attendance became sporadic during these times of abuse, and her grades, which were once good, dropped dramatically. Teachers spoke to her about her obvious depression and the events of her home life, but no one pursued the problem—not even the school counselor to whom she was eventually referred.

To Ladonna, safety meant escaping from the abusive environment in which rape, molestation, deprivation, and addiction were rampant. To flee, she married Larry, the first man who showed interest in her. He, too, had an undisclosed history of violence and addiction. However, Ladonna was too focused on escaping her own torture to ask many questions about his life and habits. She didn't know about his mounting criminal assault charges, drug dealing, and usage. She just knew he promised to take her out of her house and into his. And so she went. She married Larry at the age of fifteen and a half.

It wasn't long before Ladonna found out that rape was also part of her new life, as were many of the things she thought she could escape—such as violence, addiction, and too many children. Practically before she knew it, Ladonna had six children, and the cycle of poverty and violence had been established in her own home. Each time she tried to leave the relationship, Larry threatened to kill her or one of the children.

Ladonna's early childhood abuses had set up a pattern of low self-esteem and hopelessness. As a result, it didn't occur to Ladonna that anyone might be able to help her escape. No one had helped her when she was younger; no one responded to the obvious signs that something was wrong in her life. So she did not reach out beyond her biological family. And those in her family with whom she talked were not helpful because they shared the same hopelessness.

Years of countless rapes and beatings left Ladonna wanting another way out, so she found a man who offered to help her escape. Just as in her youth, Ladonna felt any way out involved a man taking her from her miserable life into a promised life. Steve convinced her that Larry would only kill her, not the children. He said that if she escaped with him, she could come back later for her children.

So Ladonna snuck off with Steve while Larry was at work, and she left her children behind. Steve took her to another city to "protect her" from Larry, but soon the cycle of violence and poverty began all over again. Steve was a heavy drug dealer and user. In order for him to maintain his drug habit, he needed Ladonna to "earn income" for him. So she started performing sex acts to enable Steve's drug addiction.

Ladonna's thoughts about these sex acts mingled with flashbacks of her early childhood abuse and marital rapes and produced an imagery so powerful and disturbing she needed help to get through what she was doing. She, too, began to use drugs and alcohol. Steve continued to bait her by telling her that as soon as they saved enough money, they would get her children back. But the drugs ate up all their income, and the children never arrived. As both of their drug dependencies increased, the sex trade no longer provided an adequate income.

One night, Steve convinced Ladonna to help him rob someone for drug money. The robbery did not go as planned, so Steve took the man into the alley and shot and killed him. Ladonna went to prison for second degree manslaughter.

Despair ridden, Ladonna realized her children were as trapped as she was—destined to repeat her life as they lived out a rerun of her childhood. But more despair was just around the corner. While in prison, Ladonna was diagnosed with HIV. Somewhere between rapes, IV drug use, and sex trade work, she had contracted a life sentence. Considering her twelve-year prison sentence, would she live long enough to find real and lasting love?

Another inmate told her she didn't have to wait. So Ladonna began a relationship with Shirley—another drug user and violent lover. For ten years, they were lovers in prison. Shirley, like Ladonna's previous men, controlled her every move. When Ladonna objected, Shirley beat her. Ladonna lived with the same fear she had felt since her grandmother began abusing her as a child.

Shirley completed her prison sentence and was released. She found an apartment and began taking meager, low-paying jobs while she waited for Ladonna's release. When Ladonna was released, the only place she had to go was the apartment Shirley had established. Ladonna had long since lost contact with her family. She had not contacted her children in the twelve years since her prison term began. In fact, as far as she knew, her children were not even aware she had been in prison.

*Life on the outside with Shirley did not offer the "love" Ladonna had hoped to find. Both of them quickly lapsed into drug and alcohol abuse. As a result, Ladonna's immune system became dangerously depleted. She was losing ground in her battle against HIV. Because she had neither insurance nor money, she could not obtain treatment.*

*Shirley continued to be violent with Ladonna. As her health failed, so did Shirley's tolerance. One day, during a beating, Ladonna stabbed Shirley and fled. It was a superficial wound, inflicted without forethought, but it served as a wake-up call for Ladonna. She didn't want anymore violence, especially not if it landed her back in prison, only to die there. Ladonna fled to a domestic-violence shelter, where she found sanctuary, sobriety, and support.*

*Today, Ladonna has full-blown AIDS and lives in a case-managed AIDS group home. She has just located her children and wants to rebuild her relationship with them during the time she has remaining.*

Ladonna's life offered many intervention opportunities for counselors. Most of these opportunities were missed by those few counselors she did encounter during her fifty-plus years. Elementary, middle, and high school counselors all failed to respond to the obvious clues in her life. Even in prison, no counselors asked what aspects of her experience had led her to such extremes. Other missed opportunities included the free clinics she might have visited while she was in the sex trade, as well as other health workers along the way who could have had a peek at her life and problems.

Ladonnas exist everywhere, with stories that span the decades of their tortured lives. *Counseling Victims of Violence* offers interventions that can bring hope to the Ladonnas who are praying you will help them. Will you have the skills necessary to help them in their recovery when they arrive at your office?

# CHAPTER 2

# The Psychodynamics of Trauma

VICTIMIZATION OF ANY KIND leaves its fingerprints upon the soul of the victim. Clinical evidence has suggested that physical and psychological well-being of violent crime survivors are affected by their experiences of violence (Schiraldi 2000; Walker 1991). Therefore, a humanitarian response to the epidemic of violence in this country is to provide trained counselors who are equipped with the tools needed to defuse the victims' symptoms and reduce their psychic injuries.

To do this, we must understand trauma and its effects. We need a practical approach to assessing the damage done by trauma. Because not all victims respond in the same ways to trauma—even when they experience the exact same types of trauma—a clinician must know how to assess their experiences of victimization. Before we can actually begin to assess the victims, we must understand the types of trauma disorders and stress reactions that victimization can produce.

We look first at an overview of trauma-related disorders and then in greater detail at the most prevalent reaction to trauma: posttraumatic stress disorder. The chapter concludes with sections about the psychobiology of trauma disorders, secondary victimization, the grief process, and theoretical approaches to treatment.

## Trauma-Relevant Disorders

Victims who have experienced a perceived life-threatening event, numerous adult traumas, or reoccurring abuse as a child can exhibit a range of mental-health disorders. The field of victimology, which has been recognized for a couple of decades, offers insight into these disorders. The disorders themselves are merely starting points from which to look for symptoms commonly associated with similar traumas. However, it is important that each victimization case be considered individually. Individual diagnosis and resulting outcomes can be affected by the following factors:

- Ego strength
- Resilience
- Victimization history
- Previous mental-health disorders
- Coping style

The disorders described below are often associated with traumatic coping responses. Although we are used to thinking of them as "disorders," I suggest you also think of them as "responses" to violence and trauma. Doing so can help you see the coping response within each disorder, and understand why the etiology was developed in terms of the traumatic response. (For more information about any of these disorders, please consult the *Diagnostic and Statistical Manual of Mental Disorders IV.*)

### DEPRESSION/MOOD DISORDERS

Mood disorders are often related to traumatic exposure (Hulme 2000; McCauley et al. 1997; Jumper 1995; Briere 1992). One common reaction to trauma is depression. This can occur immediately following the event. If treatment is not provided, the victim can acquire a mood disorder at a later time. Emotional withdrawal, often seen as depression, is one common coping style following an act of violence.

### ADDICTION/SUBSTANCE ABUSE

Addiction is often a medicating reaction that is related to an untreated mood disorder or depression. We now know that not treating crime victims' emotional wounds can result in substance-related issues if the victim uses drugs as an inappropriate coping mechanism. Many victims self-medicate, but not all go on to develop substance abuse disorders. The counselor should not only look for the symptoms of full addiction, but should be on the look out for any maladaptive use of a substance. Early intervention can prevent addiction.

## NARCISSISTIC PERSONALITY DISORDER (NPD)

NPD is often related to childhood neglect, abuse, or trauma. However, there are some exceptions, and a reverse relationship does not exist. Single-incident victimizations experienced by adults do not normally produce NPD. Any personality disorder diagnosis should, at the least, serve as a red flag for potential early childhood abuse or neglect. In the case of a personality disorder, the victim's childhood should be intensely examined (with the use of an appropriate assessment tool) for neglect, abuse, or trauma. Narcissism, as a coping response, appears as an intense self-focusing reaction. Early childhood trauma exposes the child to feelings of "no self-focus" by the abusing or neglecting caregivers. The child's needs are grossly ignored and unmet. What seems to be an over-inflated ego in narcissism is really the absence of a self-construct that should have developed during the period when the child was neglected or abused.

## POSTTRAUMATIC STRESS DISORDER (PTSD)

The extent to which a person experiences PTSD is related to the nature of previous childhood traumas and/or the intensity of trauma experienced as an adult. The more trauma a person has experienced, the stronger the PTSD reactions can be. The features most associated with PTSD include numbing and hyperarousal, both of which are sources of coping. Numbing helps the person distance from the overwhelming affect associated with the trauma. Hyperarousal gives the victim a sense of acute awareness that feels like "safety." (Because PTSD is the most prevalent reaction to intense trauma, it is covered in more detail below.)

## BORDERLINE PERSONALITY DISORDER (BPD)

Much like NPD (discussed above), any personality disorder diagnosis should alert the counselor to use an appropriate assessment tool to identify possible early childhood trauma or neglect. Borderline personality disorder, in particular, is a noteworthy diagnosis that is frequently associated with early onset neglect, abuse, or trauma (Cole and Putnam 1992). The particular features of this disorder point to maladaptive coping attempts, such as frantic efforts to avoid abandonment, over- or under-idealizing and devaluing others, self-damaging impulsivity, suicidal behavior, intense anger, and emotional instability. This diagnosis can complicate a treatment regime, which can be as problematic for the counselor as it is for the patient.

## OBSESSIVE-COMPULSIVE DISORDER (OCD)

OCD falls within the category of anxiety disorders. Trauma—whether early onset or mixed with adult traumas—can result in OCD behaviors. The victim attempts to use repetitive thoughts or behaviors as a coping response to neutralize the intensity of the traumatic memory.

## DISSOCIATIVE DISORDERS

Dissociative disorders represent the most complicated and severe reaction to trauma. These disorders are noted for their amnesic and fragmenting qualities. They operate as resistance to the trauma by disconnecting the event from memory. This is a highly developed coping mechanism for unassimilated and overwhelming trauma (Putnam and Trickett 1993; Briere 1992; Cole and Putnam 1992; Summit 1983) and requires intense intervention for the assimilation of the traumatic memories. The presence of a dissociative disorder warrants ruling out early childhood, long-term abuse because many victims acquire this disorder from those types of experiences. Additionally, many persons with dissociative disorders also have some of the other disorders listed here as trauma disorders.

Many dissociative disorders are acquired as an ultimate attempt to cope with ongoing and unrelenting victimization. Some dissociative disorders can be experienced as adult onset, especially following a major disaster. A counselor should know the difference between child-onset and adult-onset dissociative disorders. Additionally, many counselors find themselves inadequately trained to treat difficult cases of dissociative disorders. If you have not been trained, you should seek supervision through the treatment process.

## ADDITIONAL DISORDERS

Some specialists in the field of victimology add the following disorders to the list of trauma disorders. We will not discuss these disorders in detail, but readers may want to familiarize themselves with them.

○ Conversion disorder

○ Somatoform disorder

○ Acute stress disorder (a precursor to PTSD)

## Posttraumatic Stress Disorder

PTSD is the most frequently diagnosed disorder resulting from violence, especially when the violence or disaster was perceived by the victim as life-threatening. For this reason, an entire section on PTSD is included in this book. The prevalence of this disorder in the treatment of victimization warrants its inclusion as a primary diagnosis related to victimization, violence, and trauma. A counselor working in the field of victimology will invariably need to understand and treat this disorder.

### DESCRIPTION OF PTSD

PTSD has been described as "a normal reaction to exposure to traumatic and abnormal life events" (Niles 1990). Experiences outside of normal daily life that can lead to trauma include the following:

○ Rape

○ Domestic violence

○ Child abuse or neglect

○ Assault

○ Robbery or property crime

○ Other acts of violent crime

○ Seeing someone killed

○ Living through a disaster

○ Serious harmful threats made to one's children, self, or family

○ Witnessing traumatic events

○ Family member(s) involved in a disaster, homicide, or suicide

From this list, we can see that many types of violent crimes and disasters can be correlated with "an abnormal life event" that results in a PTSD diagnosis. Just how "affected" would a person be by one of these events? We know that the extent of PTSD depends on the level of trauma the victim has experienced (i.e., in this event and previous events) as well as the victim's coping style. Because coping styles vary from person to person, victims may have different reactions to the same type of trauma. Someone with a poorly developed coping approach will not handle a trauma as well as someone with a strong coping approach will.

## PTSD SYMPTOMS

The primary symptoms of PTSD include reoccurring thoughts, avoidance, numbing, and hyperarousal.

### *Recurring Thoughts*

Victims with PTSD can experience reoccurring thoughts and dreams about the precipitating act of violence. While sleeping, they are likely to dream about it. During the day, they can have reoccurring thoughts about acts they experienced or images they saw related to the violence. They can get lost in time and may sense the violence is happening again, right in that moment. Flashbacks to the sights, sounds, smells, tastes, and tactical experiences can happen, as well. This can lead to emotional reactions when victims are around things that represent the act of violence. This can also occur around the anniversary date of the event. Because PTSD is an anxiety disorder, and most anxiety disorders have some connection to future events as a source of anxiety, PTSD victims have a foreboding feeling about their future. They may fear everything will be cut short by violence. Because the trauma happened once, they are anxious about it happening again. This can take the form of anticipatory reoccurrence; they may worry excessively that they will never marry, have a successful career, or live long enough to fulfill their own dreams.

### *Avoidance*

As a result of their anxiety, victims may avoid people, places, or things that remind them of the violence. They use avoidance to stay away from the emotions associated with the trauma and from the memory of the trauma itself. The primary avoidance is related to the emotional content of the traumatic experience. Some individuals may have an amnesic quality and may not be able to remember parts of the traumatic event. This, too, happens so they can avoid the emotional content of the experience. Because of these symptoms, victims go through periods of withdrawal from people and activities. It is not uncommon for them to become reclusive. They are notably not as active in their lives as they were prior to the traumatic event.

### Numbing

Avoidance and withdrawal can be associated with the generalized numbing a person with PTSD feels. One of the most prevalent symptoms associated with PTSD is a numbing of feelings and responses. Persons with this numbing have decreased interest in the outside world because they do not experience the normal range of emotions. Numbing can appear as blunted or flat affect, with a limited range of emotional reactions. Victims often complain most about the absence of any kind of feeling. They describe this numbing as a "disconnection from others," even those they love. They feel a detachment from any type of emotional intimacy.

### Hyperarousal

Added to all the symptoms and difficulties listed above is the reaction of hyperarousal, or higher than normal levels of agitation. The effects of hyperarousal are very intrusive. Because PTSD is an anxiety disorder, it results in high cortisol production, which increases agitation. Cortisol and adrenaline production occur as part of the physiological response to internal imagery resulting from the victimization. This is an automatic biological function in which the body responds to the internal imagery as if it were happening in the present moment and the body releases cortisol and adrenaline as it did during the original trauma. Victims can experience unfounded anger related to the agitation. Disrupted concentration is likely to affect their work, career, or education.

Hyperarousal affects victims' ability to sleep; they have nightmares and disturbing dreams, and they do not sleep deeply due to the startle reflex. An exaggerated startle response is part of their hypervigilant approach to safety, and this is often embarrassing to them during their daily activities. For example, a loud noise or an approach from behind can result in a fear-based or combative reaction. Also, physiological reactions, such as sweating, trembling, or heart pounding, can occur when they become scared, which, in turn, can set off another cortisol or adrenaline episode.

## ONSET, RISK FACTORS, AND PROCESSING RELATED TO PTSD

PTSD onset can occur at the time of the trauma or can develop afterwards as a delayed onset. It can be experienced for varying lengths of time following the traumatic event. Different variables, as previously discussed, can determine the response to trauma, including how long a victim takes to reduce symptoms. It is important to know what factors can increase the probability of acquiring PTSD and what factors can influence the outcome of processing and treating PTSD.

Just who will go on to develop PTSD from a traumatic experience? A number of factors are related to a person's vulnerability for developing this disorder. Consequently, it makes sense that these factors may also be related to reactivation of PTSD for those who are later revictimized. A counselor should include the following factors in a detailed history when victims are screened. (You can find more information about screening materials in the next chapter on assessments.)

- Magnitude, duration, and type of traumatic exposure
- Earlier age when exposed to the trauma
- Lower level of education
- Severity of initial reaction
- Peri-traumatic dissociation
- Early childhood conduct problems
- Childhood adversity
- Family history of psychiatric disorders
- Poor social support after a trauma
- Personality traits such as hypersensitivity, pessimism, and negative reactions to stressors
- Depression in women increases vulnerability for developing PTSD
  (Kessler et al. 1995)

Researchers have studied some of the risk factors associated with the development of PTSD. For example, Niles (1990) reported that research revealed the following associations:

○ Higher levels of exposure to violence (combat/physical and abusive/psychological) are associated with higher levels of psychosocial problems.

○ Higher levels of PTSD are associated with higher levels of substance abuse.

○ Left untreated, PTSD becomes more severe with age.

○ Age, race, and gender influence the severity of PTSD (exposure at an earlier age can increase severity).

Niles (1990), as well as McCann and Pearlman (1990), suggested that PTSD is a universal bio-psychosocial process with unique individual reactive characteristics. In this context, the counselor's accurate diagnosis of PTSD and corresponding intervention strategies are major factors that influence victims' post traumatic stress responses. This is important because PTSD can be missed by the therapist if substance abuse or personality disorder factors mask the underlying problem.

### REACTIVATION AND EVENT TRIGGERS

Repeated exposure to trauma increases the chances of PTSD and will often reactivate the disorder if it existed previously. In addition, if PTSD is not initially treated, it is more likely to reactivate upon re-exposure.

Unfortunately, with PTSD, a never-ending cycle of events and reminders can jerk victims back into the midst of their traumas. Often these are reminders of a previous victimization that act as "triggers" to reactivate old symptoms, and sometimes they are new acts of violence. For example, if a person who was raped as a teen has her house robbed as an adult, her PTSD reaction may return. This reaction manifests as a psychological response to something that resembled the traumatic event. It evokes the reaction that was prevalent or should have been prevalent at the time of the trauma. The victim could have a reaction to the robbery that is more in line with a rape reaction. Victims are often shocked when they are thrown back into PTSD symptoms. Even if the victim perceives the crime as "not that traumatic" on the surface, the PTSD reaction may tell a bigger story.

Understanding reactivation and event triggers helps counselors make sense of intense reactions related to the PTSD diagnosis. Counselors can then help a victim develop coping strategies for these triggers. Triggers include but are not limited to the following:

○ Anniversary of the crime, abuse, or death. As the anniversary draws near, the reaction can increase, even taking on the intensity of the original reaction to the actual trauma. Victims have indicated that this seems to be their "automatic internal time clock." Often they will begin responding to this internal time clock long before they associate their anxiety, tension, and fear to the anniversary date itself.

○ Holidays and family events. Holidays and other family events (e.g., births, deaths, and weddings) can elicit strong recurring emotional responses. During holidays, in particular, victims may draw closer to feelings of suicide than at any other time of year. This can occur even if the victim has been doing well for many months. Seasons of "good will and peace on earth" remind victims of what they have endured and how the violation of their safety undermined their previous perception of a humane and kind world.

○ Auditory and visual reminders. Often victims will see or hear something that reminds them of their trauma. This could be a sound or a phrase or an image of a person, place, or thing. Taste, touch, and smell can recreate reminders of the traumatic event. This is especially true for victims of sexual abuse and family violence.

○ Interactions and/or confrontations with the abuser. The abuser or criminal is frequently not incarcerated. The abuser may come and go within the victim's life, especially if the victim has not disclosed the victimization, which is likely to occur in some forms of familial robbery, rape, incest, or physical abuse. Sometimes the abuser is on the run and has not been caught. The sheer agony of seeing or hearing the abuser will often trigger traumatic emotions associated with the abuse.

○ The "system." This could be the courts, police, appellate system, mental-health system, media, or another type of system that causes the victim to relive the traumatic events. Insensitive treatment and unfair laws or guidelines related to bond reduction, parole, or sentencing all are factors in a victim's ability to work through the trauma and reduce PTSD symptoms. The victim may be forced to be a part of the system for a number of years, especially if the abuser is trying to get free and the victim is striving to block the abuser's release. It may be necessary to speak at parole and other hearings to keep the abuser incarcerated. Although wishing to forget and get on with life, the victim may recognize the need to remain an active part of the victim advocacy system, even at the risk of retarding the healing process. Additionally, all types of media events (e.g., newspaper articles about the case or similar cases, news broadcasts, sensationalized talk shows, and violent movies) can play havoc with a recovering survivor's emotions. Victims are drawn to inform themselves about cases similar to their own even though their attraction can lead to reactivation of PTSD symptoms. The system and its various parts are a strong reactivation trigger in a victim's life.

## The Psychobiology of Posttraumatic Stress

Have you ever wondered why an adult survivor of incest or the victim of severe physical abuse is later physically assaulted again, and then goes on to be the victim of two date rapes? Why is it that, once someone has been victimized, the chances of becoming a victim again are so much greater? Does even a single act of victimization place someone at risk for future victimizations? As counselors, we see repeated patterns of victimization that are hard to understand. Just what is behind these repeated victimizations: coincidence or biology?

### MECHANISMS FOR CONTROLLING PAIN

The serial patterns of abuse we see are created because chronic trauma produces both body and brain reactions from an overabundance of stress. When the victim feels threatened, the body produces natural pain killers (analgesics) that have an impact on both physical and emotional pain. The brain has two separate mechanisms for controlling emotional and/or physical pain. We will look at how these mechanisms function.

The first mechanism involves a release of endorphins while one is under stress. When a painful emotional or physical input reaches the body, it triggers activity in the autonomic nervous system, and the body releases chemicals that arouse one to action. In a positive sense, this alerts the victim to danger. However, if this bodily reaction puts too much stress on the victim's system, it can counter the person's alertness to danger.

The second mechanism involves a "blocking" of painful input at the spinal cord level. This mechanism has analgesic or pain killing effects on the emotional reactions in the form of dissociation (McConnell 1986). If the brain is too stressed during trauma, it reacts by decreasing the overall pain and hyperarousal the victim is feeling. Although this helps to calm the victim, it creates a catch-22 because the person's awareness of danger is decreased through numbing and dissociation. One of the side effects of this analgesic is that it interferes with the storage of traumatic memories. This occurs in much the same way you would find it difficult to remember what happened if you drank too much.

Many victims in whom this second mechanism is active react to violence or unsafe situations by remaining numb, frozen, or unresponsive to their fight/flight system. Victims who are numb from chemical flooding, and who have few adult healthy coping strategies, are at particular risk of further victimization and less likely than people with healthy coping strategies to respond to a (possible) current victimization by fleeing.

## MEMORY ORGANIZATION, STORAGE, AND RETRIEVAL

Trauma affects how the brain organizes a memory, stores that memory, and later retrieves it. This ultimately influences how the victim perceives the events leading up to, during, and after the trauma. It also determines whether memories are stored in the same order they occurred, which in turn dictates how the victim must access the memories in order to retrieve them. We often see memory storage problems in rape victims, who are confused about what happened first, second, and last in the traumatic event. These problems also can be a hurdle in the counseling session when the victim is trying to process events that seem scrambled. Problems of memory organization, storage, and retrieval can also affect court testimony and the victim's believability.

## THE EFFECTS OF PHYSIOLOGICAL ACTIVITY ON TRAUMATIC PROCESSING

Violence affects the victim's ability to process traumatic experiences. This is due, in part, to the numbing and dissociation that the chemical reactions produce in the body, as we previously discussed. Treatment of trauma-related disorders largely focuses on helping the victim "process trauma," but this poses a challenge because the trauma itself has made it difficult for the victim to process, assimilate, and integrate the memory of the violence.

As a result, the victim can neither process the trauma nor add new coping mechanisms to assist with the symptoms.

Victims who do not or cannot process their violent experiences replay then over and over again in their daily consciousness. This process, referred to as "trauma replay," keeps the trauma replaying like a video in the mind, while the body continues to have physiological reactions. Each time the event is mentally replayed, the body reacts as if it is occurring in present time.

Violent memories that are unprocessed can become apparent to the counselor through the victim's compulsion to repeat the trauma. For example, the victim may place himself or herself in unsafe situations in which violence is likely to happen. Although this may appear to the counselor as an act of self-sabotage, it can be the victim's attempt to work through what has not been assimilated from the traumatic experience.

Traumatic processing can be particularly challenging for the victim who was also abused as a child. This victim probably has the physiological reactions from chemical flooding and also grew up in what is referred to as a "state of dependent learning." A state of dependent learning produces delays in personality development, obstructs healthier ways of keeping oneself safe, and prevents the use of appropriate coping mechanisms for dealing with stress. Such higher functioning mechanisms, which would greatly assist in counseling and recovery, are frequently absent from these types of victims. The only way these victims know how to respond to current violence is by reactivating the past dependent learning, even if its ways are uncomfortable, dangerous, or inadequate. This is also called "automatic responding."

## Defensive Coping

We have seen how the various trauma disorders tend to embody different coping mechanisms. It is also helpful to consider how each of the following specific defensive coping styles serve a protective function for the victim.

### Denial

Denial can be a powerful defensive coping mechanism. Established early on in the trauma event, denial helps to insulate the victim from the reality of a traumatic event.

### Dissociation

Dissociation is an inventive way victims distance themselves from an abusive event. During the abuse itself, victims emotionally remove themselves from the event, usually by visualizing themselves as being somewhere safe in order to protect their emotional core during the victimization. Putnam's (1985) definition of dissociation as an altered state of consciousness included symptoms of depersonalization and de-realization, which describe the protective function of dissociation.

### Self-Fragmentation

In self-fragmentation, victims internalize separate concepts about self. They may develop a self-construct that consists of the "pure" self before victimization and the "dirty" self after victimization. They internalize this breaking apart of self, which results in a disharmonious view of self.

### Arousal

The hyperarousal of victims can be seen in the ways in which they become acutely aware of others, their environment, and their own personal safety schemas through an increased autonomic response.

### Repression

Through repression, the victim works subconsciously to keep memories of the trauma from coming to the surface or conscious level. In this way, denial can stay intact, and memories can be held at bay.

### Splitting

Splitting allows the victims to divide the abuse into two concepts: the abuse or abuser and the person in their lives who could not possibly abuse them (even if that person *is* the abuser).

## Secondary Victimization Impact on Trauma

As if trauma disorders and the difficulties of processing trauma were not enough, the victim soon recognizes that victimization does not end with the initial act of violence. The many injustices that occur to victims after the crime are often referred to as "secondary victimizations." But don't let the name and ranking of "second" lead you to think that these types of pain are not as traumatic as, and do not evoke traumatic reactions similar to, those of the original victimization.

Secondary victimizations can be inflicted by

- family members, relatives, and close friends
- teachers, school counselors, and school administrators
- employers and coworkers
- acquaintances and neighbors
- pastors, clergy, and other friends in their faith
- therapists, social workers, and counselors
- hospitals, doctors, and their personnel
- the criminal-justice system, police, and attorneys
- the media, including newspaper reporters, camera crews, and investigators
- impersonal sources, such as "the newspaper at large"
- victim advocates; victim counselors; and those employed through victim systems, programs, and means of compensation

Many victims have indicated that secondary victimizations are more painful in many ways than the actual abuse because they are inflicted by people in care-giving roles who recognize the victims' vulnerability, yet abuse them anyway, or by systems the victims thought were put in place to relieve pain, not enhance it. At other times, the pain is inflicted by others in close relationships with the victim who assume the victim "is over" the abuse, "should move on" with life, or has overreacted to the trauma. Pain is inflicted when careless statements are made or inferred; the victim's pain is overlooked, minimized, or even ignored; or the victim is blamed for the trauma. In fairness to those who inflict this pain, we should acknowledge that they are usually unaware of what it does to the victim. This type of victim-blaming results from unsupportive reactions from others.

These types of responses also shape the victim's memory of the traumatic event. The responses actually become part of the memory associated with the trauma. Whether a recovery environment is supportive or unsupportive has direct consequences on the impact of the trauma on the victim.

Although systems don't necessarily reflect a highly personalized relationship with the victim, they can inflict as much harm as persons who have an emotional relationship with the victim. These systems are often geared toward victim advocacy, and the victim has placed trust in them. A victim's pain can be revisited each time that person has to go to court—which, for some, can go on for a lifetime. For example, Susan went to her state capital more than fifteen times, at her own expense, to prevent the release of the two men who murdered her deaf-mute father. Although her father had been dead for more than fifteen years, she experienced the same PTSD reactions each time she went before the parole board to plead against the release of these murderers. Likewise, Wendy had thought for years that the fate of the man who murdered her nine-year-old daughter was sealed with a death sentence. However, to her shock, ten years later, his sentence was overturned and a new trial was ordered. Wendy had to not only relive the murder, the facts, the photographs, and the trial, but also to face the possibility this man might be released.

The notification process, which does not effectively serve the victim, is also a type of secondary victimization. In the recent past, many victims were not notified about parole hearings and their entitlement to speak against the release of their abusers. Some were also not notified when parole was granted and their abusers were set free to stalk them. Or they were notified only after the abusers were released, so they had no time to emotionally prepare themselves. The shortfalls of the notification process have been a thorn in the flesh of many victims.

Fortunately, state legislation efforts have focused on developing a system to notify victims of hearings, new court dates, and appeals. Now victims are notified about the status of their cases and other legal procedures of interest to them. They are informed about how they can participate in the legal process, either by attendance or by giving a written account of their opinions concerning the case. Notification is given when the release of a perpetrator is pending. Each state is responsible for developing their own system for this. Most states have a system in place and continue to assess how to improve this process. These processes have assisted in reducing feelings of victimization at the hands of the criminal-justice system.

## Posttraumatic Stress and the Grief Process

PTSD and other trauma-related disorders are not diametrically opposed to the grief process. It is important that a therapist understand grief and loss are not relevant only to death. All victims must work through a grief process, whether the trauma has resulted from homicide, robbery, sexual abuse, or another event. Although family members of homicide victims need to grieve for obvious reasons, even victims of robbery and rape need to grieve what they have lost, whether it be their ability to trust others or something else. Because of this, we will look at the similarities and differences between grief and PTSD.

### GRIEF REACTIONS

William Worden in his book *Grief Counseling and Grief Therapy* (1991) broke down the grief manifestation reactions into the following categories: feelings, physical sensations, cognitions, and behaviors. As we will see, these categories mimic some PTSD reactions.

Grief feelings include sadness, anger, guilt, self-reproach, anxiety, fatigue, loneliness, helplessness, shock, yearning, emancipation, relief, and numbness.

Grief physical sensations include hollowness in the stomach, tightness in chest or throat, oversensitivity to noise or startle response, sense of depersonalization, breathlessness, weakness in muscles, lack of energy, and dry mouth. Often these physical sensations are not recognized because the focus is on the initial and most obvious physical problems. Many victims and counselors are surprised to learn the extent of the medical problems that are later attributed to and connected to the trauma. Medical problems include stress-related illnesses, as well as injuries resulting from blunt trauma (e.g., physical beatings) or from internal damage caused by penetration.

Grief cognitions include disbelief, confusion, preoccupation, sense of presence, and visual and auditory hallucinations. Other serious cognitions are associated with specific categories of victimization, such as incest and long-term abuse.

Grief behaviors include sleep and eating disturbances, absentminded behavior or dissociation, social withdrawal, dreams of the event, avoiding reminders of the event, searching or calling out, sighing, restless overactivity, crying, visiting places or carrying objects that are reminders of the person or event, treasuring objects that are reminders of the event, and remembering how one felt before the event or what one lost because of the event.

Grief is a natural reaction to loss. PTSD is a natural reaction to an abnormal type of loss. Victims can experience both of these reactions to loss. Their grief is a natural byproduct of their loss, and they may also react to the abnormal life experience associated with their victimization. In situations of traumatic or catastrophic loss, the bereaved person may demonstrate both traumatic stress reactions and bereavement phenomena (Raphael 1997).

When looking at both PTSD and grief, we can see the wide range of similarities that exist in the victim's experience. This would lead a counselor to ask, "Where does grief end and PTSD begin?" Grief can occur in varying degrees of severity, from a normal to a complicated grief reaction. Likewise, as we have seen, PTSD has varying degrees of severity that range from mild to chronic. Both grief and PTSD can be viewed on a single continuum—where normal grief is on the low end, complicated grief in the middle, and PTSD on the high end.

**GRIEF** ⟶ **COMPLICATED GRIEF** ⟶ **PTSD**

So what is "normal" grief, and what does a victim need to do to grieve over victimization? The normal tasks of grieving can be summed up through the following six "R" processes:

1. Recognizing the loss
2. Reacting to the separation
3. Recollecting and re-experiencing the deceased and the relationship
4. Relinquishing old attachments
5. Readjusting to move adaptively into the new world without forgetting the old
6. Reinvesting
    (Rando 1993)

These six processes are associated with successful grieving. But not all grieving goes smoothly. When grieving gets derailed, the result is complicated grief, or mourning. Complicated mourning represents a compromise or failure during one or more of the six "R" processes. Sometimes this type of complication is referred to by the following terms: traumatic, absent, abnormal, distorted, maladaptive, morbid, truncated, atypical, intensified, prolonged, unresolved, neurotic, or dysfunctional (Grief Research Website, www.grief.org.au).

Complicated grief is more intense and lasts longer than normal grieving patterns. It is characterized by an intrusive preoccupation with the event or person and results in significant problems that affect social, occupational, or other areas of functioning. Notably, the victim may engage in atypical behavioral functioning (e.g., reckless behavior, heavy drinking, sleep disruptions, problems in close relationships, and preoccupation with death and loss). As we can see, all of these symptoms mimic some of aspects of PTSD.

Victims with complicated grief often describe the experience as "feeling stuck," as if they are not progressing and moving forward in their grief. They feel overwhelmed by a stagnant process of stand-still grief. Yale University's department of psychiatry website describes complicated grief reactions as "having acute separation distress, intense pangs of yearning, a lack of purpose, a disturbing sense of feeling detached from others and numbness." This description is very close to the description of PTSD given earlier.

Earlier, we noted risk factors that contribute to a vulnerability for developing PTSD and that are related to the extent, intensity, and duration of abuse. Similar factors are related to the development of complicated grieving. Additionally, the victims' personal mechanisms for coping with emotional and physical pain influence their grief reactions. Raphael and Minkov (1999) summarized the following risk factors for complications in bereavement that are similar to those for PTSD:

○ Perceived lack of social support

○ Other concurrent crises or stressors

○ High levels of ambivalence in the relationship of the deceased

○ An extremely dependent relationship

○ Circumstance of death which are unexpected, untimely, sudden, or shocking

For all these reasons, it is often difficult for counselors to know where complicated grief ends and PTSD begins. When trying to ascertain grief levels, we do not measure the act of abuse, but rather the victims' reactions to the trauma. Gauging the reactions, not just the events, helps us differentiate normal grief reactions from complicated grief or PTSD reactions.

Victims fear abnormal reactions. If what they are experiencing is out of the norm, then who will know how to help or treat them? Helping victims see grief reactions to loss as "normal" and PTSD as a "normal" response to trauma can reassure them that what they are experiencing is not, in fact, abnormal. They can then see how grief and PTSD often manifest similar symptoms, and that grief goes hand-in-hand with any type of loss. Thus, a psychoeducational approach to understanding normal reactions to both loss and abnormal loss can be an effective intervention.

## The Treatment of Trauma

### THEORETICAL APPROACHES

Since many trauma disorders also have their roots in personality disorders (i.e., which is psychopathology), approaches to treating them vary widely. For example, how NPD and BPD are treated differs from how you would treat PTSD. Because of this, counselors might need to consider various treatment approaches when treating a personality disorder along with PTSD.

Foundational researchers in the field of victimology, McCann and Pearlman (1990), suggested that mental-health professionals' approach to working with PTSD victims must incorporate the victims' experiences as survivors. This is good advice because it means our treatment approach to PTSD must focus on each individual's response to the trauma they have experienced. The individualistic response is best understood through a review of each victim's symptomatology.

Understanding the treatment issues involved in PTSD is paramount for any counselor working with victims of violence. It is a highly probable diagnosis for those who have been through perceived life-threatening experiences. If a counselor lacks treatment knowledge about disorders often associated with trauma, I suggest obtaining training specifically in PTSD because of the frequency of this disorder in victims.

Counselors who feel confident in treating PTSD tend to approach the treatment process from their own modality of training. The following list represents commonly used approaches to PTSD treatment. If none of these is within your modality of treatment knowledge, you may want to consider selecting one or more of the following chapters in *Effective Treatment for PTSD: Practice Guidelines from the International Society for Traumatic Stress Studies* (Foa, Keane, and Friedman 2000) for further training:

Bisson, McFarlane, and Rose. "Psychological Debriefing."

Cardena, Maldonado, Van der Hart, and Spiegel. "Hypnosis."

Chemtob, Tolin, Van der Kolk, and Pitman. "Eye Movement and Desensitization and Reprocessing."

Courtois and Bloom. "Inpatient Treatment."

Friedman, Davidson, Mellman, and Southwick. "Pharmacotherapy."

Kudler, Blank, and Krupnick. "Psychodynamic Theory."

Rothbaum, Meadows, Resnick, and Foy. "Cognitive-Behavioral Treatment."

## COUNSELING SERVICES

Victims may need various types of counseling services to help them through their recovery period. Some of these types of services may not be offered by you or your agency, but may need to be sought out as outside referrals.

### Individual Counseling

Private individual counseling allows the client to personally deal with issues related to the trauma. This can be to process the events of the traumatic experience, for symptom reduction, to treat other comorbid conditions that are affecting the victim, to work an aspect of the grief process, to strengthen coping resources, to address relationships impacted by the victimization, to examine the victim's altered worldview of themselves, to address safety issues, or any other issue that the victim needs to work on related to the trauma or their functioning level.

### Pharmacological

Victims who have PTSD or PTSD features and other comorbid conditions frequently require medication. As mentioned previously, untreated PTSD often results in substance abuse, so medication should be considered (Brady et al. 2000).

### Family Therapy

The victim is often in need of support and assistance from their families. However, the victim's family may be having their own reactions to the victim's trauma. Helping families support one another through the recovery may be paramount in giving the victim the personal support they need from within the family structure.

### Group Therapy or Peer Support

When the victim is ready, group therapy or a peer support group may be intensely helpful. The support of other victims who have gone through the same thing the victim has experienced is exceptionally beneficial, as is the reduction in symptoms that usually results from the use of a support group. Victim groups that are most therapeutically helpful are those that are victimization-specific. Victims are grouped by their experiences or diagnosis. Generalized victim groups are often traumatizing for the least traumatized victim. For instance, consider a mugging victim having to listen to a homicide survivor's story of the murder of their loved one. Therefore, I recommend putting victimization groups together.

### Spiritual Counseling

Victims can struggle to understand how a benevolent God can allow their victimization. Faith and spiritual struggles are common even for those who attend regular spiritual services. Victims of faith can have dramatic setbacks as a result of insensitive statements made by untrained spiritual advisors. Finding trained spiritual counselors who understand victimization and it's impact can provide comfort, support, and closure for the victim.

### Expressive Arts

Auxiliary therapies that help victims express trapped feelings can be helpful. These can include art, music, dance, retreats, ropes courses, and other types of body work, such as massage. Some victimization types may not be ready for these or their use may be unadvisable (these are listed in the specific victimization chapters).

### 12-Step Groups

Victims who may have addictive tendencies that have been aggravated by the trauma may benefit from 12-step groups. These addictive tendencies may include drugs, alcohol, relationships, gambling, food, or sex.

## Conclusion

The disorders described in this chapter give the counselor a foundational understanding of how victims are affected by their traumatic experiences. Although trauma disorders can be extensive, knowledge about the disorders, the psychobiology related to these disorders, their triggers, the grief process, and common treatment approaches can help prepare counselors for the treatment process. Understanding the psychodynamic process of trauma is the first step in formulating a treatment plan. The next step is to understand the importance of the assessment process and how to select appropriate assessment tools. The outcomes of these assessments help guide the treatment process. This is covered in the next chapter.

### RECOMMENDED READING

Catherall, Don R. *Family Stressors: Intervention for Stress and Trauma* (Series in PsychoSocial Stress). New York: Brunner-Routledge, 2005.

Herman, Judith Lewis. *Trauma and Recovery.* New York: Basic Books, 1997.

Horowitz, Mardi J. *Treatment of Stress Response Syndromes.* Arlington, VA: American Psychiatric Association, 2002.

Johnson, Kendall. *After the Storm: Healing after Trauma, Tragedy and Terror.* Alameda, CA: Hunter House Publishers, 2006.

Johnson, Kendall. *Trauma in the Lives of Children,* 2nd Edition. Alameda, CA: Hunter House Publishers, 1998.

McCann, I. Lisa, and Laurie Ann Pearlman. *Psychological Trauma and the Adult Survivor: Theory, Therapy, and Transformation.* Philadelphia, PA: Brunnel/Mazel, 1990.

Parkinson, Frank. *Post Trauma Stress: A Personal Guide to Reduce the Long-Term Effects and Hidden Emotional Damage Caused by Violence and Disaster.* Tucson, AZ: Fisher Books, 2000.

Vasterling, Jennifer J., and Chris R. Brewin. *Neuropsychology of PTSD: Biological, Cognitive, and Clinical Perspectives.* New York: The Guilford Press, 2005.

Volavka, Jan. *Neurobiology of Violence.* Arlington, VA: American Psychiatric Association, 2002.

Williams, Mary Beth, and Soili Poijula. *The PTSD Workbook: Simple Effective Techniques for Overcoming Traumatic Stress Syndromes.* Oakland, CA: New Harbinger Publications, 2002.

Young, Bruce H., and Dudley D. Blake. *Group Treatment for PTSD: Conceptualization, Themes and Processes.* Ann Arbor, MI: Braun-Brumfield, 1999.

## RESOURCES

The National Center for PTSD
(802) 296-6300    ○    www.ncptsd.va.gov

The National Center for Victims of Crime
(202) 467-8700    ○    www.ncvc.org

International Society for Traumatic Stress Studies
(847) 480-9028    ○    www.istss.org

Anxiety Disorder Association of America
(240) 485-1001    ○    www.adaa.org

PTSD Alliance
(877) 507-PTSD (507-7873)    ○    www.ptsdalliance.org

Trauma Info Pages
www.trauma-pages.com

PILOTS Database
www.biblioline.nisc.com

Grief Recovery Institute
www.grief-recovery.com

The Trauma Center
(617) 232-1303    ○    www.traumacenter.org

# CHAPTER 3

# The Assessment

ASSESSMENTS CAN BE CONSIDERED the genesis of the counseling process. We use assessments to focus our intervention and counseling approaches. Assessments are typically accomplished by a structured clinical or diagnostic interview, a self-report questionnaire filled out by the victim, or both.

## Overview of the Functions of Assessment

Assessment tools provide many different functions. The overall purpose of any type of assessment is to gain insight into the extent and nature of the victim's adjustment problems and that person's exposure to trauma. Assessments help the counselor gauge the specific manifestations of the victim's response to trauma.

Assessments can assist the counselor to accomplish the following:

○ Determine the presence and severity of the range of adverse trauma reactions

○ Substantiate changes that have occurred because of trauma

○ Provide diagnostic information about the disorder

○ Measure symptom acuity

○ Track changes in severity or duration of symptoms

○ Measure affective, perceptual, and thematic experiences

○ Provide a comparison of how well a victim is doing at any given point in time (e.g., before counseling, during, and at termination)

○ Assist in choosing types of treatment modalities
(Blake, 1993)

## THE MISUSE AND ABUSE OF ASSESSMENT

While assessments can assist counselors, they must also be aware of the limitations and misuse of assessments. Blake (1993) identified the three greatest problems associated with use of assessments:

○ Reliance on one or two psychological measures to make long-term treatment decisions

○ Informal test administration and scoring that does not meet test protocols

○ Use of assessment tools by counselors who are not qualified by degree or experience, and (if not qualified) working without appropriate supervision

## TRAINING TO USE ASSESSMENT TOOLS

If a counselor has not had training in the use of these instruments, that person should seek supervision or take instrument-specific testing courses to become certified and competent before attempting to use any instruments. Many assessment tools come with information describing how to use them. Some list supportive workshops that provide explanations about the test protocol. Workshops often incorporate current case studies and other research that help the counselor better understand the purpose and applications of the instrument.

## Selecting Assessment Tools

While not all counselors use assessments frequently, if you become involved in the treatment of victims of violence, you will most certainly need to possess the skills to assess and test. The wide range of trauma disorders in this client population warrants the use of assessments, and often the use of more than one type of assessment.

The information gathered from assessments ultimately will direct the intervention, short- and long-term counseling processes, counseling approach, and social services needed to support the victim through recovery. Therefore, finding several assessment instruments that together deliver the comprehensive information you will need to treat the victim should be the first step in developing your arsenal of counseling tools.

Because such a wide range of instruments is available, you must first decide what information you want to acquire from the assessment. The assessments listed at the end of this chapter are all designed to help you determine the extent of the trauma and the specific areas affected by the trauma. Briere (1997) suggested using multiple sources of information rather than taking all diagnostic information from a single assessment. In fact, sometimes it is more appropriate to use an instrument not just to make a diagnosis, but also to alert the counselor to potential problems that merit further evaluation. Briere recommended counselors look for formats that assess pre-trauma functioning as part of the overall picture of trauma and functioning. He also stressed the need for greater diagnostic sensitivity to the pre-cursors and sequelae of victimization. He encouraged counselors to use observation as a means of assessment because victims who have suffered trauma may elevate scales on tests that were normed without taking into consideration the influence of trauma, and thus can lead to misdiagnoses and ineffectual treatment formulations.

## SPECIAL CONSIDERATIONS AND OTHER OPTIONS

One option for counselors is to refer the victim to a psychologist who has experience testing in a number of areas. However, if finances are an issue for the victim, it is often less expensive for the counselor to do the assessments than it is for a licensed psychologist to do a battery of tests.

Be aware that some psychophysiological and neurobiological tests require administration by a doctoral level practitioner. Check the guidelines of the instrument closely. In these cases, if you feel you need the results of that specific assessment tool, it is best to refer the client to a psychologist.

## DISRUPTION SYMPTOMS

Trauma victims bring some unique qualities to the counseling assessment. As indicated in the previous chapter on psychodynamics, trauma is associated with some predictable disruption symptoms. These clinical disruptions should be considered when selecting trauma assessment instruments.

In fact, many of the disruptions routinely seen in trauma survivors are included in trauma assessment tools. Tests geared toward PTSD will most likely have scales related to these types of disruptions.

You will need to scan the assessment tool to see what relevant results it is designed to report. Some of the disruptions you should consider are briefly described in the following sections.

### Perceptual/Cognitive Disruption Symptoms

These types of disruptions are often seen in PTSD and represent some of the more disturbing symptoms of the disorder. Assessment tools can often measure the symptoms and intensity of the disturbing symptomatology.

Perceptual and cognitive disruptions include internal and external cues that produce visual, auditory, and kinesthetic symptoms that are intrusive (Burgess, Harman, and Kelley 1990). Symptoms can include the following:

○ Flashbacks

○ Enuresis

○ Startle responses

### Biological Disruption Symptoms

These types of disruptions are often related to the physiological reactions victims have to intense or prolonged stress exposure. Assessment tools help to identify physiological markers that can be targeted for symptom relief.

A variety of biologically induced symptoms can occur, including the following:

○ Increased autonomic nervous system arousal (hyperarousal)

○ Somatic disturbances resulting in neuro-behavioral problems

○ Generalized somatic disturbances

### Interpersonal Disruption Symptoms

These types of disruptions are often related to the effects of trauma on personal relationships. Assessments tools that point to interpersonal problems can help counselors increase skill levels in relationships.

A variety of interpersonal symptoms can occur, including the following:

○ Excessive fear of others

○ Inability to assert and protect oneself

○ Repetition of aggressive sexualized behavior toward others

○ Inability to develop intimate emotional relationships

### Behavioral Response Disturbance Symptoms

These types of disruptions are often related to reduced coping and lowered functioning levels. Assessment tools can point to interventions that can address aggression, addiction, and occupational functioning.

A variety of behaviorally induced symptoms can occur, including the following:

○ Aggressive or antisocial behavior patterns

○ Substance abuse

○ Suicidal behavior

○ Impaired social functioning and social withdrawal

○ Isolation

○ Decreased school and work performance

○ Lack of peer relationships

○ Reduced social adjustment

○ Reduced ability to attain occupational achievement
(McCann and Pearlman 1990)

## Cultural and Other Influences

Counselors need to be familiar with the cultural norms that may affect certain assessment tools, inventories, and scales. Many instruments are normed for American culture and do not take into account the belief systems, behaviors, and traditions of those who are from other cultures or countries. These instruments can deliver skewed results for persons from cultures who have belief systems that trigger a flag in the assessment tool. You should thoroughly research these issues. Finding culturally informed assessment tools for clients from specific ethnic and cultural groups may be challenging. However, the publisher of an assessment can inform you about whether or not the instrument was normed in a way that took into account cross-cultural considerations. This can also apply to gender norms.

Norming for special populations can also influence the usefulness of certain assessment tools. Norming in this case takes into consideration what is normal for that specific population, but might not be normal in all populations. For example, an assessment tool may measure military PTSD, but not crime-related PTSD. Some specialty assessments look at trauma differently in children, couples, and families, as well as in cases of traumatic bereavement. You should be alert to these types of specialized instruments in case you need to find an instrument for a certain population, as well as to be sure that the instrument you do select is appropriate for the client.

## Assessment Tools, Instruments, Inventories, and Scales

In researching assessment tools that would be helpful for the population of victims of violent crime, I uncovered hundreds of assessment tools. It is beyond the scope of this book to elaborate on all these tools. Therefore, I have compiled a list of assessment tools that covers a multitude of different issues for which victims might need assessment and that specifically relate to trauma disorders. I tried to list some assessment tools that cover both PTSD reactions and other trauma disorders.

Please keep in mind that this list by no means covers all the types of assessments available for a multitude of disorders and needed measurements. For example, I did not include a substance abuse tool. Many counselors already use their own specifically selected substance abuse tests. If you are not already using a substance abuse screening tool, pick one that looks comprehensive and add it to your list of possible assessment tools. And the same goes for other specialty topics not covered in this list.

The following instruments and assessment resources are grouped by category and are listed alphabetically within category. Website addresses are provided where available so you can further study these potential tools.

GENERAL ASSESSMENTS APPROPRIATE FOR TRAUMA

The National Center for PTSD (www.ncptsd.org)
- ○ Beck Depression Inventory
- ○ Dissociative Experience Scale

- Impact of Event Scale
- Mississippi Scale for Combat-Related PTSD

PILOTS Database Instruments Authority List (www.ncptsd.va.gov/pub lications/pilots/Instruments.pdf)

- PTSD Reaction Index
- PTSD Self Report
- PTSD Symptom Scale
- State-Trait Anxiety Inventory
- Traumatic Events Screening Inventory

Psychological Assessment Resources, Inc. (www.parinc.com)

The Trauma Center (Bessel van der Kolk) (www.traumacenter.org/assess ment.html)

- Modified PTSD Symptom Scale
- Structured Interview for Disorders of Extreme Stress (SIDES) and Self-Report Instrument for Disorders of Extreme Stress (SIDES-SR)
- Trauma Antecedents Questionnaire (TAQ)
- Trauma Focused Initial Adult Clinical Evaluation

Western Psychological Services, Inc. (www.wpspublish.com)

- Clinician Administered PTSD Scale
- My Worst Experience Scale
- Trauma Assessment Inventories
- Trauma and Attachment Belief Scale
- Trauma Symptom Inventory

## ASSESSMENTS SPECIFICALLY FOR TRAUMA

Adolescent Psychopathology Scale

Checklist for Child Abuse Evaluation

Child Abuse Potential Inventory

Child Sexual Abuse Inventory

Detailed Assessment of PTSD

Devereux Scales of Mental Disorders (children)

Hare Psychopathology Check List (Rev. 2nd Ed.)

MMPI-A

MMPI-2 Adult Interpretive System

Multi-scale Dissociation Inventory

OMNI-IV Personality Disorder Inventory

Personality Assessment Inventory

Trauma Symptom Checklist for Children

Trauma Symptom Inventory For Psychopathology

## COUNSELING-RELATED ASSESSMENTS

Children's Depression Inventory

Clinical Assessment of Depression

Hamilton Depression Inventory

American Psychiatric Publishing, Inc. (www.appi.org)

Structured Clinical Interview for DSM-IV Dissociative Disorders (SCID-D)

## OTHER ASSESSMENTS

You should also have on hand or create your own medical inventory checklist of various medical disorders, especially those seen frequently in trauma victims. (See the section on incest in the chapter on sexual trauma for the kinds of medical disorders in these victim populations.) It is also helpful to have some type of grief inventory, because most victimization theories are based on the concept of loss.

## Conclusion

The importance of assessment for directing intervention and the counseling process cannot be overstated. Victimization that leads to trauma disorders often creates the need for a complicated treatment regime that can only be sorted out by acquiring information from assessments. This chapter provides a small sample of the many types of assessment tools that are available to help you gather information to provide treatment to victims of violent crime. The publishers of these tools can help you select the right instruments for your needs. Training on how to use the instruments is often available. Check with the organization or publisher for information about training.

### RECOMMENDED READING

Friedman, Matthew J. *Post Traumatic Stress Disorder: The Latest Assessments and Treatment Strategies.* Kansas City, MO: Compact Clinicals, 2003.

### RESOURCES

The National Center for PTSD
(802) 296-6300    ○    www.ncptsd.va.gov

The National Center for Victims of Crime
(202) 467-8700    ○    www.ncvc.org

PILOTS Database
www.biblioline.nisc.com

The Trauma Center
(617) 232-1303    ○    www.traumacenter.org

# CHAPTER 4

# Stalking and Cyberstalking

STALKING EXPERIENCES bring with them a horrifying experience of "Who is this and why are they doing this to me?" Victims of stalkers sometimes know their perpetrators, but often do not. Victims are left with a sense of trying to fight off or prevent something they cannot even name or identify. The powerlessness is often overwhelming for victims of stalkers. Even celebrities now take their stalking episodes extremely seriously because stalkers have the power to terrorize their victims.

## Stalking

Based on statistics from 1996:

- An estimated 1,006,970 women and 370,990 men were stalked.
- One out of every 12 women and 1 in 45 men will be stalked during his or her lifetime.
- 77 percent of females and 64 percent of men know their stalker.
- 81 percent of women who were stalked by a current/former husband or cohabitating partner were also physically assaulted, and 31 percent were also sexually assaulted by that partner.
- The average duration of stalking is 1.8 years.
- If stalking involves intimate partners, the average duration increases to 2.2 years.
- 61 percent of stalkers made unwanted phone calls, 33 percent sent

or left unwanted letters or items, 29 percent vandalized property and 9 percent killed or threatened to kill a family pet.

○ 28 percent of females victims and 10 percent of male victims obtained a protective order; 69 percent of female victims and 81 percent of male victims had the protection order violated.

(Tjaden and Thoennes 1998)

### VICTIM'S STORY                                             *KAREN*

*A couple of years after I divorced my husband, I made the decision to move from the area. I was planning to go to an area in Washington state, and my ex-husband knew about my plans. At the last minute, I ended up going to another location in California, where I got an apartment. My daughter was three at the time.*

*After we had been living there for two months, I began dating a guy. One day, he was waiting for me to come home from work and he was sitting outside my apartment. Later he told me he spoke with a blond-haired man who claimed to be my husband. He said he was looking for me.*

*I showed my friend several photos I had of different men with blond hair. They were pictures of friends and relatives, and one photo was of my ex-husband. I created a sort of "line-up" of blonde-haired men. He pointed to the picture of my ex-husband.*

*Within two months, my ex-husband had tracked me down—not to Washington state where he thought I was going, but to the place I ended up. He began calling, showing up at work, leaving notes, and following me. After less than three weeks, I packed up what I could carry in a Toyota and headed to a relative's house in another state.*

*When we finally went to court, my ex-husband denied ever being in the state of California. I was very unnerved that he could track me and just show up on my doorstep. I still wonder if he will find me today.*

### BACKGROUND INFORMATION

Stalking is defined by The National Center for Victims of Crime Stalking Center website as "any unwanted contact between a stalker and their victim which directly or indirectly communicates a threat or places the victim in fear." Only in recent years has stalking been labeled as a distinct class of deviant behavior. Before it was labeled "stalking," it was merely referred to as harassment or a behavior linked with domestic violence (Meadows 2001).

Movies such as *Fatal Attraction* and *Cape Fear* have helped us understand the impact stalking can have in people's lives and the extent to which stalkers will go. Celebrities themselves have brought the issue to light when they have prosecuted their stalkers and lobbied for better protection. Stars such as Monica Seles, Jerry Lewis, Michael J. Fox, Madonna, and Elle MacPherson have all exposed their fear of the stalkers in their lives. As a result, we live in a society that is fairly attuned to at least the basic concept of stalking, if not the specific details involved.

Nevertheless, technology and other modern conveniences have allowed stalking to go even further. Stalking no long just involves a stalker physically showing up at your home or work. Stalking now includes using the USPS, instant messaging services, and florists as means of making contact. Hidden cameras can give stalkers a video advantage, as can surveillance software installed in a victim's computer. Stalkers can even use GPS to track a victim if they hide a device on the victim's car. Distinguished from cyberstalking (see below), use of a GPS is now considered a form of physical stalking "that uses technology in order to stalk." Today's stalker clearly has many advantages in tracking his victim that he did not have in the past.

Stalkers can be male or female; victims, likewise, can be male or female. The statistics show that more victims are women and more stalkers are men, so we will use the corresponding pronouns here. Stalkers are categorized into two types:

1. *Love stalkers* represent 20 percent to 25 percent of stalkers. They are fixated on another person even though they do not have a relationship with that person. The person could even be a complete stranger. Some love stalkers go after celebrities, but many stalk everyday citizens.

   Notably, most of these stalkers are mentally ill—most frequently schizophrenic. Others live primarily through fantasy-type relationships, and expect their victims to play out the fantasy as well. They believe a relationship really will develop. When it does not develop, they may engage in threats, intimidation, and even violence. Their goal is to have any kind of relationship with the victim, whether it is positive or negative.

2. *Simple stalkers* represent 75 percent to 80 percent of stalkers. Often they were previously involved in a friendship or romantic relationship with the person they stalk. This category overlaps with domestic-violence relationships and stalking that occurs in dating relationships. In domestic-violence situations, the victim runs a 75 percent chance of being stalked (National Center for Victims of Crime, Stalking Resource Center website).

While love stalkers are often schizophrenic, simple stalkers can have a range of psychological issues. These include emotional immaturity, lack of social/dating skills, powerlessness, unsuccessful relationships due to inappropriate behavior, high levels of jealousy, and low self-esteem. They attempt to manage their low self-esteem by controlling their victim through stalking and trying to dominate that person. Doing this creates a sense of powerlessness in the victim and allows the stalker to view the victim as a possession.

Simple stalkers tend to engage in common patterns of stalking. The stalking cycle begins when the victim rebuffs the stalker. The stalker then begins wooing the victim with love letters and gifts, and then turns to intimidation when the wooing does not work. Contact increases and becomes more intrusive until it is threatening. Stalkers who reach this level can, and often do, end up committing violent acts and even murder. Stalkers resort to these means when they cannot get the victim to do what they want, and thus they do whatever it takes to regain a sense of dominance.

A stalker's unreasonable thinking can go from "I will show you how much I love you" to "You will come to love me, too" and end with "If I can't have you, no one will." Although progressions of this sort are common, each stalking case is different. Some move rapidly through the entire cycle, while others skip the middle phase and go straight to the more dangerous end. What a stalker will do and when he will do it are totally unpredictable, which makes stalking especially dangerous (National Center for Victims of Crime, Stalking Resource Center website).

Unfortunately, many people think stalking is not risky or unsafe. Therefore, they overlook or ignore the earlier phase of the stalking cycle and are taken off guard when it reaches a dangerous level. During the early phase, it is important for the victim to develop a safety plan. Understanding the difference between imminent danger and eventual danger is crucial. Unfortunately, victims often view the danger as remote when, in fact, the cycle has already escalated and they are in imminent danger. As a result, they do not act quickly enough to protect themselves. By the time they realize the true level of dangerousness, it can be too late.

Victims lack the education and resources to help them handle stalkers in the most appropriate manner so they can protect their own physical well-being. The types of steps victims can take when dealing with a stalker are described in the following sections.

## WHAT TO DO WHEN FACED WITH EVENTUAL DANGER

Acting in a timely manner when faced with eventual danger can sometimes prevent the development of imminent danger. Victims who suspect stalking should begin a safety-oriented and legal process that involves the following actions:

1. File a restraining/protective order
2. Become familiar with state stalking laws
3. Document the stalking events
4. Report stalking events
5. Develop a contingency plan for safety

Carrying out these steps and procedures is necessary for the victim as well as for the legal system that enforces the stalking laws.

### Restraining/Protective Order

These legal documents order the stalker to stay away from the victim and to stop all contact. These orders are obtained through either a court process or through the magistrate's office. There is, of course, no guarantee a stalker will respect the order. A broken order can be dealt with by having the stalker arrested and jailed. However, to be protected, the victim *must* prosecute each time the stalker violates the order.

### Stalking Laws

Although most states have stalking laws, enforcement of these laws (as in the case of domestic-violence laws) is another issue. Regardless, the victim needs to find out what the laws are in that person's state and carefully determine how faithfully local law enforcement responds to and enforces the laws. In the middle of a 911 call is not the time to find out one's city has a poor follow-through rate with respect to stalking response and prosecution. The local prosecutor's office or a victim advocate can give the victim a copy of the stalking laws and update the victim about how well the laws are enforced.

### Documenting the Events

Documentation of stalking events goes a long way in the legal process. It is crucial that a victim understand how important it is to begin this process right away. As a counselor, you need to continue to encourage the victim to keep diligent notes and to bring that person to counseling so you can check that he or she is following through. These documents can be shown to law-enforcement officers, to the magistrate, or during any court proceedings that occur because of the stalking. Documents are also useful for any future complaints, evidentiary findings in court, and establishing credibility. They can also be helpful in the case of a serial stalker who is stalking other victims.

Documentation can include a stalking incident log (see facing page), photographs of damaged property, photos of any bodily injuries, saved voice mails, recorded answering machine tapes, letters, or items sent to or left for the victim. The documented items should be removed from the victim's house to a safe and secure location so they are not damaged or stolen prior to use in court (National Center for Victims of Crime, Stalking Resource Center website).

### Reporting All Stalking Events

No matter how ridiculous the victim feels about continually calling law enforcement for each event, it is important to do so. These calls are all written as reports and are admissible evidence in court. A victim may wait too far into the stalking cycle to report the events. Or the events keep occurring, and the victim becomes too embarrassed to report each event. To avoid such problems, the counselor should quiz the victim about her consistency in reporting. The counselor can even offer to have the victim make the phone calls directly from the counseling office if some events were not reported.

Reporting is the only way to create a paper trail for prosecution. Prosecution can stop the stalking completely if the stalker is jailed; short of that,

## Stalking Incident and Behavior Log

It is critical that victims of stalking maintain a log of stalking-related incidents and behavior. Recording this information will help to document the behavior for restraining order applications, divorce and child custody cases, or criminal prosecution. It can also help preserve your memory of individual incidents about which you might later testify.

The stalking log should be used to record and document all stalking-related behavior, including harassing phone calls, letters, e-mail messages, acts of vandalism, and threats communicated through third parties. When reporting the incidents to law enforcement, always write down the officer's name and badge number for your own records. Even if the officers do not make an arrest, you can ask them to make a written report and request a copy for your records.

*Important note:* Since this information could potentially be introduced as evidence or inadvertently shared with the stalker at a future time, do not include any information that you do not want the offender to see.

Attach a photograph of the stalker, photocopies of restraining orders, police reports, and other relevant documents. Keep the log in a safe place and tell only someone you trust where you keep your log.

Documenting stalking behavior can be a difficult and emotionally exhausting task. A local advocate in your community can provide support, information about the options available to you, and assistance with safety planning.

| Date | Time | Description of Incident | Location of Incident | Witness Names (Attach Address and Phone #) | Police Called (Report #) | Officer Name (Badge #) |
|------|------|------------------------|----------------------|--------------------------------------------|--------------------------|------------------------|
|      |      |                        |                      |                                            |                          |                        |
|      |      |                        |                      |                                            |                          |                        |
|      |      |                        |                      |                                            |                          |                        |
|      |      |                        |                      |                                            |                          |                        |
|      |      |                        |                      |                                            |                          |                        |
|      |      |                        |                      |                                            |                          |                        |

Source: Copyright © 2002 by the National Center for Victims of Crime.

it can send the stalker a consistent message that every contact will be reported and will have consequences for him.

### Developing a Contingency/Safety Plan

At the first sign of stalking, the victim needs to spring into action because an eventual danger can become imminent at any time. The victim needs to have immediate access to critical phone numbers. The following numbers should be programmed into her cell phone and home phone: law enforcement, 911, domestic-violence shelter, magistrate's office, prosecutor's office, family and friends, fire department, next door neighbors, place of employment, and anyone else she thinks she might need in an emergency. Additionally, she should write down her car license plate number, make, model, and serial number, and keep the information where it is easily accessible (National Center for Victims of Violence, Stalking Resource Center website).

A counselor should spend a session with the victim developing this safety plan. It helps to make the victim truly conscious of the seriousness of her situation. During the safety plan session, a counselor can walk the victim through a scenario and help her decide what to do at each step. This includes discussing whether she will stay or whether she will flee, how she secures her environment, how immediately she phones the police, whom she phones next, where she will go in her house until a helper shows up, what she will take with her into that room, and anything else that can help her think through the likely scenarios. The safety plan should also clarify the point at which she will no longer be safe in her own home and will seek shelter elsewhere. It is good to make some of these decisions in advance. The counselor should put all of the decisions in writing, have the victim sign the document, and give her a copy that she can place somewhere safe yet accessible.

Additionally, the victim should keep a packed suitcase at another location that will be easily accessible if she needs to flee quickly. She should keep some money in reserve and should keep on hand such items as medications, credit cards, social security card, her passport if applicable, and her birth certificate. Neighbors should have access to the victim's house (e.g., keys, security codes) so they can check on things if the victim flees.

The victim should have the same types of items packed for her children, including identification. People whom the victim has identified as safe people (e.g., family, friends, employers, law enforcement, and a victim advocate, if the victim is using one) should be alerted when she is in danger or when she has decided to flee.

### Prevention

The Stalking Resource Center advises victims to take various steps while the danger is still eventual in order to prevent escalation:

- Install solid core doors with dead bolts. If the victim cannot account for all keys, change the locks and secure spare keys.
- If possible, install adequate outside lighting and trim back bushes around the residence and driveway.
- Keep an unlisted phone number. If harassing calls continue, notify law enforcement. Keep a written log of any harassing calls and any answering machine tapes or voice mails with the stalker's message.
- Treat any and all threats as legitimate, and notify law enforcement immediately.
- The victim should frequently change travel routes and other habits (e.g., the way to work, the stores where she shops, what time she goes to the gym).
- Notify a safe person about the situation. Provide information such as a photo or description of the stalker, the types of vehicle(s) he uses, and any other facts about him.
- Inform the landlord or on-site manager and provide a picture and information about the suspect.
- Have co-workers screen all personal phone calls and visitors.
- The victim should try to have someone with her when she is not at home or work. She should try to stay in visible public areas while she is out. She should limit the time she spends walking or jogging outside, especially when alone.
- If the victim needs help, she should know to scream "FIRE" to get immediate attention, because more people respond to "FIRE!" than to "HELP!"
- If possible, the victim should have an answering machine connected to a published phone line, so she can record the stalker's

messages and turn the recording over to law enforcement. The victim should also have a private, unlisted line for friends and family. The stalker may not realize she has another line.

## WHAT TO DO WHEN FACED WITH IMMINENT DANGER

Victims must also know what to do in case of imminent danger. As previously mentioned, many victims do not plan ahead, so when a crisis occurs in the stalking cycle, they have no idea what to do. If victims have adequately prepared, and many of the items listed above are already in place, dealing with imminent danger will be easier. However, if they have not prepared or have underestimated the safety issues of stalking, they will find themselves in trouble when a crisis occurs.

Having a safe place to go is the first necessity for a victim when danger becomes imminent. Safe places include domestic-violence shelters, residences of family or friends, police stations, and public areas where stalkers are less likely to act out.

If the victim cannot leave her residence to go to a safe place, then she should call law enforcement or 911. A victim who does not have a home phone or cell phone can usually obtain a free phone from law enforcement or from a domestic-violence shelter. These phones are programmed to dial only 911 or local law enforcement. They ensure that the victim can reach law enforcement at any time (National Center for Victims of Crime, Stalking Resource Center website).

## CRISIS INTERVENTION

Some victims describe stalking as "soul-destroying" (Little 1999), and they have significant psychological reactions to it. Others do not. Depending on the nature and extent of their reaction to the event(s), victims can show signs of PTSD (Kamphuis and Emmelkamp 2001). The concept of a "stalking trauma syndrome" has been developed to describe types of PTSD symptomatology (Collins and Wilkas 2001). A counselor needs to be alert to any kind of traumatic emotional evidence that can guide the crisis intervention and short-term goals.

If the victim is not showing signs of PTSD, the counselor may need to help her grasp the possible dangers of stalking. As mentioned earlier, one of the most difficult realities for some victims to accept is that stalking is dangerous and the level of stalking they are experiencing can increase rapidly and put them at risk. During crisis intervention, you need to assess whether the victim is at the level of eventual or imminent danger. The victim may need help understanding the difference between eventual and imminent danger.

At this point, you should also help the victim document the events that have occurred, if she has not already done so. However, if the victim is traumatized from the stalking and shows signs of PTSD, she may not be able to undertake documentation efforts at the time of the crisis intervention. In this case, you may have to try to reduce the victim's PTSD symptoms, while at the same time showing her how to begin to safeguard her life. This complexity can be difficult for both counselor and victim because some of the PTSD symptoms may hamper the victim's ability to move forward, concentrate, and be proactive.

During crisis intervention, it may be necessary, with the victim's consent, to engage a law-enforcement victim advocate to walk her through the process of getting a copy of the laws on stalking, acquiring a restraining order, and reporting the events. The advocate should also give the victim a list of emergency numbers and shelters available, and inform her of her rights. You can be present with the client as she meets with the victim advocate. Victims are frequently overwhelmed with this kind of information and have low retention for it, so you may want to offer to take notes. Doing this frees you from becoming too involved with the law-enforcement aspect of crisis intervention. The victim, in turn, can use you more exclusively for PTSD symptom reduction and emotional support than for dealing with legal aspects.

Crisis intervention can exceed one session. It can, in fact, take a number of sessions over a period of weeks to stabilize the victim and set into motion the needed services and safety plans. You may need to see the client more than once a week during the crisis-intervention period. The risk is just too high to delay helping the victim put into action her safety plan.

Some research has indicated that the best approach for helping stalking victims is an intensive case management program that integrates victim-centered crisis intervention, advocacy, and multi-agency service coordination (Diehl-Spence 2004). This is worth exploring with the victim during the crisis-intervention process.

### Client Concerns

○ May not yet be concerned that stalking is threatening

○ Unaware of interventions that can be used in stalking episodes

○ Fear the stalking will advance

○ Afraid to disclose stalking episodes to family and friends/ employer

○ Not wanting to "make a big deal" of the stalking by reporting it

○ Concern how the stalker acquired personal information

### Secondary Victimizations

○ Loss of work time in order to deal with stalking episodes

○ Cost involved in changing phone numbers or installing new, or more secure, locks

○ Trouble obtaining needed assistance in order to make the stalking stop

○ Encountering law-enforcement officers who are untrained in dealing with stalking

○ Inconvenience of having to use shelter care or other safety plan locations

○ Loss of a sense of safety

### Social/Public Services Needed

○ Victim advocate

○ Law enforcement

○ Magistrate/court services for restraining order

○ Domestic-violence shelter for safe housing

○ Counselor for crisis intervention

○ Ongoing counseling

○ Attorney

○ Relocation services (if needed or applicable)

○ State crime compensation (if victim meets criteria)

○ Local agencies that may help in safeguarding victim's home with locks, etc.

## SHORT-TERM COUNSELING

The victim should be assessed at the outset of short-term counseling. The results of the assessment will guide your short-term counseling objectives. If any PTSD or other anxiety disorders are noted, these will need symptom management, as will any pre-existing mental disorders or patterns of chronic and untreated victimization. Most likely, issues will focus on safety, fear, and regaining a sense of mastery.

Stalking is invasive. At any time, the victim could be viewed by the stalker: He could be watching from across the street, be behind her in the grocery store, or just randomly show up wherever she goes. This provokes feelings of powerlessness as the victim tries to make the episodes stop, but initially cannot. Powerlessness evokes fear and vulnerability. The victim may feel as if "paranoia" is setting in because she is constantly thinking something bad is happening. Insomnia related to anxiety may occur. The fear, paranoia, and vulnerability eventually lead to anger because the stalking is out of her control.

If stalking episodes continue or increase, PTSD symptoms may also increase. Each concurring stalking episode can increase the fear, anxiety, and pain associated with the uncertainty that is manifested in PTSD.

The client may voice anger at the lack of laws against stalking, untrained law enforcement, or perceived lack of support by others. Having to pay for a new phone number, installing locks, or moving can evoke a sense of utter violation. The concern that her employer will lose patience or that safe persons will grow weary of the episodes can become very real. Victims have been fired when stalkers make contact at work. Safe persons sometimes bail out when stalking continues too long or touches too close to home or when stalkers ignore restraining orders.

You should check with the victim during the session about the status of her safety plan. If her support is beginning to unravel, you can intervene emotionally as well as help her strengthen the plan. You can contact the advocate if the victim's needs change. At this stage, group counseling can be added so the victim receives support from others who are being stalked or who have lived through stalking. The group may also acquaint the victim with new approaches in safety planning that can bring her fresh hope.

*Client Concerns*

- ○ Fear of escalating violence
- ○ Fear of retaliation for reporting episodes
- ○ Fear of losing job or safe persons
- ○ Fear of having to go to court to prosecute
- ○ Fear of harm to her children (if applicable)
- ○ Increase in PTSD symptoms and lack of self-management

*Secondary Victimizations*

- ○ Having to continually file episode reports
- ○ Lost time or income from work to file reports and deal with episodes
- ○ Loss of support by employer or safe persons
- ○ Encounters with undertrained law enforcement or poorly enforced stalking laws
- ○ Possible lack of psychological support groups for stalking

*Social/Public Services Needed*

- ○ Victim advocate and court support
- ○ Law enforcement
- ○ Domestic-violence shelter for safe housing
- ○ Other alternatives for safe housing
- ○ Counselor for short-term counseling
- ○ Group counseling for support
- ○ Attorney
- ○ Relocation services (if needed or applicable)
- ○ State crime compensation (if victim meets criteria)

## LONG-TERM COUNSELING

Stalking victims, to date, are not usually seen long term unless the stalker is not captured and the stalking eradicated. If the stalking continues long term, support counseling may also continue. However, if the victim comes to counseling with PTSD symptomatology from previously untreated victimization, what would otherwise be simple PTSD can turn out to be complicated PTSD requiring long-term treatment. Assessment of the victim will clarify this status.

If the stalker had actual physical contact with the victim or threatened her with a weapon, additional counseling may also be required. If the stalking escalated to physical violence (e.g., robbery, assault, or rape), longer counseling may be necessary. Exposure to these kinds of multiple crimes can also be treated with appropriate support groups (e.g., sexual assault groups) as well as individual counseling.

Other comorbid mental illnesses can develop secondary to PTSD or to any stress associated with the victimization. Such mental illnesses include but are not limited to the following:

- Major depression
- Other anxiety disorders
- Psychotic disturbances
- Bipolar disorder
- Personality disorders
- Any disorder of acute or extreme stress, such as a dissociative disorder

### Client Concerns

- Fear of escalating violence
- Fear of continued stalking
- Fear of retaliation for reporting episodes
- Fear of losing job or safe persons due to continuation of stalking
- Fear of having to go to court to prosecute
- Fear of harm to her children (if applicable)
- Increase in PTSD symptoms and lack of management of PTSD

### Secondary Victimization

- Simple PTSD escalating into complicated PTSD
- Having to continually file episode reports

○ Lost time or income from work to file reports and deal with episodes

○ Loss of support by employer or safe persons

○ Encounters with undertrained law enforcement or poorly enforced stalking laws

○ Lack of psychological support groups for stalking

### Social/Public Services Needed

○ Victim advocate and court support

○ Law enforcement

○ Domestic-violence shelter for safe housing

○ Other alternatives for safe housing

○ Counselor for long-term counseling

○ Group counseling for support

○ Attorney

○ Relocation services (if needed or applicable)

○ State crime compensation (if victim meets criteria)

## RECOMMENDED READING

Bates, Lyn. *Safety for Stalking Victims: How to Save Your Privacy, Your Sanity, and Your Life.* Lincoln, NE: Writer's Showcase Press, 2001.

Lissette, Andrea, and Richard Kraus. *Free Yourself from an Abusive Relationship.* Alameda, CA: Hunter House Publishers, 2000.

Meloy, J. Reid, ed. *The Psychology of Stalking: Clinical and Forensic Perspectives.* San Diego, CA: Academic Press, 1998.

Meloy, J. Reid. *Surviving a Stalker: Everything You Need to Know to Keep Yourself Safe.* New York: Marlowe & Company, 1998.

Schaum, Melita, and Karen Parrish. *Stalked: Breaking the Silence on the Crime of Stalking in America.* New York: Simon & Schuster, Inc., 1995.

Wilson, K. J. *When Violence Begins at Home: A Comprehensive Guide to Understanding and Ending Domestic Abuse,* 2nd Edition. Alameda, CA: Hunter House Publishers, 2006.

**RESOURCES**

Working to Halt Online Abuse    ○    www.haltabuse.org

Cyber Angels    ○    www.cyberangels.org

Safety Ed International    ○    www.safetyed.org

The National Center for Victims of Crime, Stalking Resource Center
(202) 467-8700    ○    www.ncvc.org

National Coalition Against Domestic Violence
(202) 544-7358    ○    www.ncadv.org

National Domestic Violence Hotline
(800) 799-SAFE (799-7233)    ○    www.ndvh.org

## Overview of Stalking

*Crisis Intervention:* Unaware that stalking is threatening, afraid to disclose stalking or "make a big deal" about it, concern how stalker acquired personal information, fear of stalking advancing into violence

*Short-Term Counseling:* Fear of escalating violence, retaliation for reporting episodes, losing job or support of safe person, fear of having to go to court to prosecute, fear of harm to her children, concern over increase in PTSD symptoms

*Long-Term Counseling:* Most stalking victims not seen in long-term counseling unless stalker is not captured or stalking does not stop; if robberies/assaults/rapes occurred during stalking, victim may require long-term counseling

*Secondary Victimizations:* Loss of work time in order to deal with stalking episodes, cost involved in changing phone numbers/installing locks, encounters with law enforcement untrained in stalking, inconvenience of having to use shelter care or other safety plan locations

*Social/Public Services Needed:* Victim advocate, law enforcement, magistrate/ court services for restraining order, domestic-violence shelter for safe housing, counselor, attorney, relocation services if needed, state crime compensation if victim meets criteria, local agencies that may help safe proof a victim's home with locks, etc.

## Cyberstalking

Cyberstalking, like stalking, is a terrorizing experience for victims. Many victims do not know the person who is approaching them online. The fear in cyberstalking is not only that a stalker can damage a victim's computer, but also that cyberstalking can become stalking in a very short period of time. The possibility that the crime might become physical leaves its victims in great fear.

○ Currently, more than 80 million adults and 10 million children have access to the Internet in the United States.

○ Estimates of the number of cyberstalking victims in the United States range between tens of thousands and hundreds of thousands. (U.S. Department of Justice Report 1999)

○ Cyberstalking is a growing problem, with undertrained law enforcement and insufficient victim support. (National Center for Victims of Crime, Stalking Resource Center website)

**VICTIM'S STORY**                                           *KIM*

*I began to get e-mails from a guy I did not know. I asked him how he got my e-mail address, and he named someone whom I did not know. He continued to e-mail me, so I asked him to stop. At that point, he got mad.*

*I began to get other e-mails from other men after that, which I assumed were all from him. At first, they were just mean. Then they became sexually explicit. Then they became threatening, telling me he was following me and was going to hurt me. I would get twenty or more a day.*

*He eventually found my phone number and address. I had to move. But he found my next address! I found stuff about me posted all over the Internet. It was sexual stuff and false information. This went on for years. I reported it, but until he really threatened me, it was just a misdemeanor.*

BACKGROUND INFORMATION

Cyberstalking is defined as "use of the Internet, e-mail, or other telecommunication technologies to harass or stalk another person" (National Center for Victims of Crime, Stalking Resource Center website). This is not to be confused with receiving unwanted mass e-mails from companies or individuals, often to referred to as "spamming," although cyberstalkers sometimes use those methods as well. Cyberstalking is calculated and individually focused, so it resembles a form of physical stalking. It should be noted that just as is the case with physical stalking, cyberstalking victims are predominantly female.

Unfortunately, the laws against cyberstalking are not nearly as developed as those against physical stalking. Most states currently require that the victim be directly threatened with violence, otherwise cyberstalking is not seen as a direct threat. There are some states that will act on a threat that is implied, such as that made in an e-mail. Nonetheless, cyberstalking can be a prelude to real stalking, and many victims have seen the results of a stalker moving from their computer to their front door.

In some cases, cyberstalking has replaced physical stalking. It has made it easier to harass victims and given stalkers more anonymous ways of hiding, at least initially. Various anonymizing software programs exist that protect stalkers. These include anonymous remailers that shield the sender's identity and send out e-mails through different servers, which then instantly erase the digital tracking; and Stratfor's Shredder, which overwrites deleted files so they cannot be read and prevents law enforcement from tracking information on a computer. Coupled with a lack of laws and of trained law enforcement, these developments have created a conducive environment for stalking. All that is necessary is a computer and modem and potential victims who hang out in chat rooms and use Internet relay chat lines, message boards, or newsgroups. Most stalking stems from chat room and news group usage.

Like physical stalkers, cyberstalkers have their own techniques. These include the following online activities:

- ○ Sending a computer virus
- ○ Sending mail bombs that shut down the victim's e-mail by overloading it
- ○ Sending obscenities or threats through e-mail
- ○ Posting false statements about the victim in chat rooms the victim frequents
- ○ Setting up webpages with personal information about the victim, and asking readers to contact the victim

○ Pretending in frequented chat rooms that the victim has injured or  victimized the stalker, thus ruining the victim's reputation

(National Center for Victims of Crime, Stalking Resource Center website)

The Stalking Resource Center reported that one of the first cyberstalking episodes to be prosecuted involved a man who solicited the rape of a woman who had rejected him. The man impersonated her in chat rooms and online bulletin boards, where he posted her phone and address and asked to be raped according to her sexual fantasy. Needless to say, various men came to her door in response to her personal ad and wanted to follow through with her supposed request.

Cyber victims have difficulty being taken seriously when they do report to law enforcement. Undertraining in this area among law enforcement has left a gaping hole in victim services. This is due to the fact that some state and federal stalking laws require that the stalker make a direct threat of violence again the victim. However, other laws only require that the alleged stalker's conduct constitute an "implied" threat (National Center for Victims of Crime, Stalking Resource Center website).

Likewise, counselors may have a tendency to dismiss this form of stalking as less threatening than physical stalking. Nevertheless, the effects of cyberstalking can be just as traumatic as they are for other types of crimes. Counselors must be mindful that their treatment approaches are based on a victim's perception and response to victimization. Thus, your intervention and counseling should be based on the victim's reaction to cyberstalking.

## HOW TO PREVENT CYBERSTALKING

A person can take action early in order to curb the beginnings of cyberstalking and prevent future stalking. The Stalking Resource Center advises taking the following actions:

○ If one is using the Internet, choose a gender-neutral screen name (e.g., "Hiker," "Bookworm," "Pasta Lover," or any name that does not reveal whether one is male or female).

○ Do not give a password to anyone, especially not to someone from whom an instant message (IM) has been received.

○ Children should be advised not to give out personal information (e.g., their real names, addresses, or phone numbers).

○ Do not give credit card numbers or other identifying information as proof of age to access or subscribe to a website that is run by an unfamiliar company.

○ Use free e-mail accounts (e.g., Yahoo or Hotmail) to send messages in news groups, subscribe to mailing lists, enter chat rooms, fill out forms, or correspond with unfamiliar individuals.

○ Never give out a primary e-mail address to anyone one does not know, and advise others who have that e-mail address not to give it out to anyone without permission.

○ Check out the chat rooms or news groups that are of interest by silently observing before posting any messages.

○ If participating in these kinds of online activities, only type what would be said in person to someone. Often overdisclosures that would not occur in person are made through e-mail.

○ Never respond to an e-mail from someone who is unfamiliar because the reply verifies the e-mail address.

○ Each month, type one's name into an Internet search engine to see what information, if any, comes up. To have one's name removed from any directory, contact the search engines in which one is listed and request the name be deleted.

(National Center for Victims of Crime, Stalking Resource Center website)

## HOW TO STOP CYBERSTALKING

If cyberstalking has already begun, it may be more difficult to stop. The following actions are suggested:

○ If victims are under eighteen, they should tell their parents or another adult they trust that they are being contacted, harassed, or threatened. Parents and other adults must know what is going on to be able to help and support.

○ If one is getting harassing e-mails, one should get a new account or request a new log-on name and password from the Internet service provider (ISP). One should close one's old account. Learn how to use the filtering capabilities of e-mail programs to block certain e-mail addresses.

○ Save every piece of communication from the cyberstalker. Save all of the header information in e-mails or news group postings. Print a hard copy, and copy the communication to a disk as well, for documentation.

○ Start a log of each communication and take notes to explain the situation in detail. Victims should document how the harassment is affecting them and what steps they are taking to stop it.

○ Once and only once, victims should contact their harasser directly and state in simple, strong, and formal terms to stop contacting them and/or posting anything about them. State that the communications are unwanted and inappropriate and that further action will be taken if they do not stop. E-mail a copy to the ISP system administrator. Save copies of these communications and note them in a log.

○ If victims receive abusive e-mail, they should identify the domain and contact the ISP. Most ISPs have an e-mail address (e.g., abuse@ domain name or postmaster@domain name) that can be used for complaints. If that does not work, victims can usually find contact addresses by going to http://www.networksolutions.com/cgi-bin/ whois/whois and doing a "who is" search for the ISP. If e-mail complaints don't work, make a phone call. Save copies of these communications, and note all contacts in a log.

Keep in mind, however, that this may be just a short-term fix or may even exacerbate the situation if the stalker discovers the ISP has been notified. Under these circumstances, the stalker may attempt to retaliate or pursue stalking off line. Victims need to be aware that, regardless of whether online stalking has stopped, the stalker may have obtained personal information via the Internet or through other sources. Appropriate safety planning is warranted, as described above for stalking.

○ Contact the local police. Report every incident of online abuse and provide the police with copies of evidence. Save copies of any police incident reports, and note each contact to law enforcement in a log. If the stalker lives in a different state from that of the victim, victims should also contact their local office of the FBI (George Mason University Sexual Assault Services 1999).

## CRISIS INTERVENTION

Cyberstalking can be a faceless crime. In many cases, victims never know who their stalkers are, unless the stalkers begin sending photos of themselves. It can be spooky for victims to not know who their stalkers are. At any time, victims are aware that the stalking can move from cyberspace to doorstep. If victims have no idea who their stalkers are, they will also have no idea when the stalkers have landed in their lives.

As in the case of physical stalking, while working with a victim, the counselor may need to help her differentiate between eventual and imminent danger. Because any kind of stalking can move quickly from eventual to imminent, the counselor needs to cover both of these intervention practices with the victim.

As mentioned previously, with the victim's consent, a counselor may want to contact a victim advocate to begin education about cyberstalking and to initiate law-enforcement involvement, as needed. You should also consult the information on physical stalking (presented earlier in this chapter) for use with cyberstalking victims. As described in that section, you can be present with the client as she meets with the victim advocate. Victims are frequently overwhelmed with this kind of information and have low retention of it, so you may want to offer to take notes. Doing this frees you from becoming too involved with the law-enforcement aspect of crisis intervention. The victim, in turn, can use you more exclusively for PTSD symptom reduction and emotional support.

Crisis intervention can exceed one session. It can, in fact, take a number of sessions over the following weeks to stabilize the victim and set into motion the needed services and safety plans. You may need to see the client more than once a week during the crisis-intervention period, because too much is at risk if you delay helping the victim put her safety plan into action.

### Client Concerns

○ Fear of cyberstalking turning into physical stalking or violence

○ Fear of lack of support by agencies or family and friends

○ Fear of loss of computer use, especially in the case of home-based businesses

○ Fear of cyberstalking expanding to families or children

○ Increase in PTSD symptoms

### Secondary Victimizations

○ Lack of professionals trained to handle cyberstalking

○ Law-enforcement agencies under-equipped to track stalkers (if applicable)

○ Poorly enforced cyberstalking laws

○ Lack of community resources, such as support groups

### Social/Public Services Needed

○ Victim advocate/court support

○ Law enforcement

○ Domestic-violence shelter for safe housing (if events escalate)

○ Other alternatives for safe housing

○ Counselor

○ Group counseling for support

○ Attorney

○ Relocation services (if needed or applicable)

○ State crime compensation (if victim meets criteria)

## SHORT-TERM COUNSELING

The assessment(s) you performed can guide the treatment planning for short-term and long-term counseling, if applicable. The client's issues will probably include fear of the unknown, vulnerability, and safety. Knowing that a faceless perpetrator could easily appear at her doorstep, and not even be recognized as such, can leave the victim feeling like a "sitting duck." In addition, if any PTSD or other anxiety disorders were noted, these will need symptom management. Any pre-existing mental disorders or untreated chronic victimization patterns will also need treatment.

Victims of cyberstalking are more likely to feel the crime has been minimized and they are not being taken seriously than are victims of physical stalking. A victim's fear may be heightened if she thinks law enforcement has not intervened adequately. In fact, law enforcement may not have addressed the problem, thus increasing the chance that off-line incidents of violence may occur. Lack of training in law-enforcement agencies can prevent them from understanding how quickly cyberstalking can become physical stalking. In addition, many law-enforcement agencies do not have state-of-the-art technology to track cyberstalkers. Instead, victims are often given simplistic intervention advice, such as "turn off your computer and avoid your e-mail." The ease with which personal information can be obtained online, the lack of security measures offered in cyberspace, and under-equipped law enforcement all place cyberstalking victims at a grave disadvantage.

Victims also may have less extensive social support from friends and family than other crime victims often have. A counselor can check local resources to see if any support groups are available for cyberstalking victims, or the counselor might consider starting one.

### Client Concerns
- Fear of cyberstalking turning into physical stalking or violence
- Fear of lack of support by agencies or family and friends
- Fear of loss of computer use, especially in the case of home-based businesses
- Fear of cyberstalking expanding to families or children
- Increase in PTSD symptoms

### Secondary Victimizations
- Lack of professionals trained to handle cyberstalking
- Law-enforcement agency under-equipped to track stalkers (if applicable)
- Poorly enforced cyberstalking laws
- Lack of community resources, such as support groups

### Social/Public Services Needed
- Victim advocate/court support
- Law enforcement
- Domestic-violence shelter for safe housing (if events escalate)
- Other alternatives for safe housing

○ Counselor for short-term counseling

○ Group counseling for support

○ Attorney

○ Relocation services (if needed or applicable)

○ State crime compensation (if victim meets criteria)

### LONG-TERM COUNSELING

Like stalking victims, cyberstalking victims are not usually seen in long-term counseling unless the stalking does not cease. If the stalking continues, it is conceivable the victim will need support counseling throughout the entire episode.

However, if the victim comes to counseling with PTSD symptomatology from previously untreated victimization, what would otherwise be simple PTSD can turn out to be complicated PTSD, requiring long-term treatment. Assessment of the victim will clarify this status.

Other comorbid mental illnesses can develop secondary to PTSD or to any stress associated with the victimization. Such mental illnesses include, but are not limited to, the following:

○ Major depression

○ Other anxiety disorders

○ Psychotic disturbances

○ Bipolar disorder

○ Personality disorders

○ Any disorder of acute or extreme stress, such as a dissociative disorder

#### *Client Concerns*

○ Fear of cyberstalking turning into physical stalking or violence

○ Fear of lack of support by agencies or family and friends

○ Fear of loss of computer use, especially in the case of home-based businesses

○ Fear of cyberstalking expanding to families or children

○ Increase in PTSD symptoms

### Secondary Victimizations

- ○ Lack of professionals trained in cyberstalking
- ○ Law-enforcement agencies underequipped to track stalkers (if applicable)
- ○ Poorly enforced cyberstalking laws
- ○ Lack of community resources, such as support groups

### Social/Public Services Needed

- ○ Victim advocate/court support
- ○ Law enforcement
- ○ Domestic-violence shelter for safe housing (if events escalate)
- ○ Other alternatives for safe housing
- ○ Counselor for short-term counseling
- ○ Group counseling for support
- ○ Attorney
- ○ Relocation services (if needed or applicable)
- ○ State crime compensation (if victim meets criteria)

## RECOMMENDED READING

Bocij, Paul. *Cyberstalking: Harassment in the Internet Age and How to Protect Your Family.* Westport, CT: Praeger Publishers, 2004.

Meloy, J. Reid. *Violent Attachments.* Northvale, NJ: Aronson Publishers, 1992.

Orion, Doreen. *I Know You Really Love Me: A Psychiatrist's Journal of Erotomania, Stalk, and Obsessive Love.* New York: MacMillian Publishers, 1997.

## RESOURCES

Online Privacy Alliance   ○   www.privacyalliance.com

National Criminal Justice Reference Service Victims Page on Stalking
www.ncjrs.org/vicstlk.htm

Privacy Rights Clearinghouse   ○   www.Privacyrights.org

Network Solutions WHOIS
www.networksolutions.com/ci-bin/whois/whois

### Anti-Stalking
www.antistalking.com
www.stalkingbehavior.com
www.stalkingvictims.com

## Overview of Cyberstalking

*Crisis Intervention:* Not recognizing cyberstalking as threatening, fear of cyberstalking turning into physical stalking or violence, lack of support by agencies and by family and friends, fear of cyberstalking expanding to families or children, increase in PTSD symptoms

*Short-Term Counseling:* Cyberstalking not taken seriously by law enforcement, poorly enforced cyberstalking laws, cannot protect themselves if they don't know who the stalker is, lack of support by friends and family, fear of cyberstalking turning into physical stalking or violence, loss of computer use, increase in PTSD symptoms

*Long-Term Counseling:* Cyberstalking victims are not normally seen in long-term counseling unless the stalker is not caught or the stalking does not stop; need to treat ongoing PTSD symptoms, need to assess for comorbid mental illness that might be complicating the victim's reactions to cyberstalking

*Secondary Victimizations:* Lack of professionals trained about cyberstalking, law enforcement under-equipped to track stalkers, poorly enforced cyberstalking laws, lack of community resources such as support groups

*Social/Public Services Needed:* Victim advocate and court support, law enforcement, domestic-violence shelter for safe housing if events escalate, other alternatives for safe housing, counselor, group counseling, attorney, relocation services if needed, crime compensation if victim meets criteria

## PART II

## Specific
## Victimization
## Categories

# CHAPTER 5

# Property Crime and Robbery

○ In 2001, the number of property offenses and robberies rose to 10,412,395, including burglaries, larceny, motor vehicle theft, and arson offenses.

○ In 2000, 6.1 million households in the United States were vandalized.

○ Close to 50 percent of robberies are committed with firearms.

(National Center for Victims of Crime website)

**VICTIM'S STORY**                                    *MARTINA*

*While in college I was living in a basement apartment. The back door went into an alley; the door lock was loose, and the windows had inadequate locks. My roommates and I continued to ask the landlord to fix these things, but he didn't.*

*One day, while we were in class, someone broke in and took our TV, radios, phone, and CD players. The thief selectively went through our CDs and took the ones he wanted. He took steak from the freezer and food from the pantry. He was obviously there awhile.*

*We begged the landlord again to fix things. All he did was put one more screw in the lock. A week later, while I was sleeping, someone broke the window and came in. When I woke up, he ran out. But he left behind his size-15 shoe print!*

*Shortly thereafter, the nightmares began. I was trembling so much I couldn't fall asleep until 5:00 A.M. And I startled easily. Because I wasn't sleeping, I cut classes. I couldn't concentrate and I felt depressed and weepy. I did horribly that semester, and my parents said I was "lazy." They didn't understand what the break-in did to me. I felt it could happen all over again at any time.*

## Background Information

Robbery is a form of theft and is distinguished from its lesser form, known as larceny, by the presence of threat or force. The FBI Uniform Crime Report defines robbery as the "taking or attempting to take anything of value from the care, custody, or control of a person or persons by force, threat of force, or violence, and/or by putting the victim in fear" (FBI 1996).

Property crimes are often lumped together with burglaries or robberies because, even if a person is robbed on the street, some form of property has been stolen. But property crime can also extend to vandalism or arson in the home. Robbery is also identified by the degree of force used or threatened. Therefore, most armed robberies are considered more forceful and threatening than are robberies without a weapon.

Robberies can occur in a victim's home, on the street, at a business or workplace, on a bus, or in a park. Household burglary ranks among the more serious felony crimes, not only because it involves illegal entry into one's home, but also because a substantial proportion of the violent crimes that occur in the home take place during a burglary incident. Thus, burglary is potentially a far more serious crime than its classification as a property offense indicates. Three types of burglaries exist:

1. Forcible entry: Force is used to gain entry (e.g., breaking a window, breaking a lock on the door)

2. Attempted forcible entry: Force is used as an attempt to gain entry

3. Unlawful entry: Someone without legal right to be on a property gains entry even though force is not used; the probability that a burglary will be reported to the police is related to various aspects of the burglary:

   ○ The kind of intrusion
   ○ Who committed the intrusion
   ○ Whether a household member was present

○ Whether a violent crime was committed during the robbery

○ Whether anything was stolen

○ If something was stolen, the value of the property

(U.S. Dept. of Justice, Office of Justice Programs, Bureau of Justice Statistics 2001)

According to data from the early 1990s, forcible entries were reported almost twice as often as were nonforcible entries. Robberies committed by relatives (including spouses and ex-spouses) were reported to police more frequently than were those committed by strangers. However, not all victims felt robbery in a home by a relative constituted a crime. Robberies in which violent crime was involved were reported in higher numbers than were those in which no personal violence occurred. Unlike victims of rape or other assaults, robbery victims were less likely to know their assailant; in one study, only 26 percent of victims knew the perpetrator (Reiss and Roth 1993).

How likely victims are to report property crimes is most closely related to the emotions they experience. Property crime victims who notify police to so for one of three reasons:

1. They are cognitively motivated by reward and cost considerations

2. They are affectively motivated by the emotions of victimization

3. They are socially motivated by societal concepts of victimization

Of these three, social influence has been shown to be the best predictor of reporting (Greenberg and Beach 2004).

Robbery can be both a property crime and a personal crime. It is likely to result in personal violence and harm because almost 50 percent of robberies are done with the use of a firearm. Studies have shown that robbers who carry a gun are more likely to complete their robberies than robbers who are unarmed. Any resulting gun injuries have a high probability of being lethal; in fact, the fatality rate for gun robberies was found to be ten times the rate of robberies with other weapons (Cook 1991). Guns typically are used to attack certain types of victims (e.g., groups of male teenagers or businessmen) who would be relatively invulnerable if a weapon were not used (Roth 1994). Not surprisingly, robbery is one of the most feared crimes in the United States because of its threat of potential violence. Moreover, robberies outnumber rapes and homicides.

The crimes of robbery and breaking and entering violate more than just a person's domain. Victims of robbery feel violated in much the same way as do rape victims. In both cases, the boundaries of safety are violated. In robbery, victims may suffer because their personal life has been laid bare; their personal possessions and papers have been ransacked, their prized objects or heirlooms have been stolen, and a part of themselves, their history, or heritage has been wiped out in a single incident of violence. Because many robbery victims feel an impending danger and are unable to regain a sense of security, they choose to relocate to other housing. This, for many, is a violation of their homestead and their free choice to maintain a home in a place of their choosing. In the case of aged victims who are forced to leave a home they have lived in for many years, the incident can lead to premature death (Waller 1985).

Compared with many other types of victims, property crime and robbery victims are less likely to know their perpetrator. This creates the anxiety of the "unknown." Victims do not know what to expect in the future from someone they do not know. In addition, almost 50 percent of robberies are committed by more than one perpetrator, which may increase the victim's fear that one of those assailants will try to commit another robbery.

Some aspects of robbery are known to increase PTSD reactions in victims. Face-to-face confrontations, especially those involving a weapon, can evoke severe PTSD reactions. Debriefing and integration are often necessary for store clerks or hotel personnel who have been held at gunpoint, locked in vaults, or tied up and abandoned. Other victims can have similar reactions simply as a result of being faced with a weapon during the event.

Unfortunately, robbery is often downplayed, especially when personal violence does not occur. In fact, robbery is one of the most frequent—yet most neglected—traumas (Waller 1985). As a result, the need robbery victims have for counseling following their victimization is often overlooked. They may be less likely than other trauma victims to be referred to a victim advocate or to be given community resources for follow-up care. This could be one reason only 4 percent of robbery victims in one study were found to have been treated by mental health–care providers (Miller, Cohen, and Wiersema 1996).

Whether or not a victim was actually harmed during a robbery or property crime, that person may suffer from the threat of violence or from the sense of violation as a result of coming home to a house that was robbed. The vision of one's home as a crime scene can cause PTSD reactions in much the same way as experiencing the actual violence can. PTSD symptoms can also be reactivated in robbery victim who were previously victimized. Therefore, all robbery victims need to be assessed for stress reactions, regardless of whether the crime occurred face-to-face.

## Crisis Intervention

The overall loss to robbery victims is quite large. As much as 85 percent of a victim's loss is nonmonetary (Reiss and Roth 1993). These losses include emotional suffering, pain, risk of violence or death, and an overall reduction in quality of life. According to Waller (1985) victims can suffer from crime in six ways:

1. Loss of property and money

2. Personal injury

3. Feelings and behaviors that occur because of PTSD

4. Effects of the crime on family and friends of the victim

5. Inconveniences caused by the state's actions to identify, convict, and hold an offender accountable

6. Lack of access to specialized services for victims

All of these ways a victim can suffer represent issues the victim needs to discuss and process. Early counseling sessions usually focus on issues of loss and the resulting symptoms of PTSD or other stress disorders.

The emotional trauma, or "invisible wound," is the least evident, but often most brutal, effect of the crime. Being robbed or discovering one's home was robbed are terrifying experiences. Most victims react with shock and then fear, not knowing if the criminal has left the premises. They may remain shocked or numb, appear disoriented, and have trouble relaying information to the police. During the crisis, victims may find it difficult to notice everything that was stolen. They focus on an item that was most important to them—even if it is not important to the investigation—such as an heirloom or something of sentimental value that was taken.

Following the loss of items of sentimental value or heirlooms, victims need to engage in a grieving process. Some clinicians do not realize how deeply victims can react to the loss of heirlooms or other property. Sentimental possessions mean much more to a victim than the equivalent cash. For example, the photo of a deceased loved one or a wedding ring is irreplaceable if lost.

The process of grieving must accompany any loss if the victim is to successfully work through the feelings associated with that loss (see the section in Chapter 2 on the grief process). Of course, the length of time it takes to grieve the loss of material property is normally less than that for the loss of a person. Nevertheless, the robbery victim's grief in response to the loss of heirlooms or other attachments must not be overlooked.

If the victim's home was damaged by breaking and rampaging, the victim may feel a heightened degree of fear. Visible signs of violence, such as cushions slit with a knife or bullet holes in the wall, instill a vivid picture of the act of violence in the victim's mind that is especially disturbing (Waller 1985).

It is important for counselors to encourage victims to notify law-enforcement officials. The possibility of recovering stolen possessions without law-enforcement efforts is remote. However, a victim's right to decline to report a crime must be respected. Victims may decide to report it later when they begin to deal with the incident more cognitively or at some time during the counseling process.

After a robbery, when victims feel a sense of personal boundary violation, they will probably want someone to stay with them. Or, they may want to stay with friends or family until the police indicate it is safe for them to return. However, one must be aware of the possibility of secondary injury to the victim by inept caregivers who dismiss the victim's concerns, minimize the crime, or generally do not understand what a victim goes through following a robbery (e.g., saying, "at least it was only material things stolen and not your life").

Some things victims can do at the time of crisis intervention include changing their locks, repairing windows, having security devices installed, and ordering security inspections. They may want to organize a neighborhood watch program (i.e., in which property is marked for identification), if one is not already in place. Some choose to purchase a guard dog for their homes. All these actions assist victims in reestablishing security and safety. However, victims suffering from PTSD may be unable to accomplish all the necessary tasks involved in recuperating from a robbery. A counselor, family member, or victim advocate can assist such victims with all these matters.

### Client Concerns

- ○ Return of stolen possessions
- ○ Inventory of what was stolen
- ○ Wondering if the criminal is off the property
- ○ Wondering if the criminal will return
- ○ Wondering if insurance will cover the stolen articles
- ○ Wondering if anything could have been done to prevent the robbery
- ○ Installing security devices
- ○ Personal safety
- ○ Fear of repeat robberies or robberies as revenge for reporting the incident

### Secondary Victimizations

- ○ Replacement cost of articles stolen
- ○ Loss of articles of sentimental value
- ○ Cost of security devices
- ○ Cost of a gun or other weapon purchased for protection
- ○ Missed time at work
- ○ Insensitive law enforcement, family, and friends
- ○ Cost of relocating; change in lifestyle

### Social/Public Services Needed

- ○ Crime investigator
- ○ Victim advocate
- ○ Inspection of safety and status of house and assessment of reentry possibilities

○ State crime compensation

○ Crisis-intervention counseling

○ Medical treatment (if injured during break-in)

## Short-Term Counseling

Short-term counseling will probably continue to focus on aspects of the victim's safety. Victims may want to replay the crime over and over in their minds in order to cognitively reframe it. They may want to incorporate new elements, such as how different safety devices might have deterred the crime, how they could have interacted with the robber, and what they would do should future victimizations occur.

As the shock and numbness of the event begin to subside, victims' anger will begin to increase. Their anger may be directed at the criminal for the articles stolen, at the criminal-justice system for not apprehending the criminal, at a family member for not securing the house, or at friends for inappropriate responses or lack of support.

You can help the victim direct anger toward positive change—personally as well as in the environment. The victim's anger can be the motivation to start a neighborhood watch or other preventive programs. Anger channeled toward positive action can help to prevent an irrational and potentially dangerous retaliation.

A general sense of not being safe, not having control over one's domain, uncertainty about the future, and fear of possible additional victimizations are normal reactions for victims of robbery. Children can suffer from an increased feeling of not being safe and can be afraid of being left alone at night or entering the room that was robbed.

Victims can harbor harsh feelings about comments made by law-enforcement officials or family regarding "what they could or should have done to prevent the robbery." Such reactions of others can trigger victims' guilt, especially in cases in which face-to-face confrontation occurred and in which children were present or could have been harmed in the robbery.

If victims are involved in a court hearing, they may be unfamiliar with the procedures and may need the assistance of a victim advocate to help them through the process. They may be concerned about retaliation by the criminal and future safety after the criminal is released. Often when the property is retrieved, it is not returned to the victim immediately. It is held for trial, which can mean waiting several months or longer before possession is regained.

### Client Concerns

○ Safety

○ Retaliation

○ Victimization by another criminal

○ Learning how the criminal-justice system operates

○ Return of property

### Secondary Victimizations

○ Dealing with the criminal-justice system

○ Lack of support from family and friends over an extended period of time

○ Increased insurance premiums

○ Unreturned property

○ Missed time from work for court appearances or court-related business

### Social/Public Services Needed

○ Victim advocate

○ Short-term counseling and support programs

○ State crime compensation

○ Neighborly services for safety equipment installation

○ Insurance company contact

○ Assistance with moving (if appropriate)

## Long-Term Counseling

Victims of robbery are usually not seen over a long period, unless additional crimes (e.g., murder, rape, or assault) were also involved or if previous PTSD symptoms were reactivated. An additional reason robbery victims are not usually seen in long-term counseling is that society minimizes the effect of robbery, and therefore many victims are not willing to continue to express distress. Moreover, many areas do not have support groups geared toward robbery victims. As a result, robbery victims are mixed with other types of victims, often rape and assault victims, and they may not feel their issues are adequately addressed in the group.

Unfortunately, robbery victims often feel invalidated in their victimization when they are faced with or hear about more violent types of crime. They naturally want to minimize the robbery they experienced when faced, for example, with a woman weeping about rape. However, serious trauma does occur in robbery cases, and victims can exhibit PTSD symptoms.

If the victim was held at gunpoint, or if someone was murdered during the robbery, long-term counseling intervention is warranted. A homicide survivors' support group is often helpful for a victim who witnessed a murder during the course of a robbery; a rape support program can be helpful if the victim was raped during a robbery. In these specialized support programs, the victim can work not only on violence issues (e.g., rape or murder), but on the issues surrounding the robbery itself. (See the chapters on assault, sexual trauma, and murder.)

## RECOMMENDED READING

Davis, Robert C., Arthur J. Lurigio, and Wesley G. Skogan. *Victims of Crime.* Thousand Oaks, CA: Sage Publishers, 1997.

Feroce, Richard D. *You Can Fight Back: How to Protect Yourself, Your Family, and Your Property against Crime.* Boca Raton, FL: Cool Hand Communications, 1995.

Lein, Laura. *Property Crime Victims: An Analysis of Needs and Services.* Austin, TX: Lyndon B. Johnson School of Public Affairs, 1992.

MacDonald, John Marshall. *Armed Robbery: Offenders and their Victims.* Springfield, IL: Charles C. Thomas Publishing, 1975.

Yager, Jan. *Victims: A Moving Portrait of Crime Victims Including Victims of Homicide, Aggravated Assault, Robbery, Rape & Burglary.* Stamford, CT: Hannacroix Creek Books, 2005.

## RESOURCES

The National Center for Victims of Crime
(202) 467-8700
www.ncvc.org

National Center for PTSD
(802) 296-6300    ○    www.ncptsd.va.gov

National Organization for Victim Assistance
(703) 504-5462    ○    www.trynova.org

***Anti-Stalking Websites***
www.antistalking.com
www.stalkingbehavior.com
www.stalkingvictims.com
www.vaonline.org (victim assistance online)

Crime Victims    ○    www.witnessjustice.org

Privacy Rights Clearinghouse    ○    www.privacyrights.org

## Overview of Robbery

*Crisis Intervention:* Shock, numbness, disorientation, heightened sense of fear, beginning of the grieving process, notification of law-enforcement agencies and insurance companies, boundary violation, changing locks and/or installing safety devices, general safety issues

*Short-Term Counseling:* Safety issues; replaying of event; cognitive reframing of event; anger at systems, self, and the criminal; revenge or retaliation; lack of support from friends

*Long-Term Counseling:* Most victims do not engage in long-term counseling

*Secondary Victimizations:* Cost of replacing stolen articles, loss of nonreplaceable articles of sentimental value, cost of safety devices, increase in insurance premiums, lost wages, insensitive law enforcement or criminal-justice system

*Social/Public Services Needed:* Crime investigator, insurance adjustor, victim advocate, state crime compensation, safety inspection services, crisis intervention counseling, short-term counseling and/or long-term counseling

# CHAPTER 6

# Hate Crimes

A HATE CRIME refers to the victimization of an individual based upon that person's race, religion, national origin, ethnic identification, gender, or sexual orientation (National Center for Victims of Crime website). The crime can take such forms of assault, property damage (e.g., defacing property, arson) robbery, mugging, rape, and murder. In the case of a hate crime, the attack can be characterized in the following ways:

- Specifically directed attacks against certain populations
- Physical, emotional, verbal, or sexual in nature
- Often premeditated
- Influenced by a gang or group emotionalism
- Perpetrated by strangers (e.g., mugging or property crime)

Astonishingly, more than 600 hate groups were active in the United States in 2000 (Southern Poverty Law Center 2000). Some studies indicate that membership in hate organizations (especially those with a racist agenda) is on the rise (Perry 2000). The Internet's capacity to quickly deliver hate messages to new audiences may be one factor accounting for this trend (Blazak 2001).

Hate crimes are seven times more likely than general crimes to involve attacks against a person and are also more likely to involve multiple offenders (Levin 1992–1993). The primary hate crime is assault, followed by property crime (McMahon, West, Lewis, Armstrong, and Conway 2004).

Assaults associated with a hate crime are twice as likely to cause injury and four times as likely to involve hospitalization, compared with general assaults (Levin and McDevitt 1993).

Various theories have been put forth in an attempt to explain why hate crimes are committed. Ethnocentrism refers to a group's proclamation of its culture as the standard against which the cultures of all other groups should be measured. With this perspective, members of a group regard themselves as intellectually, psychologically, and physically superior to others (Atkinson, Morten, and Sue 1998). Other theories focus on the imbalance of power, resources, or opportunities as the key factor leading to rivalry and bias (Walker and Smith 2002). The commonality of these theories seems to be a belief system that allows or encourages hate crime activities.

The Hate Crime Act of 1990 helped to establish hate crimes as a specific form of victimization and created a standardized process for determining if an offense is a hate crime. The FBI (1999) specified that a crime must be motivated by bias to be considered a hate crime and identified five other factors that determine a hate crime. Specifically, the victim of a hate crime

1. belongs to a targeted group

2. has an active role or an advocacy role in the community

3. represents the victim's group in the community

4. has a previous record of victimization

5. has a pattern of visitation to a high-tension community

Four other factors that determine a hate crime are related specifically to the perpetrator. In these cases, the perpetrator

1. makes gestures, comments, or written statements supporting bias

2. shows interest in the crime's impact on the victim

3. is a member of a hate group

4. has a record of previously perpetrating hate crimes

According to the FBI, other considerations when determining if a crime is a hate crime include the following:

○ Significance of the date or place of the crime

○ The community reaction

○ History of similar incidents in the same place or at the same time

○ Presence of items, markings, graffiti, or symbols portraying bias

○ Difference in status between victim and perpetrator

○ History of established animosity between the victim's and perpetrator's respective groups

○ Lack of alternative explanations for the crime
  (FBI 1999)

Unfortunately, the identification of a hate crime depends heavily on how law enforcement interprets the event (Bell 2002). Law enforcement must identify a crime as a hate crime in order for it to be classified and prosecuted as one. The data collection in these types of cases hinges on how the crimes were identified and reported. Therefore, the actual number of hate crimes that occur could be much higher than what is identified and reported.

Because hate crimes can comprise such a broad category of victimization, clinical assistance should be geared to both of the following:

○ The category of victim (e.g., gay, ethnic)

○ The type of victimization (e.g., assault, robbery, rape)

Treatment approaches will differ from victim to victim, depending on the individual's victim type and the nature of the victimization. Therefore, the different categories of hate crime victimization have been broken down in this chapter so as to better help counselors assist these victim populations.

Because hate crime violence is not primarily a category of victimization, but rather refers to a population of victims, you should consult the chapter that covers the type of victimization perpetrated against a victim (e.g., assault, rape, domestic violence), as well as the information listed here about various hate crimes. This chapter covers issues unique to two categories of victims (i.e., for ethnically, racially, or religiously based crimes; gender-based crimes) in the three stages of treatment (i.e., crisis intervention, short-term counseling, and long-term counseling).

## Ethnically, Racially, or Religiously Based Violence

○ 30 to 50 percent of Latina, South Asian, and Korean women have been sexually or physically victimized.

○ In 2002, 50 percent of hate crimes were motivated by race, 18 percent by religion, 17 percent by sexual orientation, 14 percent by ethnicity, and 1 percent by other.

○ 805,513 African Americans were victims of violence in 2001.

○ 637,000 Latinos were victims of violence in 2001.

(National Center for Victims of Crime website)

### VICTIMS' STORIES

The news is full of stories about hate crimes based on the ethnic, racial, or religious identity of the victims. The following are two brief examples:

One afternoon, in the parking lot of a supermarket in California, Eddy Wu, a 23-year-old Chinese-American, was carrying groceries to his car when he was attacked by Robert Page, who stabbed him twice. Chasing Wu into the supermarket, Page stabbed him two more times. Wu suffered serious injuries, including a punctured lung. In his confession, Page, an unemployed musician, said, "I didn't have anything to do when I woke up. No friends were around. It seemed no one wanted to be around me. So I figured, 'What the f—, I'm going to kill me a Chinaman.'" He also said he wanted to kill an Asian because Asians "got all the good jobs." Page pleaded guilty to attempted murder and a hate crime and was sentenced to 11 years (Audit of Violence Against Asian Pacific Americans 1995).

In Colorado, a campus chapter of the American Arab Discrimination Committee received threatening letters and telephone calls when it sought to organize an Arab awareness week. In an apparent attempt to discourage the effort, the president of the chapter was assaulted on campus by two individuals (American-Arab Anti-Discrimination Committee 1996).

### BACKGROUND INFORMATION

Racial violence has long been a part of American history. Arson, bombings, threats, assaults, acts of vandalism, and even murder have been perpetrated simply because of a person's ethnic background or race. While Black history month is a celebration of the contributions made by African-American individuals to American society and culture, it also serves indirectly as a reminder of the racial violence and prejudice that have occurred. Other cultural groups have their own stories of bigotry and separation based on their ethnicity.

What once was called "bigotry" is now also referred to using terms such as "cultural prejudice," "transgenerational hatred," and "ethnoviolence." A single event of violence is referred to as ethnoviolence, but violence on a larger scale is referred to as genocide. The Holocaust and more recent events in Kosovo, Bosnia, Croatia, Nairobi, and Rwanda are examples of mass murder of ethnic groups conducted under the guise of ethnic cleansing. In the case of Rwanda, the term "tribal bloodletting" has been used instead of genocide (Hughes 2004). Some American history books use expressions such as "personal issues within countries" or "civil war" to avoid speaking about genocide and possibly in an attempt to reduce guilt felt regarding the crimes.

Ethnically and racially based crimes are perpetrated by people who are almost invariably prejudiced against more than one group (Nguyen 1992). Racist organizations tend to have a world view (Blee 2002) that does not include embracing the diverse society in which we live. White supremacists groups (e.g., the Ku Klux Klan, Aryan Brotherhood, the Order, the Sword, the Arm of the Lord, and neo-Nazi groups) blatantly display their hatred for selected groups or populations and are sometimes referred to as "domestic terrorists." African Americans have traditionally been the primary target of racial violence (Bishop and Slowikowski 1995).

The FBI's report (1996) on hate crimes indicated that persons engage in these crimes because of their views about race, ethnicity, sexual orientation, or religion. According to the FBI, most hate crimes are motivated by race. Second to racially motivated hate crimes are hate crimes motivated by religious bigotry, with the highest rate of crime against Jews. The third major category of hate crimes are those motivated by a victim's sexual orientation. The fourth category of hate crimes are motivated by a victim's ethnicity or national origin, with the highest percentage directed toward Latinos. Other ethnically targeted groups include Cambodians, Laotians, Koreans, Chinese, Vietnamese, and Iraqis.

Ehrlich (1990) cited the following three types of violations that fuel ethnic violence:

○ Violation of territory/property ("us against them beliefs")

○ Violation of the sacred (values, beliefs, customs)

○ Violation of status (perceived normalcy)

Ethnically and racially based crimes, compared with other types of crimes, are more likely to be perpetrated at random by complete strangers (Levin 1993). While one can try to lessen the odds of victimization in many types of situations, potential victims can do little to avoid the severity of an attack based on ethnicity or race. Moreover, greater societal disruption results from random acts of violence than from violence that is more personally directed (McDevitt 1989).

Whereas other types of assault usually involve one victim and one perpetrator, ethnically and racially based crimes usually involve more than one perpetrator. Many victims of other types of crimes know their perpetrator, but most victims of ethnically and racially based crimes do not (Berk 1990).

According to one study, victims of ethnically and racially based hate crimes suffered 21 percent more adverse psychological and physiological symptoms than did victims of the same crimes that did not involve prejudice. Additionally, the reactions of bystanders contribute significantly to a victim's post-crime psychological adjustment (Denkers 1999). A bystander's nonjudgmental attitude can reinforce a victim's sense of innocence (Frazier 1990), which is important in the recovery process from ethnically and racially based crimes.

Ethnic minorities seek counseling far less frequently than do whites. According to Sue (1998), this trend has been attributed to several factors:

○ Ethnic match (ethnically dissimilar client and therapist)

○ Service match (lack of ethnically specific services)

○ Cognitive match (client and therapist do not think in the same manner)

Because so many "types" of victims could conceivably be listed with respect to ethnic, racial, or religious violence, it is beyond the scope of this chapter to address all possible groups or their specific and unique needs. This chapter on hate crimes is designed to draw attention to this form of victimization in general and to increase awareness among counselors about the general issues these victims face.

In recent years, increasing attention has been given to the need for cultural competence and multicultural counseling skills (Sue 1998). Cultural factors such as race, gender, sexual orientation, national origin, and disability have been found to play a role in the therapist-client relationship and the effectiveness of treatment (Atkinson, Morten, and Sue 1998). Therefore, counselors should be trained in the skills and competencies that allow them to work effectively with individuals from diverse cultural backgrounds.

Nevertheless, the ability of counselors to understand and help clients from different ethnic and racial groups can be hindered by a lack of research in this area (Sue 1999). Most psychological research focuses on members of the mainstream culture. Thus, counselors should research areas that may influence their approach to individuals from other racial and ethnic groups.

Often when counselors think of racial and ethnic groups, they think first of those who have recently migrated to the United States from abroad. However, it is equally important to be sensitive to the diversity that exists within American-born populations. African Americans, Asian Americans, and Native Americans are examples of groups that deserves cultural sensitivity and respect in the counseling setting, but do not always receive it. While some of the challenges immigrants face do not apply to racially and ethnically diverse Americans, the cultural characteristics of all individuals are equally important when it comes to the counselor's effective intervention.

## CRISIS INTERVENTION

Crisis intervention can focus on such issues as reporting, obtaining needed services, communication challenges (if applicable), victim's belief system about outside assistance, stabilization, illegal status (if applicable), and fear about being a racial, cultural, or religious target.

In addition to the issue of a counselor's cultural competence, victims of ethnically, racially, and religiously based hate crimes face problems in reporting abuse and obtaining services. This can be true for victims born in the United States as well as for those from abroad. The victims' beliefs about the crime, law enforcements' proclivity for racial profiling, the reporting process, and effects on other family members are factors that can impede or delay intervention. Members of ethnic, racial, or religious groups that are portrayed negatively in the news media may try to avoid reporting because of a perceived bias about their race, religion, or nationality. These groups include Middle Easterners, especially since 9/11, and African Americans in some cities where racial tensions are high. Some Asian Americans have felt "labeled" since World War II and the Vietnam war.

For some immigrants, communication in English is difficult and inhibits them from making their needs known to authorities or to counselors. This issue is particularly crucial to address during crisis intervention, when victims may be hysterical or in shock. Without an interpreter, they may be unable to receive services or may receive inadequate services.

Stabilization is a core focus of crisis intervention and may need to be attempted even if communication is poor. Educating the victim about available services is important, especially if the individual feels displaced or doubts whether Americans or the American system will be concerned about the victimization. Victims from other countries may underestimate this country's response to immigrants. American-born victims may be aware of other racial, religious, or ethnic groups that have been mistreated or profiled by the system and doubt their ability to obtain effective assistance. Working to bridge any gap in communications is especially important because all aspects of the crisis intervention and counseling process hinge on the ability to communicate.

Some victims may be afraid to report if they have illegal immigration status. Latinos may feel especially targeted for immigration investigations. By showing acceptance to the victim and reinforcing his or her right to proper treatment, you can help the individual reach out and accept services that are available. Many cities now target their services for specific minority groups. For instance, many rape centers have brochures in various languages. Some Latino communities have Latino mental-health counselors, health clinics, and other services.

All phases of the intervention need to deal with the issue of fear. People can more easily face the fact they were victims of a random crime than the idea that they were targeted because they were from a culture, religion, or race the perpetrator hated. Because African Americans have been the primary target of racial hate crimes, they may need specific interventions to deal with the fear of being a walking target. Ethnic and racial victims may be especially fearful of being a target because they are often visually identifiable as ethnically or racially different. This can be due to skin color, facial features, or clothing. Some religious groups can also be identified by their clothing or other items. With no way (or necessarily desire) to conceal their ethnic, racial or religious identity, they feel exposed and vulnerable to repeated acts of violence. This is, of course, the message perpetrators of these crimes want to give to their victims.

### Client Concerns
- Being deported (if in the United States illegally)
- Lack of ability to communicate effectively
- Fear of retaliation to the victim or victim's family
- Fear of lack of concern or fear of not being believed
- Not understanding U.S. laws, systems, or services
- Having to accept laws, systems, or services that are contrary to the victim's cultural or religious beliefs

### Secondary Victimizations
- Prejudice by system caregivers
- Communication problems based on language skills
- Loss of income because of victimization
- Loss of income to send to family members in other countries
- Retaliation, sometimes by the victim's own family, for reporting
- Shame about the victim's culture or country of origin
- Feeling "second class"

### Social/Public Services Needed

The social services used for any other type of victimization can be used with victims of ethnically or racially motivated crimes. Search your community to see what specific ethnic or racial service centers are available for the victim's needs. If specific services are not available, you may want to initiate group therapy with the use of an interpreter. Be aware of services that could inadvertently violate the victim's belief system.

## SHORT-TERM COUNSELING

Short-term counseling may focus on issues carried over from crisis counseling, such as continued communication problems, continued fear of immigration investigation (if applicable), and continued disillusionment with or disbelief in the American system. Additionally, understanding immigration patterns, different coping and reaction styles, cultural dynamics, and the victim's confusion about the counseling process can present challenges for the counselor during short-term counseling.

The counseling process itself can be confusing to some clients if they do not understand your program, theories, or therapeutic approach. This confusion can be compounded if you are unaware of the client's cultural family dynamics, beliefs, or roles. Thus, for you as a counselor from one culture to work effectively with a client from a different culture, it is important to have specific didactic and experiential knowledge about the client's culture. This is particularly important when counseling extends past crisis intervention into short- or long-term counseling. You may need to do research into a client's culture, focusing on such factors as values, belief systems, rituals, ceremonies, superstitions, and family systems. You should become aware of ways in which you might unintentionally violate a client's customs or beliefs.

Ethnically, racially and religiously based crimes include many types of victimization (e.g., rape, arson, assault, robbery, and murder). However, the client's coping style when faced with these crimes can be greatly influenced by that person's ethnicity, race, or religious background. For example, clients from different cultures may exhibit PTSD reactions that are based more on their coping styles than on biological reactions to the trauma. In other cases, culturally diverse clients may have similar PTSD reactions, but differ with respect to how they present their PTSD symptoms or the kinds of social support systems they need.

Members of some groups do not believe in showing emotion readily, no matter what they are feeling. These individuals may have an emotional state what counselors would consider "flat affect," but which is normal for them. For example, Asians are often very composed and show little facial affect. Members of some religious groups also emphasis peaceful exteriors, which can be misread by mainstream culture counselors. Counselors need to keep in mind that the presentation of trauma can be different for people from different cultures.

Some clients may not recognize the victimization as a crime, especially if spousal abuse, elder abuse, or child abuse are not considered violations in their culture. In some cultures, any reporting of domestic violence is seen as an ultimate betrayal because it strips the male head of household of his authority. If you as a counselor do not understand any of these types of cultural factors that may be influencing a client, you will be hindered from providing effective counseling.

Also crucial to working with clients from some ethnic groups is an understanding of "chain migration." In these cases, the extended family in another country pools its limited financial resources to send one member to the United States to find a job. That person sends money to support the relatives and to enable others to immigrate to this country (Buchanan 1979; Laguerre 1984; Seligman 1977). The new arrivals often share living quarters until they can locate separate housing. This is seen heavily in Latino cultures. Moving out of this situation can be particularly important, for instance, if a child is being abused by an extended family member who financed the child's caregiver immigration to the United States. Understanding chain migration can also be important in cases of domestic violence, or in the case of crimes resulting in the loss of money earmarked to be sent back to the native country.

Some ethnic minorities have undergone violence and persecution in their own countries, only to find it here as well. They may feel disillusioned with the "American dream" and be unwilling to reach out for help. Some who do reach out meet with prejudice within the systems of criminal justice, law enforcement, and mental health. Others fear they will be turned in to immigration officials, so they are reluctant to receive services or report a crime.

Many prejudices exist toward ethnic, racial, and religious groups. Most group members are well aware of the stereotypes, negative images, and profiling associated with their group. Because of these prejudices, many do not reach out for help following victimization.

Finally, a lack of English language skills may not allow for formal counseling sessions. It may also inhibit the use of group therapy or other types of therapy normally used with victims of violent crime.

### Client Concerns

- Language barrier that prevents ongoing counseling
- Language barrier that prevents participation in group therapy or other treatment programs

○ Culture does not accept the concept of counseling

○ Financial loss

○ Prejudice from system caregivers

○ Fear of retaliation against self or family

○ Fear that relatives in the native country may insist the victim come home because of victimization in the United States

○ Shame about the culture or country

○ Not understanding U.S. laws, systems, or services

*Secondary Victimizations*

○ Language barrier

○ Lack of insurance or ability to provide for self while recuperating

○ Financial loss

○ Loss of trust in the United States and the "American dream"

○ Being reprimanded by family for reporting

○ Not understanding U.S. laws, systems, or services

*Social/Public Services Needed*

The social services used for any other type of victimization can be used with victims of ethnically, racially, or religiously motivated crimes. Search your community to see what specific ethnic or racial service centers are available for the victim's needs. If specific services are not available, you may want to initiate group therapy with the use of an interpreter. Be aware of services that could violate the victim's belief system.

## LONG-TERM COUNSELING

Long-term counseling may focus on issues carried over from short-term counseling. Additionally, helping clients understand the concept and benefits of long-term counseling and the purpose of group counseling can help keep the victim in the healing process. The counselor's challenges may include developing a therapeutic relationship with other family members as a way of understanding the cultural dynamics and to establish alliances and work toward educating the client and family about the legal system and their role in it.

Understanding the culture of your client is important in ascertaining the possibility of long-term counseling. The concept of counseling itself may be novel for certain populations and may be interpreted as a sign of weakness, an affront to maleness, or lost status as the head of household. Therefore, long-term counseling may not be a realistic option for clients from certain cultures that disapprove of it.

Group counseling with clients from similar cultures who have experienced similar victimizations may prove successful. The language barrier may be less of an obstacle in group sessions than in individual counseling sessions. Another option is to find a counselor from the same ethnic background to run the group. Not only will such a group supply victimization support from other victims, but cultural support as well.

An important aspect to consider in long-term counseling is the possibility of building a solid relationship not only with the victim, but with the family. This strategy is especially important if the client comes from a culture in which the entire family is seen as a unit. Individual identity is not considered as important in many cultures as it is in the American culture. What an American counselor may term "enmeshment" can be viewed as the stable condition of the family unit in another culture. This can be seen in races and cultures in which multiple generations tend to stay and live together. Asian, Latino, African American, Middle Easterner, and Native American families, as well as families from various religious groups, often have several generations living together.

Educating clients from other countries about how American laws are intended to help the victim, how the legal system is designed to catch the perpetrator, and how services equip the victim with the necessary tools for healing can give the client a clearer picture of what each system is designed to provide. Helping victims work through their problems with the legal system can go a long way toward "opening up" the American system to clients who are unfamiliar with it or have become disillusioned with it. In addition, you can train them how best to prevent further victimization, role model acceptance of other cultures, and demonstrate nonprejudicial behavior. Counseling, advocating for, and working with culturally different clients is an affirmative way of getting to know the world around us. Helping these clients through the pain of victimization—whether it be in their new land or within their own country—is a kind hand extended.

### Client Concerns

- ○ Language barrier that prevents ongoing counseling or group counseling
- ○ Culture does not accept the concept of counseling
- ○ Loss of "maleness" or status as head of household if a male victim accepts counseling
- ○ Prejudices from system caregivers and criminal-justice system
- ○ If money to be sent to family in native country is stolen, there are financial losses to both the family here and abroad
- ○ Fear of retaliation against self or family
- ○ Not understanding U.S. laws, systems, or services
- ○ Lack of transportation to stay involved in long-term counseling

### Secondary Victimizations

- ○ Language barrier
- ○ Lack of insurance or ability to provide for self while recuperating
- ○ Financial loss
- ○ Loss of trust in the United States and the "American dream"
- ○ Being reprimanded by family for reporting
- ○ Time off work and additional financial loss for counseling sessions and court appearances

### Social/Public Services Needed

The social services used for any other type of victimization can be used with victims of ethnically or racially motivated crimes. Search your community to see what specific ethnic or racial service centers are available for the victim's needs. If specific services are not available, you may want to initiate group therapy with the use of an interpreter. Be aware of services that could violate the victim's belief system.

#### RECOMMENDED READING

Carter, Robert. *Hand Book of Racial-Cultural Psychology and Counseling, Theory & Research.* New York: John Wiley & Sons, 2005.

Hamm, M. *American Skinheads: The Criminology and Control of Hate Crime.* Westport, CT: Praeger Publishers, 1993.

Kivel, Paul, and Allan Creighton with the Oakland Men's Project. *Making the Peace: A 15-Session Violence Prevention Curriculum for Young People.* Alameda, CA: Hunter House Publishers, 1997.

Perlmutter, Phillip. *Legacy of Hate: A Short History of Ethnic, Religious, & Racial Prejudice in America.* Armonk, NY: M.E. Sharpe, Inc., 1999.

Ponterotto, Joseph. *Handbook of Multicultural Counseling.* Thousand Oaks: CA: Sage Publishing, 2001.

Suall, I., and T. Halpern. *Young Nazi Killers: The Rising Skinhead Danger.* New York: Anti-Defamation League, 1993.

Sue, Derald Wing, and David Sue. *Counseling the Culturally Different: Theory and Practice.* New York: John Wiley & Sons, 1999.

## RESOURCES

National Institute against Prejudice and Violence    ○    (410) 830-5170

National Hate Crime Hotline    ○    (206) 350-HATE (350-4283)

The National Center for Victims of Crime
(202) 467-8700    ○    www.ncvc.org

Male Survivors    ○    www.malesurvivor.org

The National Center for PTSD
(802) 296-6300    ○    www.ncptsd.va.gov

### Native-American Abuse
www.tribalresourcecenter.org

### African-American Abuse
www.dvinstitute.org

### Latino Abuse
www.justicewomen.com
www.dvalianaza.org

### Asian-American Abuse
www.atask.org
www.aworc.org

## Overview of Ethnically,
## Racially, and Religiously Based Violence

*Crisis Intervention:* Affective, cognitive, and behavioral constriction; having witnessed destruction or genocide in the victim's native country (if applicable); relocation to a different culture (if applicable); difficulty in reporting a crime because of language barriers (if applicable); afraid of deportation (if applicable), fear about being a racial or cultural target

*Short-Term Counseling:* May be disillusioned with America because of crime; feeling targeted because the victim is perceived as different; does not understand U.S. laws, systems, and services (if applicable); coping mechanisms influenced by cultural belief system

*Long-Term Counseling:* May not engage in long-term counseling because of cultural beliefs; bridge relationship between victim and counselor by involving extended family members; education about laws, systems, and services

*Secondary Victimizations:* Abuse ignored because the victim is not American (if applicable), limited community resources available in different languages (if applicable), prejudice by resource providers and systems, financial losses because of lost work time

*Social/Public Services Needed:* The same social services that would apply to anyone suffering particular types of victimization (see charts for robbery, sexual abuse, homicide, and other crimes), interpreter and group counseling geared toward a particular ethnic population might be needed

## Gender-Based Violence

- ○ Of the almost 10,000 hate crime incidents reported in 2001, 14 percent were motivated by sexual orientation.
- ○ 2,210 crimes were committed against gays and lesbians in 2001.
- ○ The gay murder rate increased by 50 percent between 1998 and 2000.
  (FBI 2002)

## VICTIM'S STORY                                                    *LORI*

*I am gay. One night a lesbian friend and I were walking to a club, when a car with two men stopped and offered us a ride. I had seen these men at the club, so I assumed they were gay too. So we said yes.*

*Once inside the car, the men began to come on to us. At first, I thought it was joke because they obviously knew we were gay since they had seen us at the gay club. But they indicated they were not gay. They pulled off into a wooded area and raped us. They said they would turn us around from our gay lifestyles.*

*I felt really bad for my friend because she was a virgin. All I could think of was what this was doing to her emotionally.*

### BACKGROUND INFORMATION

In this section, we look at the role gender can play in hate crime victimization. In fact, crimes against women are the most prevalent gender-related crimes and, in some cases, are even socially accepted (Franklin, 2000). In this book, the issues of female assault, rape, and other crimes against women are covered in the chapters on domestic violence, sexual assault, and other victimization groupings because the primary victim in those categories are females. Be aware, however, that lesbians can be as much a focus of hate crimes as are gay men.

This chapter focuses on gender violence targeted at the gay, lesbian, and transgender population. In a society that is predominantly heterosexual, the gay population has been stigmatized for a number of reasons:

○ Perceived as a violation of gender norms

○ Perceived as deviating from masculine or feminine characteristics

○ Condemnation of those who do not conform to gender roles regardless of their actual sexual orientation
 (Herek 1990)

Our society clearly values heterosexuality and is less tolerant of relationships that deviate from that orientation. For some offenders, the belief that America is—and should be—primarily heterosexual is the primary motivation for gay abuse.

Gays have been abused in every conceivable manner, and this abuse is notably widespread. Even so, the homicide rate for gays and lesbians has only recently been recorded. For years, the incidence of violence against gays was probably severely underestimated. If police were unaware a homicide victim was gay, the record would not indicate a the victim's sexual orientation or that the crime may have been hate motivated. Documentation in this area is still poor.

The perpetrators of gender hate crimes often believe that society will protect them from being punished for their acts because society attaches such a stigma to the victim. Many hate crimes are committed by thrill-seeking youth who are acting out of boredom, seeking fun, or trying to feel powerful (Levin and McDevitt 1993). Violence toward gays has long been seen as a source of recreation or amusement by youth. Engaging in this type of crime is viewed as a way to increase status with peers or valid maleness, and it is seen as carrying little risk of injury and minimal risk of arrest because gays rarely report an offense.

Youth offenders are not the only perpetrators of violence against gays. Other types include reactionists, who try to protect their perceived resources from intruders by acts of violence, and "mission offenders," who aim to please to a higher authority by eradicating an inferior group (Levin and McDevitt 1993). Gay violence is often more socially accepted than other types of hate crimes and prosecution is usually weak (Anderson 1993).

Abuse of gays is not new. Gays have been a target of abuse for centuries. Gays were singled out by the Nazis for persecution and murder. In concentration camps, homosexuals were often assigned the most hideous work details and were subjected to medical experiments, including castration, hormone injections, mutilation, and exposure (Adam 1987; Plant 1986). Even today, it is noteworthy that attacks on gays are usually extremely brutal in comparison with similar attacks on non-gays. For example, whereas as a non-gay person might be simply shot, a gay person would be more likely to be stabbed a dozen or more times, mutilated, and strangled. Thus, hate crimes based on sexual orientation are associated with greater psychological distress than are crimes not motivated by hate (Herek, Gillis, and Cogan 1999).

These types of hate crimes tend to be perpetrated by strangers. This may be because it is easier to maintain stereotypes among strangers. If the abuser feels a greater emotional distance from the victim, it may be easier to physically act out hostilities (Berk 1990). Nevertheless, indications are that gay-on-gay violence is also increasing.

In the past ten years, incidents of gay violence have drawn considerable media attention. In 1992, Allen Schindler was murdered by a fellow navy member. In 1993, Brandon Teena was murdered after identifying a girl's rapist. On the *Jenny Jones Show*, in 1995, Scott Amedure admitted to a sexual attraction to another man, and that man later hunted him down and killed him. The renowned case of Matthew Shepherd's murder occurred in 1998, when he was beaten to death. After Regan Wolf, a lesbian, was attacked twice by men and beaten, she was accused by the police of faking her own beating.

Gays are often blamed for their own physical and sexual victimization. Notably, gay victims associate their gay identity with a heightened sense of vulnerability. This can challenge the victim's sense of self (Garnets, Herek, and Levy 1992) and increase issues of self-blame. Compared with general crime victims, counselors can expect to find higher levels of depression, anxiety, anger, and PSTD in gay victims (Herek et al. 1997).

In the past, gays often struggled more after being victimized than did other types of victims because they had fewer social supports. Being blamed for their own victimization isolated them from social services, community support, pastoral counseling, and other types of services, which in turn amplified guilt and self-blame. In recent years, the gay community has become increasingly active in providing its own services for victimization. Gay victims and their advocates or counselors should check what services are currently offered through the gay community for victims of violence.

## HIV/AIDS

Many victims suffer double jeopardy in one form or another. As was pointed out above, some become the objects of violence because they are both female and gay. In the case of gender-based crime, double jeopardy also occurs as a result of prejudice and crime directed at individuals who also have AIDS or are HIV-positive. AIDS, of course, is not relegated to gays, but even those with AIDS who are not gay can suffer prejudice or crime through association.

It is not clear whether the AIDS epidemic actually generated an increase in hate and violence toward gays. Some consider AIDS not so much a cause of anti-gay sentiment as a renewed justification for expressions of pre-existing prejudices. Gays and lesbians have simply become more visible through the AIDS epidemic.

In the early 1980s, society's reaction to AIDS was notably homophobic. The fear associated with the disease led to the blaming of the gay community, along with a feeling of entitlement to punish gays for violating sexual norms. Persons with HIV/AIDS became targets of violence because of their disease. This violence is linked to assumptions made about the AIDS patient's morality, sexuality, and contagion. Much like lepers in former days, AIDS patients were shunned based on misinformation about the contagiousness of the disease. Anger was directed at the "drain on society" associated with their care. Patients with other major diseases, such as cancer or heart disease, that were not associated with sexual orientation, did not face the same discrimination.

## CRISIS INTERVENTION

The focus of crisis intervention may include reduced social support; increased self-blame; higher levels of depression, anxiety, and PTSD; perceived participation in or compliance with the victimization; and partner recognition issues.

As previously mentioned, because gays are often blamed for their own physical and sexual victimization, their gay identity can add a heightened sense of vulnerability, which challenges the victim's sense of self and may increase self-blame. During crisis intervention, counselors may need to work not only with the victims' fear and vulnerability, but also with their self-constructs that have been damaged by the violence. Because depression, anxiety, anger, and PSTD may be higher in gay victims than other victims, stabilization and symptom management may play a big role in crisis intervention.

Additionally, counselors need to be aware that significant issues surround "coming out" (self-identification as being gay) for gays and lesbians. Being victims of a crime may force them into a position of "coming out" sooner than they otherwise would have, or may put them in a vulnerable position once their gayness is disclosed. Issues of vulnerability and forced "coming out" may be presented during crisis intervention, as well as other normal traumatic reactions to violence.

Gay victims often closet not only their gay lifestyle, but also their victimization. During sexual assaults, lesbians may be targeted directly for abuse because they are lesbians. A lesbian also may be raped "opportunistically" when an abuser inadvertently discovers during another type of crime that she is lesbian and sees her is an open target because she is not under the protection of a man (Garnets, Herek, and Levy 1990). On the other hand, even among gays, sexual assault against a man is generally considered impossible without consent. Counselors need to be sensitive to their clients' needs to protect their sexual orientation as part of their overall victimization history.

Gay victims may struggle not only with accepting that a rape occurred, but that it happened at all. If they did not fight or struggle, they may question their own willing participation or compliance with the violence. They may associate their rape as punishment for their gay lifestyle. (See Chapter 10 for more information about male rape.)

Painful to gay victims can be the issue of how their significant others are treated during the aftermath of victimization. The significant others of gay victims are not always treated as affected family members, as they would be in other types of crimes. Unlike immediate family members, significant others may be denied visitation in the emergency room or hospital room and may not be recognized for family treatment or therapy by counselors, social workers, or victim-assistance agencies.

Likewise, legal protection and legal recognition do not always exist for the gay population. For example, housing, employment, and other services may be overlooked or unavailable because gay relationships do not hold legal status. These kinds of issues arise during crisis intervention or as secondary victimizations in short- or long-term counseling. Confidentiality is especially important when working with gay clients because of the many ramifications that disclosure of sexual orientation can bring (e.g., loss of job, home, or children; legal prosecution).

As a counselor, you need to examine your own feelings, stereotypes, and bias about homosexuality, lesbianism, and transgenderism (Cheng 2002). If you are not comfortable with same-gender relationships, refer your clients elsewhere. The potential exists for damaging a victim further if transferred attitudes and prejudices intrude during crisis intervention or therapy. Keeping up with current information about gay identity and related mental-health issues is important.

### Client Concerns

- Disclosure of sexual orientation
- More abuse after disclosure of sexual orientation
- For male sexual abuse victims, concern about not preventing or fighting off offender
- For female sexual abuse victims, being raped by opportunists based on their lesbianism

### Secondary Victimizations

- Significant others not included in counseling or legal and medical proceedings
- Lack of adequate social services available to gays
- Prejudiced social service providers or criminal-justice system
- Victim blaming by systems designed to help
- Removal of natural children from custody after a forced "coming out"
- Committing suicide after being victimized for being gay
- Lack of support from family because of sexual preference
- Fear of disclosing victimization and how disclosure will affect gay community

### Social/Public Services Needed

The social services used for any other type of victimization can be used for gay victims. However, in addition, you may check into group and family therapy offered through the gay community.

## SHORT-TERM COUNSELING

Your assessment outcomes will assist you in determining the short-term counseling focus, especially as related to increased risk for depression, anxiety, and PTSD symptoms. It is likely that the issues from crisis intervention will continue to be the focus in short-term counseling. Therefore, short-term counseling needs to address the victim's feelings about having been targeted simply on account of sexual orientation. In addition, if the crime led to repeat incidents in the community, the victim may struggle with guilt about "causing" additional violence to other gays.

Counseling needs to address not only the violence and corresponding PTSD reactions, but also issues of social hostility, isolation, stigmatization, and oppression related to gender-based violence. You can help the victim develop a network of supportive friends and contact available services to deal with these issues.

Counselors need to be aware that, because of higher substance abuse rates among gays than non-gays (Benshoff and Janikowski 2000), and because PTSD is often associated with substance use, it may be necessary to evaluate the victim for any addictions or the beginning maladaptive use of substances to medicate the victim's anxiety.

If victims have HIV/AIDS—whether or not they were targeted because of their disease—counseling may need to include appropriate health resources or grief counseling to face issues about diminished health or dying.

Family psycho-educational issues are important. A victim's significant other and family members need to understand what the victim is feeling in order to provide support and promote post-victimization healing. However, do not overlook the need significant others themselves may have to express feelings about the crime. They are an overlooked population of secondary victims who have feelings not only about the crime, but also about why the victim was targeted. Significant others may need their own individual counseling or counseling referrals to deal with their exposure as secondary victims.

Those targeted for gay violence often feel exposed when their sexual orientation is revealed, so they limit contact with the rest of the world, which increases feelings of isolation. Men may be seen as powerless and called effeminate names, while women may be stereotyped as powerful and called "dykes." If these dynamics are ongoing, they may produce overwhelming feelings of anger in the victim and impair their ability to recover. Counselors need to help victims reduce isolation and face feelings of powerlessness.

It is important during counseling to help victims direct their anger in constructive ways. Channeling anger into activities such as lobbying against anti-gay violence or helping other victims can assist in reducing anger and can empower the victim. Self-defense classes can help victims reconstruct some avenues for safety in their life.

### Client Concerns

○ Disclosure of sexual orientation

○ More abuse after disclosure of sexual orientation

○ Overwhelming feelings of anger

○ For male sexual abuse victims, concern about not preventing or fighting off offender

○ For female sexual abuse victims, being raped by opportunists based on their lesbianism

### Secondary Victimizations

○ Fear of disclosing victimization and how disclosure will affect gay community

○ Social hostility, stigmatization, isolation

○ The effects of the crime on relationships

○ Prejudiced social-services, criminal-justice, and other systems designed to help

○ Significant others not included in counseling or legal and medical procedures

○ Youth (and others) attempting or committing suicide after the incident

○ Having to modify behavior and freedom of movement to reduce risk of further attacks

### Social/Public Services

The social services used for any other type of victimization can be used for gay victims. However, in addition, you may check into counseling, family therapy, support groups, and other services that may be available through the gay community.

## LONG-TERM COUNSELING

Just as understanding your client's culture is important in the case of ethnically and racially motivated violence, it is important to understand the social/sexual culture of your client in this long-term counseling context. As mentioned previously, because gays have an increased risk of PTSD and substance abuse, their long-term counseling needs to reflect these issues. A likely ongoing issue is victims' feelings of being targeted because of their sexual orientation and the risk they perceive they may cause to other gay persons. Educating them to understand their victimization in a social context will help them see that the crime was based on a global hatred for gays rather than on them as personal targets (Garnets et al. 1990). To this end, the gay community may have literature that can help your client understand the social issues surrounding gay violence.

An important aspect of a gay person's trauma is the issue of internalized violence. If a victim felt forced into "coming out" only because of the victimization, feelings of exposure, vulnerability, lack of control, fear of homophobia, and alienation may be increased. During long-term counseling, you may need to separate the experience of the victimization from the coming-out experience and process these issues separately (Garnets et al. 1990).

The trauma associated with the violence may become internalized in a way that associates it with the victim's homosexuality. This can increase the psychosocial problems already associated in the victim's mind with being gay, and can inhibit involvement in the gay community, where the person could get help, support, and services (Garnets et al. 1990). This can also produce family problems if the family members were unaware the victim is gay. Family counseling may be necessary, as well. In addition, tension in the relationship with the victim's significant other may need to be addressed.

For those who are gay and living with AIDS, a secondary victimization occurs when they have to contend not only with facing diminished health or death, but also with the fear, reprisal, and prejudice of the community, and possibly their medical caregivers. This can increase long-term depression, isolation, and withdrawal from others.

Assisting gay victims with family and social dynamics and helping them find constructive avenues for change with respect to how the world reacts to violence can improve their self-image and give them a greater sense of control over their lives. The community also benefits when former victims become front-runners in prevention programming.

### Client Concerns

○ Feelings of being singled out for victimization because of sexual orientation

○ Anger over victimization

○ More abuse after disclosure of sexual orientation

○ Vulnerability, lack of safety and control

### Secondary Victimizations

○ How the violence will affect current relationships

○ The effects of "coming out" on the family

○ Prejudice of medical, legal, and psychological systems

○ HIV/AIDS medical needs and prejudices

### Social/Public Services

The social services used for any other type of victimization can be used for gay victims. However, in addition, you may check into counseling, family therapy, and social services that may be available through the gay community.

#### RECOMMENDED READING

The American Social Health Association. *STD Counseling and Treatment Guide.* Triangle Park, NC: ASHA, 1995.

Creighton, Allan, with Paul Kivel. *Helping Teens Stop Violence: A Practical Guide for Counselors, Educators, and Parents.* Alameda, CA: Hunter House Publishers, 1992.

Dolan, Matthew. *The Hepatitis C Handbook.* Berkeley, CA: North Atlantic Books, 1999.

Evosevich, J. M., and M. Avriette. *The Gay and Lesbian Psychotherapy Treatment Planner.* New York: John Wiley & Sons, 2000.

Garnets, L., G. M. Herek, and B. Levy. *Violence and Victimization of Lesbians and Gay Men: Mental Health Consequences.* Newbury Park, CA: Sage, 1992.

Grodeck, Brett, and Daniel S. Berger. *The First Year—HIV: An Essential Guide For the Newly Diagnosed.* New York: Marlowe & Company, 2003.

Herek, G., and K. Berrill. *Hate Crimes: Confronting Violence Against Lesbians and Gay Men.* Newbury Park, CA: Sage, 2000.

Hoffman, Mary Ann. *Counseling Clients with HIV Disease: Assessment, Intervention and Prevention.* New York: Guilford Press, 1996.

Kivel, Paul, and Allan Creighton with the Oakland Men's Project. *Making the Peace: A 15-Session Violence Prevention Curriculum for Young People*. Alameda, CA: Hunter House Publishers, 1997.

Levin, J., and J. McDevitt. *Hate Crimes: The Rising Tide of Bigotry and Bloodshed*. New York: Plenum, 1993.

Wilson, K. J. *When Violence Begins at Home: A Comprehensive Guide to Understanding and Ending Domestic Abuse*, 2nd Edition. Alameda, CA: Hunter House Publishers, 2006.

## RESOURCES

National Gay & Lesbian Task Force
(202) 332-6483   ○   www.thetaskforce.org

The Prejudice Institute
www.prejudiceinstitute.org

Gay and Lesbian National Hotline
www.glng.org

Gay and Lesbian Alliance Against Defamation
www.glaad.org

National Center for Lesbian Rights
www.nclrights.org

The National Center for PTSD
(802) 296-6300   ○   www.ncptsd.va.gov

Trauma-Info Pages
www.trauma-pages.com

Male Survivor
www.malesurvivor.org

The National Center for Victims of Crime
(202) 467-8700   ○   www.ncvc.org

National Organization for Victim Assistance
www.trynova.org

Sexual Abuse of Males
www.jimhopper.com

Men Against Sexual Violence
www.menagainstsexualviolence.org

## Overview of Gender-Based Violence

*Crisis Intervention:* Targeted because different, targeted because of sexual orientation, fear, guilt, being blamed for one's own victimization

*Short-Term Counseling:* Sexual orientation confusion (if applicable), forced "coming out," PTSD reactions, isolation, stigmatization, oppression

*Long-Term Counseling Issues:* Understanding victimization in a social context, lack of control, homophobia, alienation, psychosocial aspects of homosexuality, PTSD reactions, personal safety, self-defense

*Secondary Victimizations:* Society's homophobia, abuse ignored, feeling forced to change personal habits (e.g., way of dressing), loss of freedom of movement, significant others not included in social services and counseling, prejudice by systems providing care

*Social/Public Services Needed:* The same types of services that would be offered to other victims of that particular crime would be offered to victims of gender-based crimes (see chapters on robbery, sexual abuse, homicide). In addition, you may want to find out what services are offered by the gay community

# CHAPTER 7

# Domestic Violence

○ Nearly 1 in 4 American women between the ages of 18 and 65 has experienced domestic violence. (Body Shop 1998)

○ In 1996, nearly one million women and 150,000 men were victims of intimate violence. (Greenfield et al. 1998)

○ Women who had protection orders in place were 80 percent less likely to be physically assaulted in the year after their attack than were women without protection orders.

○ The strongest risk factors for femicide are a perpetrator's access to a gun, a previous threat with a weapon, a stepchild in the home, and an estrangement.

○ Almost 20 percent of homeless populations are victims of domestic violence.

(National Center for Victims of Crime website)

**VICTIM'S STORY**                                    *ROSE*

*I tried to get my boyfriend to move out of my house, and he refused to move. He insisted things would work out with us. But when I insisted, he became incredibly angry. I called 911 and asked for assistance.*

*He went to my bedroom and retrieved my gun and put the muzzle in his mouth. I tried to reason with him. He slammed me into the wall and tried to strangle me. He then punched me in the temple three times, until I fainted.*

*When I woke up, and he was assured I was conscious enough, he put
the gun under his chin and fired it. He collapsed dead from one shot in front
of me and our four-year-old daughter.*

## Background Information

The National Center for Victims of Crime defines domestic violence as the
willful intimidation, assault, battery, sexual assault, or other abusive behavior perpetrated by one family member, household member, or intimate
partner against another. Some states have expanded this to include those
who are dating.

The women's movement of the 1970s brought to light the issue of
domestic violence. The first domestic-violence shelter was established in
1974. This new understanding helped many acknowledge that domestic
violence touches persons of every socioeconomic group, race, religion, and
educational status.

Today, domestic violence and its impact on the family, children, and
justice system are widely known. In fact, domestic violence was instrumental in spawning the development of victimology as a field of study and
trauma as a recognized field within psychology. As a result of these milestones, domestic-violence shelters and programs now exist in almost every
city and town across the country, offering emotional, financial, vocational,
legal, and supportive services to survivors and their children.

Domestic-violence laws continue to evolve and are providing increasing amounts of coverage for victims. These laws differ from state to state,
so counselors should check the laws in their area. Many states now have
mandatory arrest laws for domestic violence. Others have added a system
of vertical prosecution, whereby specifically trained prosecutors handle
cases from filing through prosecution. Doctors, nurses, and other medical
health practitioners are required to report suspected battering in some
states (Meadows 2001).

In some (but not all) states, the law enforcement of domestic violence
is now characterized by the following:

○ Police are mandated to arrest batterers, even if the victim does not
press charges or recants her story.

○ Abusers who have been issued restraining orders are included in a restraining order registration system that law enforcement can check.

○ Batterers who have restraining orders cannot own or possess a firearm during the duration of the order.

○ Prison sentences have been increased for domestic violence, as well as fines.

○ The visitation rights of an abuser can be cut off, supervised, or restricted when a restraining order is in effect (Meadows 2001).

In these states, if the victim refuses to testify, the testimony of the law-enforcement officer who was at the scene can still result in jail time or forced counseling for the abuser. Moreover, court advocates provided through the domestic-violence agencies who accompany the victim to court can answer questions during proceedings if asked by the judge, and the advocate can advise the victim how to answer. These promptings help keep the legal proceedings moving toward some form of intervention for the victim and legal recourse against the abuser.

In other states, however, a victim can still be forced to press charges and to testify at various stages of the process against the person with whom they live and who beats her on a regular basis. This testimony is obviously dangerous for the victim. Unfortunately, if she fails to appear at a hearing or drops the charges, she can be accused of making a false report or wasting the system's time. Victims who do follow through with the required legal procedures often find their charges are not taken seriously, especially in small towns where domestic-violence laws are lenient, or they find the system is reluctant to punish the abuser for what is often referred to as a "family problem."

Domestic violence can be particularly distressing to victims because it is perpetrated by someone they love. Hearth and home are supposed to be associated with safety and protection, but domestic violence is about power and control. Abusers typically have an abnormal degree of dependence on the women they abuse. This dependency often conflicts with their own self-image and results in loss of control and lack of emotional intimacy with the very women on whom they are dependent. Abusers have higher than normal levels of suspicion, paranoia, jealousy, possessiveness, hostility, depression, anxiety, blaming, and inability to take responsibility for their violence (Vaselle-Augenstein and Ehrlich 1993).

Society has had a double standard with respect to violence in the home and out of the home. On the one hand, violence against a stranger is considered an assault. Violence committed against a family member, on the other hand, is considered a family argument. While violence against a stranger usually ends in an arrest and the perpetrator is charged with assault and battery, a family member who commits violence is simply told to "cool down." For many years, the message to families was that battering was permitted within the family structure. Over time, programs, services, and laws have been developed to correct this imbalance. Laws now apply equally to family members and strangers.

Domestic violence incorporates any or all of the following types of abuse:

- *Psychological abuse:* Intimidating, threatening harm, harassing, harming pets or property in order to frighten or stop the victim from leaving

- *Emotional abuse:* Undermining the victim's self-image by belittling, criticizing, verbally attacking, demeaning

- *Sexual abuse:* Coercing or forcing sexual contact, including forced acts of perversion, rape (including marital), unprotected sex, pornography, and sex with others

- *Physical abuse:* Injuring the victim by slapping, hitting, kicking, tying up, punching
  (Domestic Violence Information Manual 1991)

Domestic violence can be understood in terms of the cycle of violence. This concept can be applied to any type of personal physical violence in which the victim and perpetrator are known to each other (e.g., child and parent, elder and caregiver).

The cycle of violence (see Figure 7.1) begins with an escalation of tension by the perpetrator. Victims can recognize the signs of impending violence by such abuser behaviors as hitting, blaming, demanding, and yelling. The abuser excuses his actions by saying the woman's behavior forced him

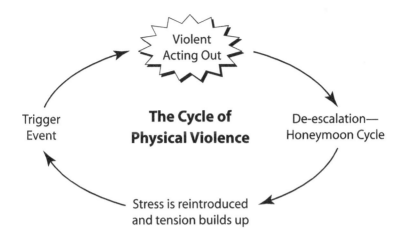

**FIGURE 7.1.** The cycle of physical violence

to become violent. The abuser may suggest the victim did not do something correctly, such as cleaning or child rearing, or that she responded to him in a way he did not like. His reaction sets into motion the actual violent event: hitting, punching, tearing, biting, tying up, beating, kicking, name calling, and sometimes murder.

Victims often have an "odd" reaction to the explosion of violent behavior. They have said they actually feel relief once the violent act is over because they know that after the built-up tension has exploded, the abuser will once again de-escalate. The victims are often correct. The abuser does begin to calm down, and following his de-escalation, may apologize and promise to never become violent again—or any other promise he knows the victim wants to hear. This is referred to as the "honeymoon cycle" because the abuser promises the victim a future with no more violence and, of course, a brighter relationship. During this cycle , the victim hopes she has seen the last of the violence. However, because this is a cycle, tension begins to escalate again in the abuser, and they are back on the merry-go-round of violence.

## THE BATTERED WOMAN SYNDROME

The "battered woman syndrome," a term coined by Dr. Lenore Walker (1979), describes the common effects of domestic violence on a woman. Many of the same symptoms are also seen in PTSD. They are especially likely to occur in relationships that are long-standing and in which the victims may have developed mechanisms for coping with the emotional abuse and constant threat of violence. Walker reminded us that these symptoms may seem maladaptive or bizarre when taken out of context. For instance, the victim may abuse alcohol or drugs as a way of coping. Her moods may swing from euphoria to uncontrollable crying, and she may experience such symptoms as dissociation, flattened affect, obsessive attention to others' moods and desires, apparently irrational fears, self-destructive tendencies, nightmares, severe depression, and even psychosis. Consequently, the degree of control the batterer exerts over the victim often produces a feeling of hopelessness that can emotionally paralyze her. She may become unable to detach herself from the situation and unable to protect her children from violence as well. In addition, it is typical for a battered woman to experience numerous physical reactions to stress, such as headaches, unexplained rashes, gastrointestinal problems, fatigue, or insomnia. These symptoms often disappear quickly when the stress of the violent relationship is removed (Gerard 1991).

Because the victim may leave the violent situation only to return again, repeated exposure to the trauma occurs. The linear process of developing PTSD may not be as noticeable in domestic violence as in some other types of victimization. This is because the starting and stopping of exposure may interrupt normal patterns of PTSD development.

Although our discussion focuses on female victims, not all victims are female. Some men are battered by spouses and girlfriends. Domestic violence can be devastating for men because they and others assume abuse toward men is preventable. When it is not prevented, the man is considered weak or passive, and these perceptions can negatively affect his self-concept, ego, and sexuality. Additionally, same-gender violence can be an issue. Gay couples are just as likely to have domestic-violence issues as are straight couples. (See Chapter 10 for more about male rape and male victimization.)

## BEYOND PHYSICAL VIOLENCE

Domestic violence is a complex system of power and control, and a victim's early exposure to violence can set a life-long pattern. Violence in intimate relationships begins in adolescence in 25 percent of cases (Martin et al. 1999; Molidor, Tolman, and Kober 2000). Yet physical violence is only one aspect of this pattern. People who abuse others use various methods to control the victim and limit that person's outside resources of help and support.

The spectrum of power and control includes intimidation, emotional violence, financial abuse, and isolation. The Domestic Abuse Prevention Project developed the Power and Control Wheel (see Figure 7.2 on the next page) to illustrate how these dynamics work in the context of an abusing relationship.

This wheel makes clear the extent to which an abuser controls every aspect of a female victim's life. Violence against a woman in a relationship makes a hostage of its victim. While the cycle of physical violence diagram illustrates the "micro" view of the dynamic processes in each act of violence, the power and control wheel helps us see the "macro" view of these processes in the context of the whole violent relationship.

## Crisis Intervention

Counselors need to be aware that many couples or individuals who seek counseling for "other" presenting problems are actually in violent relationships they have not disclosed. One in four women has experienced domestic violence; clearly, the percentage is higher among those seeking counseling. Therefore, it is important not to rule out domestic abuse in the initial evaluation of a client's problem. Especially with female clients, you should identify any violence in her past or current relationships. This will guide the kinds of assessments you choose to assist you in developing a treatment approach with this client (Gerard 1991).

While taking a history, some items that are frequently associated with domestic violence should serve as a red flag for you:

- ○ Lost pregnancies
- ○ History of emergency room usage
- ○ Disconnection or isolation from friends and family
- ○ Suicide attempts or gestures
- ○ History of previous abusive men or relationships
- ○ Prior shelter use, police protection, or restraining orders

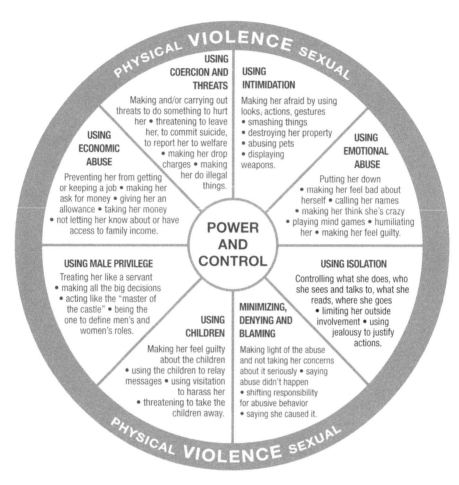

**FIGURE 7.2.**  The Power and Control Wheel. Abusers use many kinds of behavior to get and keep control over their partners. Battering is never an accident. It is an intentional act used to gain control over the other person. Physical abuse is only one part of a whole series of behaviors an abuser uses against his partner. Violence is never an isolated behavior. There are always other forms of abuse.

This diagram uses the wheel as a symbol to show the relationship of physical abuse to other forms of abuse. Each spoke represents a tactic used to gain control or power, which is the hub of the wheel. The rim that surrounds and supports the spokes is physical abuse. It holds the system together and gives the abuser his strength.

Source: Domestic Abuse Prevention Project, 202 East Superior St., Duluth MN 55802, (218) 722-2781, www.duluth-model.org.

○ Prior separations from this partner

○ History of childhood abuse, abuse of her children, or any reports to the Department of Social Services because of abuse to her children

○ Passive or dependent personality

In addition, be alert for some of the specific behaviors a victim may exhibit as she goes through the process of trying to separate herself from her abuser:

○ Not calling the police or not following through on pressing charges

○ Returning to the batterer or continuing to love the abuser

○ Unwillingness to take the advice of family and friends, failing to protect her children, feeling intimidated by friends and family who urge her to stay with abuser

The following behaviors can occur as a result of various thoughts, feelings, or beliefs on the part of the victim:

○ Fear of repercussions to self or children if she leaves the abuser; fear the abuser will follow through on threats or kill himself

○ Embarrassment for anyone to know

○ Thinking abuse is due to financial pressure

○ Belief that violence is not that abnormal or that the abuser will eventually change; religious beliefs about the sanctity of marriage

○ Fear of change of any kind
(National Center for Victims of Crime website)

Most victims will not volunteer information to the counselor about violence in the relationship when the batterer is also in the session. If you have reason to suspect abuse, arrange for a time to speak with the victim alone and allow enough time for a complete private interview. The victim may minimize the violence or be unable or unwilling to identify what is happening to her as "violence," so be direct and ask specific questions to help her focus her thoughts.

Many victims of domestic violence have also experienced abuse as children or have been in a succession of violent relationships, so they may have great difficulty with trust—including trusting a counselor. You should let the victim know you believe and support her disclosure of the violence. It is equally important to let her know the information shared will not be disclosed to the abuser without her expressed permission (Gerard 1991).

You may want to give a copy of the power and control wheel to the victim. The wheel can help her identify different categories of abuse she has experienced but that were not obvious to her. You can also give the victim a set of colored markers and have her circle the events that happened to her. She can use one color for events that never occurred, another color for events that occur occasionally, another for those that occur frequently, and another for those that occur almost daily.

If you suspect abuse on the basis of the history intake, follow up with one of the trauma assessments listed in Chapter 3. This will guide your intervention. The next step after taking the victim's history is to find out how at-risk they are by asking questions about the abuser and how volatile the home situation seems. The following questions can help you with your assessment:

- Does the abuser have access to weapons?
- What violent episodes occurred previously, and what was their outcome and severity?
- Is the abuser currently using drugs and alcohol?
- Does the abuser use intimidating behavior to control the victim and her children, such as threatening family members or making threatening phone calls?
- Is the abuser adept at utilizing and manipulating the legal system?
- Does the abuser have a previous history of mental illness? Has the abuser physically assaulted others outside the immediate family?
- Is the abuser sexually abusing his wife or children?
- Has the abuser threatened to kill himself, his partner, children, relatives, or others?
- Does the abuser have fantasies about who/how/when/where to kill someone?

○ Has the abuser harmed or tortured animals?

○ Has the abuser previously harmed pregnant women?

(Gerard 1991; Martin 1987)

If you determine the victim is experiencing domestic violence, or if she comes to counseling specifically for this reason, her physical safety is the most important factor to address in the initial contact. Although the battered person is in the best position to determine when the next incident of abuse may occur, she may underestimate the severity of past abuse and the potential for serious abuse in the future. PTSD effects can numb her ability to respond to impending danger.

It is important to validate the victim's fears about future violence and help her devise ways to feel in control again. You can develop a safety plan with the victim, including how she will escape during the next incident, where she will go, whom she will contact, and what she will take with her. The safety plan can help the victim become more realistic about the likelihood of further violence and break through some of her denial about the extent of violence in her life. (Gerard 1991). The chapter on stalking has additional information about developing a safety plan.

The victim should be given information about legal alternatives, such as calling the police and pressing charges, filing for a restraining order or injunction, and gaining temporary custody of the children. She should be referred to the local domestic-violence program so she can learn about the availability of an emergency shelter should she need one, and she should be given information about support groups for persons in violent relationships (National Center for Victims of Crime website).

It is important to keep in mind during crisis intervention counseling that the victim may not place much faith in law enforcement, police protection, or the criminal-justice system if she tried to obtain police assistance previously and did not receive the requested protection. If the victim had clashes with the police about the limited amount of protection provided, she may be reluctant to file for another restraining order. Law enforcement may also be reluctant to proceed in cases in which the victim did not press charges, repeatedly dropped charges, or did not show up for court (Gerard 1991) Victims whose domestic violence was perpetrated by a law-enforcement husband or boyfriend are especially likely to have concerns that unbiased help will not be available. In some such cases, domestic violence is actually reported to another human-service agency instead of law enforcement, due to the potential conflict of interest. Counselors who encounter a case of this nature can check out procedures in place with their local Department of Social Services.

### Client Concerns

- ◯ Physical safety of self and children
- ◯ Fear of abuser locating them
- ◯ Concern about how they will survive
- ◯ Not having a place to stay that is away from the abuser
- ◯ Not having money, a job, or work skills
- ◯ Not having transportation
- ◯ Not having legal representation

### Secondary Victimizations

- ◯ Lack of protection from law-enforcement agencies
- ◯ Lack of services available to help with transition
- ◯ Lack of work skills, money, or information about how to increase skills
- ◯ Stigmatization by label "spousal abuse victim"

### Social/Public Services Needed

- ◯ Crisis intervention counselor
- ◯ Spouse abuse shelter
- ◯ Victim advocate
- ◯ Transitional services (housing, financial aid, job skills)
- ◯ Restraining order
- ◯ Prosecutor or attorney
- ◯ Group counseling
- ◯ Police intervention
- ◯ Child protection services

○ Transportation

○ Emergency medical treatment

○ Counseling for the children

## Short-Term Counseling

It can take victims years and countless attempts before they successfully disconnect from their abusers. This can be frustrating to a counselor who does not understand the cycles and patterns of domestic violence. In fact, getting disentangled from an abuser and the effects that doing so can have on the victim can be more complicated than initially apparent.

For this reason, you may have counter-transference issues with the victim. You must examine your own feelings about victims who stay, and honestly decide whether you are the best agent to help this victim or whether you should refer her to someone with a more specific background in domestic violence. Counselor's who have their own personal history of domestic violence or their own histories of abuse as a child may have additional counter-transference issues they need to discuss in clinical supervision (Gerard 1991).

With that said, the most important goal of short-term counseling is empowering victims to make their own choices. Because the nature of domestic violence involves the abuse of power and control, victims must regain control over their lives. This can be difficult for a person who has lived for years without power, control, or decision-making choices. Encouraging the victim to make her own decisions can be a painstaking process. She may be reluctant to do so for safety reasons, may have forgotten how to be aware of what she wants, or may never have made decisions for herself before. Many battered women move from their parents' home to their abuser's home at an early age. They never live independently or learn how to support themselves financially or emotionally. Some women have very regressed personalities and passive tendencies. Decision-making skills must be learned in an atmosphere of safety and unconditional acceptance, under the guidance of a counselor who gently but firmly refuses to make decisions for the victim.

The act of attempting to take back power while a victim remains with the batterer can be dangerous. The victim must have some assurance of safety because, statistically, the most dangerous period in a violent relationship is when the victim takes back control and either leaves or starts making demands of her batterer. This represents a loss of control for the batterer. Often, batterers will do anything to regain a sense of control, including more violence. Many victims have been killed because they tried to leave or asked for a divorce. If you do not have experience helping victims leave violent relationships, you should have someone from the local shelter advise your client about the safety precautions she should take. Information about personal safety in the presence of abusers can also be obtained on from the National Center for Victims of Crime's website, under the domestic-violence category (www.ncvc.org).

Reactions to domestic violence include the symptoms often seen in PTSD, such as fear, nightmares and sleep disorders, anxiety, anger, difficulty concentrating, depression, social withdrawal, helplessness/hopelessness, numbness, and hypervigilance (National Center for Victims of Crime website). Short-term counseling should focus on issues of low self-esteem (reinforced by the abuser and perhaps by the victim's childhood), sense of self, and purpose. Likewise, unrealistic hope, isolation, emotional dependence, and the need to repeat trauma are aspects of the client's belief system that need to be challenged.

Issues that can compound the problems of domestic violence include the victim's substance abuse; previous victimizations, such as physical or sexual abuse as a child; other mental-health diagnoses in the victim, especially an Axis II diagnosis; family, cultural, or religious pressures to continue the abusive relationship; lack of economic resources necessary to maintain independent living; and an absence of life skills.

Some women recover rather quickly from the effects of violence when the threat is taken away. Others, especially women who grew up in violent homes, take much longer and may need long-term counseling. The decision to continue treatment can be based on your assessments.

Family or couples counseling related to violent relationships should not be attempted until you can be sure that the victim will be safe to speak honestly in a session. If the violence has not stopped, it is not safe for the victim to disclose information to the counselor that the abuser does not want disclosed, despite any claims he might make to the contrary. If you do not have specific training in domestic violence, you may not be the best person to judge when (if ever) family counseling should occur. Instead, separating the partners allows the victim the safety to explore her own feelings without fear of reprisal. At the same time, the batterer is forced to focus on his own behavior instead of rationalizing his violence by focusing on what the victim did to provoke him. It should be the victim's decision when she feels ready, if ever, to enter into joint counseling with her batterer.

Additionally, batterer intervention programs may be necessary and even court ordered. The completion of a battering intervention program in no way guarantees safety for the victim. Many batterers have completed the program only to begin battering again. A victim may place too much hope in behavioral change simply because he attended a batterer-counseling program. Recidivism rates in battering are fairly high (Gerard 1991).

### Client Concerns
- When or how to disclose and to whom disclosures should be made
- Regaining power and control over her life
- Inability to make decisions
- Separation or divorce
- Safety for self and children
- Job, money, and skills
- Future living arrangements
- Hyper-focus on the abuser (e.g., getting him help, how he will get along without her, his addictions)

### Secondary Victimizations
- Counselor's bias concerning domestic violence
- Victim-blaming from numerous sources
- Lack of control in decision making
- Lack of independent living skills
- Substance abuse and other addictions
- Family, cultural, or religious pressures to stay in the relationship
- Victim's own untreated mental-health issues

*Social/Public Services Needed*

○ Short-term counselor

○ Group counseling

○ Domestic-violence shelter

○ Assertiveness training

○ Offender counseling (if desired)

○ Job skills and life skills

○ Housing, financial assistance, and food

○ Counseling for children

## Long-Term Counseling

Some women show amazing resilience when removed from a violent relationship. Some women are able to bounce back and heal fairly rapidly. Others do not heal as well. Some obstacles to healing include the following histories:

○ Previous victimizations, including physical or sexual child abuse

○ Sexual assault

○ Substance abuse problems

○ Unresolved abandonment issues related to the death of a parent or divorce

○ Poor emotional, physical, or sexual boundaries

○ Passive-dependent personality types in which an inability to have faith in her own feelings or judgment keeps the victim from making decisions

○ PTSD or other trauma-related disorder

○ Low self-esteem

○ Codependency

○ Suicidal behaviors

(Gerard 1991)

Long-term counseling issues and length of time may be influenced by information gathered in the assessments. Certain diagnosis and trauma disorders can warrant long-term treatment.

Additional counseling may need to focus on trust, intimacy, shame, loss, acting out, and the ability to know what healthy relationships should look like, as well as any PTSD symptoms (see Chapter 2, "The Psychodynamics of Trauma").

Do not underestimate the victim's need for help in dealing with her rage or guilt related to violent thoughts or actions she had in response to the violence, her inability to protect her children from abuse, and secondary abuses by those outside the relationship who failed to assist her in time of need. It can be very helpful for her to become involved with a support group of women who have been through similar experiences and who are now struggling with the same recovery issues. Most battered women's programs have support groups available at no cost to the participants (Gerard 1991).

Most communities in the United States are now served by a battered women's shelter or safe home network. If you work with victims of domestic violence, you should become familiar with these programs and the services they offer. Most shelters offer safe, confidential housing for women and their children, counseling by telephone or in person, and information about specific social service resources and legal remedies available for victims in that state. In some communities, counseling services for the violent partner are offered through the battered women's shelter, as well. If not, the shelter should be able to refer the batterer to a local counselor who specializes in counseling batterers.

### Client Concerns

- Finding available shelter
- Returning to an abusive relationship
- Unsure of pressing charges
- Unsure charges will stick
- Ability to survive and support children independently
- Loving, yet fearing, the abuser
- Fear of abandonment

○ Boundaries

○ Distrust in own judgment

○ Rage

### Secondary Victimizations

○ Substance abuse

○ Inability to develop close relationships

○ Loss of trust

○ Lack of protection by systems

○ Societal bias toward domestic violence

○ Victim-blaming

○ Family and cultural or religious pressures to stay in the relationship

### Social/Public Services Needed

○ Long-term counselor

○ Group counseling

○ Assertiveness training

○ Offender counseling (if desired)

○ Housing, financial aid, food

○ Occupational training

○ Legal aid and advice

## RECOMMENDED READING

Bergen, Raquel Kennedy. *Issues in Intimate Violence*. Thousand Oaks, CA: Sage Publications, 1998.

Berry, Dawn Bradley. *The Domestic Violence Sourcebook*. New York: McGraw Hill, 2000.

Jayne, Pamela. *Ditch That Jerk: Dealing with Men Who Control and Hurt Women*. Alameda, CA: Hunter House Publishers, 2000.

Lissette, Andrea, and Richard Kraus. *Free Yourself from an Abusive Relationship*. Alameda, CA: Hunter House Publishers, 2000.

Mariani, Cliff. *Domestic Violence Survival Guide*. Flushing, NY: Looseleaf Law Publications, 1996.

Paymar, Michael. *Violent No More,* 2nd Edition. Alameda, CA: Hunter House Publishers, 2000.

Roberts, Albert R. *Handbook of Domestic Violence Intervention Strategies: Polices, Programs and Legal Remedies.* New York: Oxford University Press, 2002.

Sokoloff, Natalie J. *Domestic Violence at the Margins: Readings on Race, Class, Gender and Culture.* Piscataway, NJ: Rutgers University Press, 2005.

Stark, Evan, and Anne Flitcraft. *Women at Risk: Domestic Violence and Women's Health.* Thousand Oaks, CA: Sage Publications, 1996.

Wilson, K. J. *When Violence Begins at Home: A Comprehensive Guide to Understanding and Ending Domestic Abuse,* 2nd Edition. Alameda, CA: Hunter House Publishers, 2006.

## RESOURCES

National Domestic Violence Hotline
(800) 799-SAFE (7233)   ○   (800) 787-3224   ○   www.ndvh.org

National Coalition Against Domestic Violence
(303) 839-1852   ○   www.ncadv.org

National Council on Child Abuse and Family Violence
(800) 222-2000

National Center for Victims of Crime
(202) 467-8700   ○   www.ncvn.org

The Women's Law Project
www.womenslawproject.org

National Organization for Victim Assistance
www.trynova.org

Family Violence & Sexual Assault Institute
www.fvsai.org

Partners Against Violence Network
www.pavnet.org

## Overview of Domestic Violence

*Crisis Intervention:* Physical safety of person, validation of fear of danger, safety plan for future victimization, safety contacts, legal aid, restraining order, temporary child custody, emergency shelter, support groups

*Short-Term Counseling:* Counselor's own attitudes about violence, empowering the victim to make decisions, teaching independent life skills, grieving

*Long-Term Counseling:* Victim's own previous issues of childhood physical or sexual abuse, addictions, codependency, religious issues, financial issues, boundaries, trust, intimacy

*Secondary Victimizations:* Not recognized as a crime; no place to go; lack of job skills and money; insensitive systems, such as law enforcement or criminal justice

*Social/Public Services Needed:* Battered women's shelter, victim advocate, restraining order, job skills training, vocational rehabilitation, general education degree schooling, counseling through all stages, battered woman's support group, welfare or public housing, food stamps, aid for dependent children, children's and women's health care, medical attention

# CHAPTER 8

# Elder Abuse

○ 1 in 10 to 25 elderly are abused, approximately 2.5 million a year.

○ In 1996, 551,011 elderly experienced abuse or neglect in domestic settings.

○ In 2001, the elderly accounted for a disproportionate number of those losing at least $5,000 in Internet fraud.

○ In 2001, 40 percent of nursing home residents were reportedly victims of verbal abuse and 15 percent were victims of physical or sexual abuse.

○ As of 2000, more than 50 percent of the U.S. population was over age 50.
(National Center for Victims of Crime website)

**VICTIM'S STORY**         *LENORA*

*Lenora was 82 years old and living with her daughter and son-in-law. When her friends and family noticed a decline in Lenora's general condition that they felt was due to her living situation, they called in a social worker. However, whenever the social worker asked Lenora about the situation, she always told him things were "okay." Still, he got the definite impression they were not.*

*Lenora appeared depressed, was losing weight, had lost interest in her daily activities, had a high number of "bumps and bruises" on her body, and no longer could afford even the most inexpensive items for herself. When the social worker asked Lenora if she would rather live elsewhere, she would glance at her daughter and say, "I guess not."*

*Following a full investigation, the social worker found that Lenora was being abused. Her daughter took her entire check, fed her only once a day, refused to take her to activities such as church or a friend's home, and asked her to stay in her bedroom all day. When Lenora cried, her daughter hit her. A long history of relationship problems between mother and daughter was uncovered, stemming from when the daughter was young. Now the tables had turned. Although Lenora still did not want to leave her daughter, even in the face of abuse, she was placed with other family members.*

## Background Information

With baby boomers reaching the initial years of old age, and with their increase in overall life expectancy, the number of elderly Americans is on the increase (Griffin and Williams 1992). One benefit of this trend is an increase in services and programs. This increase came in response to the recognition of elder abuse as a victim classification.

Until recent years, people assumed the elderly would grow old safely and with the support of loved ones. In prior generations, extended family members shared the responsibility of caring for the elderly. Many elderly lived at home with their children or extended family. Or, family members came to the elder's house daily to provide care. Today, however, families are smaller and the elderly have fewer offspring to care for them. In addition, economic constraints in families and increased family mobility have dramatically affected how the elderly are cared for in later life (Griffin and Williams 1992). As a result, the elderly are frequently alone and become targeted as victims for robbery, scam artists, and assault. Those who are not alone are frequently abused by family members in their own homes or by caregivers in care facilities.

Elder abuse is greatly underreported (Hardin and Khan-Hudson 2005). As the baby boom generation ages, we can expect the incidence of abuse to rise. Notably, the frequency of elder abuse is only slightly lower than that of child abuse but is much less frequently reported than is child abuse (Hardin and Khan-Hudson 2005). Elder abuse is more difficult to identify due to the isolation of the victims, the reluctance of the elderly to report abuse, and the fear of retaliation (National Academics of Sciences 2002).

The elderly have a difficult time advocating for themselves, especially in a nursing-home or hospital environment. When elderly victims do complain of abuse, their reports often are dismissed as symptoms of senility.

Like other forms of family violence, elder abuse is rarely an isolated incident and usually follows a cyclic pattern. Because of the frailty of its victims, elder abuse is always serious and can be fatal. Like other forms of family violence, it occurs at all socioeconomic levels.

## Types of Neglect and Abuse

Categories of neglect that constitute elder abuse include the following:

1. *Active neglect:* The willful failure to provide care

2. *Passive neglect:* The inadequate knowledge or inability of a caretaker that results in non-willful failure to provide care

3. *Self-neglect:* The failure of the family to monitor an elder's ability to care for her- or himself (Commonwealth of Pennsylvania 1988)

4. *Physical abuse:* Acts committed by a relative or caregiver that result in physical injuries, unreasonable confinement, or oversedation

5. *Sexual abuse:* Any type of sexual manipulation to which an elderly person does not consent

6. *Financial exploitation:* The caretaker's improper use or misman-agement of an elderly person's funds or property

7. *Psychological or emotional abuse:* A caretaker's actions or verbaliza-tions that are designed to humiliate, provoke, confuse, or frighten the elderly person

8. *Violation of rights:* Locking the elderly in or out of their home, placing them into a nursing care facility against their will, coercion, unreasonable confinement, opening or censoring mail, refusing access to a telephone or visitors, or any other breach of rights that citizens have under state, federal, or constitutional law, including state and federal statutes (Martin 1987)

The factors that contribute to the abuse of the elderly are similar to the factors associated with family violence. Risk factors for elder abuse include the following:

○ A shared living situation, which increases the opportunity for contact and thus also conflict and tension (Lachs, Williams, O'Brien, Hurst, and Horowitz 1997)

○ Dementia, which increases the chance for physical abuse due to disruptive and aggressive behaviors that cause stress and distress to the caregivers (Dyer, Pavlik, Murphy, and Hyman, 2002)

○ Social isolation from friends and family members, which increases overall family caregiver stress and also hides behaviors of abuse from others (Compton, Flanagan, and Gregg 1997)

○ The pathology of the caregivers, which is usually associated with mental illness and/or alcohol misuse (Compton et al. 1997)

○ Abuser(s) are heavily dependent on the elder (Pillemer 2004) especially financially

In addition, Henton, Cate, and Emery (1984) described various stress factors that can contribute to elder abuse. These stress factors can include the following:

○ Lack of family support or relief support

○ Lack of social services available for the elderly

○ Family or elder poverty

○ Added responsibilities of caring for someone physically or financially; disruption of employment caused by the need to care for the elder

○ Dependence upon family members who may not be in a position financially or emotionally to meet long-term caregiving needs

○ Family members who become resentful, exhausted, and burned out

○ Previous unresolved conflicts with the elder or power struggles with the elder

○ Not receiving enough gratification from or appreciation for care giving

○ Previous history of family violence

Because violence is a learned behavior, caregivers who were abused themselves run a significantly higher chance of abusing elders in their care than do caregivers without a history of abuse. Some cases of elder abuse occur in homes with a lifelong pattern of violent relationships as seen in previous spouse or child abuse situations. If the caregiver was specifically abused as a child by the elder who is in his or her care, retribution and revenge may motivate the caregiver.

## Crisis Intervention

When working with the elderly, it is important to note certain barriers that may hamper effective intervention and treatment. These include a lack of eyewitnesses of the abuse, fear of retaliation, fear of relocation, embarrassment, fear of having to go to court, feeling that "it won't do any good to tell," religious justification, nonassertive personality, learned helplessness, and inability to realize one is being abused (i.e., too impaired mentally or physically).

These barriers may affect different levels and stages of the counseling process. Some barriers may be evident immediately during crisis intervention (e.g., lack of eyewitnesses, inability to realize one is being abused), whereas others will become apparent during short- or long-term counseling. Psychological abuse (e.g., the threat of placement in a nursing home if the victim reveals physical, sexual, or financial abuse) or the threat of having medicine withheld can be extremely debilitating, especially over the long term.

The reactions of the elderly to abuse are not unlike those of other victims. Their reactions can range from passivity to severe anxiety. They may exhibit increased confusion and disorientation, verbal withdrawal and referral of all questions to the abusing caregiver, cowering in the presence of the caregiver, and fearfulness. If the elder is suffering from an organic brain dysfunction (e.g., Alzheimer's disease), any abuse may go undetected. The inability to communicate or disoriented communication makes it difficult for others to observe the abuse. The presence of organic brain dysfunction can also increase the likelihood of geriatric euthanasia.

If the victim is in danger, removal from the situation and reporting are mandatory. It may be difficult to find another placement for an elderly person. If the elderly victim has extensive medical problems, the options may be limited to medical or nursing home placement, depending on their insurance options or ability to pay. If they are medically disabled, domestic-violence shelters may not be an option. Requesting help from family members or friends may be necessary.

During crisis intervention with the victim, it is imperative to work jointly with the family and caregivers. Intervention often involves education of the caregiver and family to help them learn about the developmental characteristics of aging and to assist them in assessing the limits of their ability to provide care. Notably, many families lack information about the aging process, the possibility of abuse by caregivers or professionals, support networks that can help them in their caregiving roles to an elder, and how to deal with the dependency issues involved in caring for the elderly.

Thus, the focus of the intervention is not only on protection of the victim, but also on improving the quality of life and coping skills of both the victim and caregivers. You may need to help the family obtain services available to the elderly (e.g., Meals on Wheels, respite care, hospice, or other community services) to relieve the stress of caregiving. You also may need to locate services directly related to the caregiver (e.g., support groups for them and counseling that helps with positive interactions and verbalizing needs). The family may need to investigate the option of protective placement (e.g., removing the victim from the care of the abuser and placing the victim in a nursing home), taking into consideration the physical condition of the victim. In this process, it is important to treat the family unit with a family-systems therapy approach.

Elder abuse victims may view the reporting of abuse as more of a punishment to themselves than a solution to their problems, especially if reporting might result in their removal to institutionalized care (e.g., nursing home, hospital, or home health care). Abuse within an institutionalized care facility is also difficult for the elderly victim to report. Most forms of abuse in this setting are geared toward overmedication or improper medication and neglect. This abuse tends to be both active (e.g., improper medication or overmedication) and passive (e.g., neglect or lack of stimulation). Crisis intervention can also entail taking legal action, such as obtaining restraining orders or bringing criminal charges against the abuser. However, these actions are rarely taken in the case of elderly victims.

Issues that can arise with elderly victims during crisis intervention include their wish to protect the abuser, especially if the person is their child. Because of ethical concerns, it is difficult for a counselor to report abuse without the willingness of the victim. Check the state laws in your area. Other important issues during treatment include helping victims come to terms with their fear of institutionalization, lack of mobility, and resulting dependency on their caregivers.

### Client Concerns

○ Fear of retaliation (applies to abuse by a relative or by staff members at an institution)

○ Fear of relocation

○ Embarrassment by being abused by a relative or child

○ Fear of having to go to court

○ Fear of institutionalization

○ Fear of further abuse or death

○ Fear of having food or medication withheld

### Secondary Victimizations

○ Feeling punished because of relocation to another caregiver

○ Cost of institutionalized care if moved from a home to a medical care facility

○ Loss of relationship with caregiver

○ Loss of health or will to live after being relocated

○ Overmedication or insufficient medication

○ Neglect, confinement, lack of mental stimulation

○ Lack of local community services

○ Lack of elder advocacy

### Social/Public Services Needed

○ Elderly advocate

○ Community services, such as Meals on Wheels, community day care center, hospice, or respite care

○ Support groups for caregivers

○ Family-systems therapy for family caregivers

○ Stress reduction education for both victim and caregiver

○ Educational groups for caregivers

## Short-Term Counseling

Assessment outcomes should guide your short-term counseling goals. Not all trauma-based assessments are designed for geriatric populations. You will need to check with the publisher of any assessment tool you use to see if it is applicable for geriatric victims. Some assessments specifically focus on measuring abuse in elderly victims.

It is often more difficult to remove elderly victims than other types of victims from abusive environments. Finding replacement care for the elderly can be challenging. Services are scarce and expensive, and both the victim and the caregiver may recognize this fact. For this reason, counselors often put extensive effort into working with the abusive family member (if applicable) to try to create a suitable environment for the victim.

Counselors are more likely in cases of elder abuse than any other victim populations to be in a position of working with both abusers and victims. Therefore, short-term counseling may focus on empowering victims through assertiveness training to help them meet their needs (if they are cognitively able to benefit from counseling). It also focuses on educating the caregiving family about how to divide workloads, handle stress, use available community services to alleviate personal stress, and become familiar with the aging and developmental processes of the elderly.

In some situations, you may feel you are dealing with two separate categories of victimization: the victims and the abusers. Abusive family members are often viewed as victims of circumstance on account of their "sandwich position." The resulting stress, and perhaps the reduced mental ability of the aging parent(s), can create an abusive experience for the caregiver. Some aging parents who are senile hit, slap, or verbally abuse their caregivers. The line between victim and offender can become blurred. In some cases, both parties are victims and both are offenders. This presents a unique challenge for the counselor who must address the needs of both parties.

If elderly victims are abused during institutionalized care, your efforts can be aimed at assisting either the elderly victims or their families in gathering resources to report the abuse. The reporting may be directed to state protective services or state regulatory commissions for medical-care professions. Help finding replacement care may also be necessary. Contacting local community services for a referral or calling state agencies for a recommendation must be considered.

### Client Concerns

Elderly client concerns:

- ○ Inability to report abuse effectively
- ○ Inability to recognize abuse
- ○ Fear of retaliation
- ○ Fear of relocation
- ○ Lack of knowledge of community services
- ○ Fear of having to go to court
- ○ Loss of relationship with the caregiver and the rest of the family
- ○ Fear of institutionalization
- ○ Fear of increased abuse

Caregiver client concerns:

- ○ Lack of knowledge of available support services and community services
- ○ Fear of removal of elderly parent
- ○ Fear of judgment of family for removal of parent
- ○ Continued physical or verbal abuse by elderly parent
- ○ Guilt and shame
- ○ Lack of knowledge concerning aging and developmental processes
- ○ Increased stress of caregiving
- ○ Loss of relationship with other family members because of increase in caregiving
- ○ Increased financial responsibilities, as well as lack of personal time alone

### Secondary Victimizations

○ Cost of care to both the elderly victim and caregiver

○ Fear of loss of relationship with caregiver and family on the part of the elderly victim

○ Loss of health and will to live if the elderly victim is relocated

○ Loss of adequate care for the elderly victim if abuse is reported

○ Cost of medical care if abuse is perpetrated by family caregiver and the elderly victim is moved to a medical facility

### Social/Public Services Needed

○ Protection services, if family cannot help

○ Hospice care

○ Respite care

○ Community services, such as Meals on Wheels, Neighborly Senior Services

○ In-home medical or nursing care (home health care)

○ Support groups for elderly

○ Support groups for caregivers and family

○ Community financial aid

○ Senior day care centers

○ Nursing home or medical residential care

## Long-Term Counseling

Long-term counseling may be viewed as adaptive, especially in the case of elderly victims who have to stay with an abusive caregiver (who may also by victimized). By helping both parties adapt to their new lifestyle and face the resulting limitations and reductions in independence, you can facilitate their long-term ability to stay together successfully.

The primary caregiver is not the only one who needs assistance adjusting. The breadwinner on whose shoulders the added financial responsibility falls and the children who must share the divided attention of the caregiver also need adaptive skills. Focusing on the extended family and using a family-systems approach to therapy are useful in this type of long-term counseling situation. Family members can be encouraged to join support groups that validate what they have lost through the caregiving of an elderly person in their home. Such groups also help caregivers see what they have gained through the presence of the elderly person in their home. In fact, the elderly offer unique gifts of retrospection, insight, and wisdom. They can add security and stability and provide friendship and camaraderie for other family members. Long-term counseling can emphasize these positives dimensions to the family unit, rather than focusing only on the burdens.

### Client Concerns

Elderly client concerns:

- Fear of becoming a burden
- Financial aspects of long-term care
- Fear of senility
- Fear of death
- Fear of institutionalization
- Fear of relocation

Caregiver client concerns:

- Unsure of ability to provide long-term care
- Financial aspects of long-term care
- Fear of senility of the elder
- Fear of death of the elder
- Loss of personal time for other family members

### Secondary Victimizations

- Emotional toll on both victim and caregiver of long-term caregiving
- Financial concerns of both victim and caregiver of long-term caregiving
- Lack of knowledge about community services

### Social/Public Services Needed

- Protective services, if family cannot help
- Community services

○ Hospice and respite care

○ Financial assistance

○ Medical care facilities

○ Support group for caregiver and family

○ Support group and counseling for victim

○ Education for both victim and family

○ Legal intervention (if necessary)

○ Senior day-care center

○ Elderly advocate

## RECOMMENDED READING

Lissette, Andrea, and Richard Kraus. *Free Yourself from an Abusive Relationship.* Alameda, CA: Hunter House Publishers, 2000.

Payne, Brian K. *Crime and Elder Abuse: An Integrated Perspective.* Springfield, IL: Charles C. Thomas Publishing, 2000.

Pillemer, Karl A., and Rosalie S. Wolf. *Conflict in the Family.* Dover, MA: Auburn House, 1986.

Sandell, Diane S., and Lois Hudson. *Ending Abuse: A Family Guide.* Fort Bragg, CA: QED Press, 2000.

Toshio, Tatara. *Understanding Elder Abuse in Minority Populations.* Philadelphia, PA: Taylor & Francis, 1999.

Wilson, K. J. *When Violence Begins at Home: A Comprehensive Guide to Understanding and Ending Domestic Abuse,* 2nd Edition. Alameda, CA: Hunter House Publishers, 2006.

## RESOURCES

Family Violence & Sexual Assault Institute
www.fvsai.org

The National Center for Victims of Crime
(202) 467-8700   ○   www.ncvc.org

National Center on Elder Abuse
(202) 898-2586   ○   www.elderabusecenter.org

## Overview of Elder Abuse

*Crisis Intervention:* Safety, working with caregivers, removal, institutionalization, preventive intervention focused on educating caregiver

*Short-Term Counseling:* Working with abusive caregiver, finding community and support services, assertiveness training for elderly victim, cognitive reframing of event for victim, some victims may not realize they have been abused

*Long-Term Counseling:* Adaptation to dependent lifestyle, finding long-term support and resources, helping victims adjust to any loss of health or physical problems from abuse

*Secondary Victimizations:* Cost of institutionalized care, over- or undermedication, lack of community services, loss of relationship with abusive caregiver

*Social/Public Services Needed:* Elderly advocate, protective services, respite care, stress-reduction education for caregiver, Meals on Wheels, support groups for victim and caregiver, financial aid, senior day-care program

# Violence Against Children

NOTHING STIRS US AS human beings and as counselors more than reports of child neglect, physical, and sexual abuse. The imagery of defenseless children being hurt, hungry, or ignored touches us deeply. Our skills in assisting them are vital to children's recovery. To be effective, we must understand the intricate details of the resulting trauma in a child's life.

## Child Abuse

- 1,400 child fatalities occurred in 2002, or 1.98 children per 100,000.
- Child fatalities due to abuse and neglect are underreported.
- Children age three and younger are the most frequent victims in child fatalities.
- Children younger than one year accounted for 41 percent of fatalities.
- Child abuse increases the odds of future delinquency and adult criminality by 40 percent.

  (National Child Abuse and Neglect Data System 2002; Widom 1992)

### VICTIM'S STORY                                    GERRY

*Unfortunately, I do remember the child abuse. My mother held me upside down by my ankle and beat me with a tree branch. Other beatings were with extension cords, whips bought in Mexico as souvenirs, belts with belt buckles, and even two-by-fours. She took me along on her sex-capades, where I saw her have sex with men.*

   *Often she left me and my little brother alone in the winter to survive by ourselves. At age six, I had to keep the fire going and make food for the two of us. She told me she had tried to abort me as a fetus. At age thirteen, I left home with her permission. The physical wounds have healed, but not the psychological ones.*

## BACKGROUND INFORMATION

Child abuse has probably become the most widely recognized form of abuse. It is a pervasive problem, spanning generations, in our country. Appalling in any and all forms, abuse toward children can include forms of neglect and/or emotional, physical, or sexual abuse, and these can manifest as a pattern of events that can begin as early as infancy or as late as the teen years. Like other forms of family violence, child abuse does not discriminate based on socioeconomic, gender, demographic, or racial factors. As a result, counselors need to be aware that child abuse is rarely a single incident, but more often a constellation of events.

Many abused children do not recognize the events as abusive or abnormal because they occur so frequently. In some cases, it is considered part of what "their family does" (Ackerman and Graham 1990). Abusing adults often convince children that what is occurring to them is "normal." As a result, children often will not disclose the abuse in a counseling session. Other deterrents to disclosure can come from the loyalty and love the child feels for the adult, or from fear the adult will punish even further for the disclosure (especially if the child has regular contact with the adult). Even if the child recognizes that what is occurring is "not right," he or she may take great strides to protect the abuser—especially if it is a family member. Therefore, eliciting disclosure can be difficult because the child does not want to incriminate a family member, especially a parent.

In the past decade, more adults have been trained to recognize the signs and symptoms of child abuse. Many career positions now require training in child abuse detection. Teachers, school guidance counselors, day care workers, and medical service providers are all possible eyes and ears to the abuse occurring to children. Referrals to a therapist or a victim advocate may be generated from sources like these.

Nevertheless, the most feared outcome of child abuse—child fatalities —continues to be underreported. Deaths are often attributed to events other than abuse (e.g., SIDS for very young children, or accidents), even when the actual cause was abuse or neglect. These undetected homicides leave children in at-risk situations in which the parents' lack of coping and parenting skills and abusive tendencies place the child at death's door.

A counselor's ability to access parenting skills is of importance in child abuse cases. A good predictor of a child's vulnerability to abuse is related to the parents' inadequacy, unavailability, or conflict, and to poor parent-child relationships (Finkelhor 1994). In most states, counselors do not have to "prove" child abuse in order to report it. Counselors are mandated by law to report if they have a "suspicion." However, other state agencies determine if abuse has actually occurred. Many counselors hesitate to report or do not report because they fear they will have to prove their allegations. The state will prove and prosecute if state investigators deem abuse to have occurred. In intra-familial settings, this occurs through the Department of Social Services, which investigates abuse allegations within families. In circumstances in which abuse is believed to have been perpetrated by a non–family member, law enforcement investigates. Depending on a state's laws, not reporting places counselors at risk as an accessory to the crime (Brown 1991). This may have implications for your malpractice insurance if you are found negligent for not reporting. Therefore, understanding not only your state laws, but also what you are looking for in a child victim is crucial.

## TYPES OF ABUSE

### Physical, Emotional, and Educational Neglect

Neglect can accompany (and often does) other forms of abuse (National Center for Victims of Crime website); therefore, if you see neglect in a child's life, it is wise to look closely for other forms of possible abuse.

Neglect can be physical, emotional, or educational in nature. Physical neglect refers to the pervasive situation in which parents or guardians do not or cannot provide basic necessities for children under 18 years old (National Center for Victims of Crime website). Physical neglect includes the following:

- ○ Refusing to seek or provide medical or psychological treatment for illnesses

○ Abandonment

○ Lack of adequate supervision to provide physical safety

○ Failing to make the home safe for the child

○ Failure to provide adequate nutrition, clothing, or cleanliness, when to do so is within the means of the caregiver

Emotional neglect includes the following:

○ Emotional abandonment

○ Lack of encouragement for or social interaction with the child

○ Lack of loving physical and verbal contact

○ Refusal to allow age-appropriate interactions with other children

○ Deprivation of love, stimulation, and security
   (National Center for Victims of Crime website)

Educational neglect includes the following:

○ Withholding school training

○ Knowing about yet allowing chronic truancy

○ Not enrolling the child in school at all, and not providing school at home or elsewhere

### *Physical Abuse*

Physical abuse is often the most recognizable form of abuse because of the physical indicators and evidence. It is defined as a pattern of injuries to a child that is non-accidental (National Center for Victims of Crime website). Some indications of intentional infliction of physical pain include the following:

○ Hitting, spanking, welts, bites, burns, broken bones, fractures

○ Internal injuries to major organs

○ Head trauma

○ Physical restraints, such as tying up the child or strangling

Some of these types of abuse can cause head injuries that result in developmental delays, learning disorders, mental retardation, or permanent cognitive impairments. Acts of physical or sexual abuse also involve emotional abuse. In fact, the emotional aftereffects of physical, sexual, and psychological abuse and neglect are just as traumatizing as the actual events.

Finding evidence of child maltreatment is an important step in intervention in a child's life. The following behavioral indicators warrant further investigation:

○ Radical mood swings

○ Sense of impending danger

○ Changes in eating habits

○ Nightmares, sleep disturbances, sleepwalking

○ Change in school performance, including a radical improvement in grades (overachieving)

○ Depression

○ Substance abuse

○ Hostile behavior or being overly withdrawn

○ Isolating self

○ Increased absenteeism from school

○ Being overly compliant

○ Bed wetting

○ Regressive or babyish behavior

○ Suicidal tendencies

○ Physical evidence and/or verbal hints of abuse

○ Startle response when someone raises a hand or arm

○ Unexplained fears

○ Repetitive and rhythmic movements (such as rocking)

○ Excessive attention to details

○ Absence of verbal, physical, or social communication with others
  (Brown 1991)

Physical indicators of abuse have a better chance of leading to intervention if they are reported early enough for a state agency to see the actual physical evidence. The following are some signs of physical maltreatment.

○ Bruising or bleeding on any areas of the body

○ Unexplained frequent injuries

○ Injuries not in normal areas for children (e.g., not knees or elbows)

○ Any type of burns or bites

○ Frequent stomachaches or digestive disturbances

○ Somatic illnesses

○ Significant weight gain or loss

○ Unexplained "battle scars" around the back side of the ears, inside the mouth, on the scalp

○ Signs of malnutrition

○ Injuries from lack of adult supervision (falling down stairs, ingestion of harmful substances)

(Brown 1991; National Center for Victims of Crime website)

Gauging the time frame and history of bruising can help to confirm stories or expose false ones. Although the coloration of bruises can only be approximated, the following can serve as a guideline:

○ Red: immediate bruise, within a few hours of injury

○ Blue: from 6 to 12 hours after the injury

○ Black-purple: from 12 to 24 hours after the injury

○ Green tint, dark: from 4 to 6 days after the injury

○ Pale green to yellow: from 5 to 10 days after the injury

Bites and burns are serious injuries and demonstrate the seriousness of the abuse. These symptoms are usually signs of escalated physical abuse that has been occurring over a period of time, and may indicate some pathology in the abuse. These should be responded to with immediate intervention.

### Emotional Abuse

Emotional abuse can be one of the most difficult types of abuse to identify because of its lack of physical evidence. It is described as the willful destruction or significant impairment of a child's competence (National Center for Victims of Crime website). Although similar to emotional neglect in that the parent is failing to provide something needed, in emotional abuse, the parent is actively participating in something damaging to the child.

Emotional abuse includes the following:

- Emotional and verbal assaults such as name calling and degrading remarks
- Physical confinement that causes psychological damage, such as being confined in a dark closet, or tied to a bed
- Refusing treatment for a child's emotional illnesses
- Allowing the continuation of antisocial behavior in the child
- Not responding by nurturance or by social service intervention to emotional or physical illnesses, such as failure to thrive in infants

### Sexual Abuse

Sexual abuse is defined as the exploitation of a child for the sexual gratification of an adult, and encompasses the terms "child sexual abuse," "assault," and "exploitation" (National Center for Victims of Crime website). Sexual abuse includes any type of molestation, penetration, or fondling, as well as exposure to age-inappropriate sexual materials, talk, or actions. Sexual abuse is addressed separately in the second half of this chapter, as well as in Chapter 10 on rape and assault.

### Characteristics of an Abusive Family

Some children are targeted for abuse based on specific risk factors associated with their families. Brown (1991) mentioned four types of family dynamics that can lead to abuse. First, the child may be unwanted. This can happen if there are too many children in the family, if pregnancy occurs too soon after marriage, if the pregnancy is difficult, or if the child is illegitimate.

Second, the child may be abnormal in some way. For example, children are more likely to be abused if they are disabled, retarded, under- or overweight, have other medical problems, are considered ugly, or were born prematurely. Third, the child may carry a negative association; for example, by reminding the parents of someone they do not like (e.g., a relative, spouse, or other child). Finally, a child's assertiveness can lead to abuse. A child is more likely to be abused if that child is highly needy, hyperactive, demanding, gifted, learning-impaired, or has other needs that engage the parents in providing more care than they consider "normal" or than they give to other children in the family.

It should also be noted that children who are abused often do not have these risk factors. In such cases, the primary factor is the presence of a potentially violent adult who is in charge of their welfare. Abusive parents can be identified by some of the following characteristics:

- Emotionally needy or immature
- Isolated from support by friends or family
- Personally abused or neglected as children, or abused or neglected in an adult relationship
- Low self-esteem
- Addicted
- Never having felt loved
- Poor parenting skills or coping skills

Violence is a learned behavior that is transmitted by example from generation to generation within families. Those who were abused may go on to abuse their own children, and those children will react and handle stress in the same way—violently (Finkelhor 1994). In this way, a dysfunctional family is created and perpetuated.

Dysfunctional families are families in conflict, often characterized by patterns of abuse, low functionality, poor boundaries, inadequate coping skills, and sometimes substance abuse histories or exposure to substance-abusing adults (Wikipedia website 2005). In a dysfunctional family, each member may negatively affect another member, creating a chain of negative effects and dependence. Some families are not only socially isolated, but the adults—who have little ability to self-soothe or meet their own needs—attempt to have their children meet their emotional needs. This has been termed "emotional incest" (Love 1990).

Most dysfunctional families do not respond well to changes in their lives or environment. These changes add stress to the family members' daily lives and may erupt in abuse toward the children. Stresses that precipitate violence can include financial problems; unemployment; changes in the family structure due to separation, divorce, or added family members; and moving or eviction. While such events do not constitute the etiology of family violence, they can have an effect on the poor functioning of the adults.

In addition to direct family influences, broader socioeconomic factors can affect families in ways that increase the risk for violence. For example, research has found that children from families with low incomes experience maltreatment at a rate that is five times higher than that for children from higher income families.

## CRISIS INTERVENTION

Child abuse is a family-systems problem. Therefore, treatment must focus on each individual family member as well as the family as a cohesive unit. Treatment must be provided to the child, abuser, spouse, and siblings. You may not be the counselor responsible for all the aspects of this counseling within the family system. If you are working with the child, it may not be appropriate for you to work with the abusing parent, for instance. They may need to be referred to someone else in your agency or practice, or to another counselor. During this time, all counselors working with the family need to coordinate services and treatment approaches. Co-joint sessions may also be an option.

During crisis intervention, mandatory reporting of the abuse to a state agency is foremost. It is common for the child to be removed from the home during abuse and while the family is undergoing treatment. This action is determined by the investigating state agency. The child may indicate a preference to remain in the family. In fact, most children opt to be with the abusive family, either because they hope the abuse will stop or because they do not recognize the behavior as abusive.

Removing the child to a foster system as a crisis intervention will have limited effectiveness if the child is subsequently returned to the abusive family environment. This is also why the entire family must undergo treatment at the same time. Likewise, removing one child from an abusive family may put the remaining children at higher risk. Their removal is likely to be investigated as well, and your assessment of all children in the home is likely to be needed.

In addition to addressing the issue of living arrangements, crisis intervention should focus on helping the child deal with feelings of loss, abandonment, guilt, fear, and stress in a new environment. Helping the child develop positive coping mechanisms for placement in a new home may ward off acting-out behaviors, subsequent truancy, and other long-term behavioral problems.

Child abuse not followed up by counseling intervention can result in serious adult disorders, providing the children live to reach adulthood. These disorders can include depressive and anxiety disorders, compulsive behaviors and addictions, codependency, learning disorders, and trauma disorders. They can also include personality disorders. In extreme cases, they include dissociative disorders. (See Chapter 2, "The Psychodynamics of Trauma," and Chapter 10, "Sexual Trauma," for more information on long-term effects of untreated child maltreatment.)

### Client Concerns

○ Perceived abandonment by family

○ Wondering when the child will be reunited with the family

○ The family blaming the child for disclosure

○ Healing from physical injuries

### Secondary Victimizations

○ Other siblings becoming the target for abuse

○ Removal from a familiar environment, adjusting to a new home and school environment

○ Loss of friends and support

○ Stress associated with repeated interviews by the court system

○ Stigma of being a foster child

### Social Services Needed for the Whole Family

○ Child protection services

○ Crisis intervention counselor

- Guardian ad litem (for child victim)
- Prosecutor or attorney (for child victim)
- Defense attorney (for abuser/family)
- Offender treatment
- Family treatment
- Sibling treatment
- If offender is arrested, may need financial assistance, new housing, job placement, etc.
- Spouse counseling
- School guidance counselor (for child victim)

### SHORT-TERM COUNSELING

Short-term counseling may focus on child- or family-oriented issues. You can help the child adjust to the new foster home environment, which may include a new school. You can also address the child's sense of blame, guilt, and poor sense of self-worth. Stress management and positive coping skills should be taught. Loss issues, bereavement, anger, and acting out behaviors may need to be addressed. Because each child reacts differently, you should be flexible and respond to the child's most immediate counseling needs.

Family-oriented issues include how the child fits into the family system. These issues can best be dealt with using a family-systems approach. In addition, counseling may need to focus on issues of codependency, problems of children of alcoholics (if applicable), and parental drug addiction. Teaching communication both as a personal construct and in the family system is important. Even younger children can be taught effective communication skills.

The child (depending on age) may be ready for a group experience with other children who have experienced the same type of victimization. If the child is too young to engage with a group, play therapy or developmental play may be helpful.

If the offender is still in the home, counseling that individual is paramount. Violence is a learned behavior, and counseling can provide alternative ways of coping that do preclude violence. Intervening to stop potential abuse of any siblings is critical. It is also important to address how the family perceives the child(ren) who was a victim of abuse. The non-abusing spouse's reaction to the removal of the child, as well as the possible removal of the offender, may involve helping that spouse come to terms with any anger and resentment toward the child or the offender. Any addictions on the parts of the offender, spouse, or siblings will also need to be treated.

During short-term counseling, building trust and rapport with the abused child and family can strengthen their commitment to treatment. It has been noted that parental social support and compliance with treatment best predict the child's benefit from treatment. However, the family and child often both suffer from PTSD. You may find PTSD more difficult to recognize in the child than in adults. In fact, little research has addressed the merits of applying adult methods of treating PTSD to children with PTSD (Ruggiero, Morris, and Scotti 2001).

Child-specific responses to trauma are not necessarily listed as PTSD reactions or symptoms, and you need to be aware of the variances between adults and children. For instance, children who have been traumatized frequently exhibit regression of previously learned skills, withdrawn behavior, and separation difficulties (Lyons 1987; McNally 1991; Perrin, Smith, and Yule 2000; Scheeronga, Zeanah, Drell, and Larrieu 1995; Vogel and Vernberg 1993). Yet, these are not listed as symptoms in the *DSM-IV* for PTSD. While you may look for symptoms of fear (prevalent in PTSD) in the child, fear is often masked by agitated behavior (Ruggiero et al. 2001). To confuse matters further, some of the symptoms of trauma exposure are the same in adults and children, such as an increase in aggressive behavior (Stern, Lynch, Oates, O'Toole, and Cooney 1995); attention problems (McLeer and Ruggiero 2000); and deficits in academic (or, for adults, vocational) performance (Rust and Troupe 1991).

### Client Concerns

- Perceived abandonment by family
- Wondering when they will be reunited with the family
- Wondering if the abuser will be part of family
- The family blaming the child for disclosure
- Continued feelings of blame or guilt
- Fear, nightmares, bedwetting
- Healing from physical injuries

*Secondary Victimizations*

- Children may view themselves as criminals because they were removed and the abuser stayed (if applicable)
- Adjusting to a new home and school environment
- Loss of friends and support
- Stigma of being a foster child
- Repeated interviews with court system
- Inability to adjust to new environment
- Experiencing new abuse at foster home

*Social Services Needed for the Whole Family*

- Short-term counseling
- Child protective services
- Guardian ad litem (for child victim)
- Prosecutor or attorney (for child victim)
- Defense attorney (for abuser)
- Family counseling
- Offender counseling
- Sibling counseling
- Spouse counseling
- Group counseling for child victim (if applicable, based on age)
- Financial assistance (if abuser is arrested)
- School guidance counselor
- Play therapy or developmental play (if applicable, based on age)
- Prevention skills

## LONG-TERM COUNSELING

Most child abuse cases are not resolved with short-term counseling. When addressing the needs of the whole family unit (i.e., siblings, abuser, spouse, and the abused child), short-term counseling may quickly become long-term counseling. Issues dealt with in short-term counseling can be carried over into the long-term process.

Additional issues that may warrant discussion include whether the abuser is incarcerated and any inappropriate blame placed on the child victim as a result. A child's appearance in court is often difficult, and you will need to prepare the child for this process. The return home of the child and reunification of the family are long-term goals, as well as a concern if the abuser is also returning home. Prevention skills should be taught to the child victim as well as siblings and spouse to lessen the likelihood of re-victimization by the same abuser or a subsequent abuser.

The literature on childhood abuse lays out the possible long-term effects of childhood abuse. Of course, once a child has received treatment, counselors feel an increased optimism for that child's well-being. Nevertheless, the development of long-term effects depends on the length, intensity, and duration of the abuse, as well as on the victim's coping skills. Therefore, you should carefully monitor the child and any siblings for chronic pathology, acting out, or the presence of "victim syndrome." Persons with victim syndrome have an ongoing view of themselves as victims. Their identity is highly related to their self-concept of being someone else's target. Monitoring of adjustment issues and of affective or depressive disorders will facilitate diagnosis and future treatment.

It is not uncommon for children to be treated at the initial disclosure of abuse, and then to return to counseling throughout childhood and adolescence. Many of the long-term effects of child abuse are connected to developmental tasks (Hulme 2004) and arise as the child ages and encounters these tasks (Cicchetti and Lunch 1995). Developmental deficits include a delay or inability to self-regulate emotions, behaviors, and sexuality in a manner that is age appropriate (DeBellis 1999), poor communication of needs and feelings, low problem-solving abilities, attachment irregularities, and social incompetence. It is usually more effective to deal with the child when developmental deficits are uncovered than to keep the child in counseling indefinitely, waiting for a deficit that needs work to be discovered.

You should explain to the family that the child can be expected to return for more counseling in a few months or years. Although the need for further counseling can appear at any time, issues of adolescence and sexuality are likely to instigate this need. During such times, short-term counseling can be reestablished.

### Client Concerns

- Being able to return home
- Abuser returning home
- Wondering whether abuser has really changed
- Wondering how the rest of the family feels about the child since disclosure
- Fear of retaliation
- Unsure of new coping and prevention skills
- Shame, guilt

### Secondary Victimizations

- May be labeled "foster child" or "abused child" on return to previous school, or other stigma
- Old friends may not renew acquaintance or may have made new friendships

### Social Services Needed for the Whole Family System

- Child protective services
- Guardian ad litem (for child victim)
- Prosecutor or attorney
- Court mediation services
- Parenting classes
- Offender reentry program
- Long-term family counseling
- Long-term sibling counseling
- Long-term child victim counseling
- Assertiveness training (child victim)
- Prevention skills

#### RECOMMENDED READING

Deaton, Wendy, and Kendall Johnson. *No More Hurt: A Child's Workbook about Recovering from Abuse.* Alameda, CA: Hunter House Publishers, 1991.

Johnson, Kendall. *Trauma in the Lives of Children,* 2nd Edition. Alameda, CA: Hunter House Publishers, 1998.

Kolko, David, and Cynthia Cupit Sweson. *Assessing and Treating Physically Abused Children and Their Families: A Cognitive Behavioral Approach* (Interpersonal Violence: The Practice Series). Thousand Oaks, CA: Sage Publications, 2002.

Kramer, Donald. *Legal Rights of Children.* Colorado Springs, CO: Shepard's/ McGraw-Hill, 1994.

Rossman, B. B. Robbie, and Mindy Susan Rosenberg, eds. *Multiple Victimization of Children: Conceptual, Development, Research and Treatment Issues.* New York: Haworth Maltreatment & Trauma Press, 1998.

Trotter, Chris. *Helping Abused Children and Their Families.* Thousand Oaks, CA: Sage Publications, 2004.

## RESOURCES

American Humane Association Children's Division  ◌  (303) 792-9900

Children's Defense Fund  ◌  (800) 233-1200  ◌  (202) 628-8787

ChildHelp USA  ◌  (800) 4ACHILD (422-4453)

Family Violence and Sexual Assault Institute  ◌  (903) 534-5100

National Center for Children Exposed to Violence  ◌  www.nccev.org

National Child Traumatic Stress Network  ◌  www.nctsnet.org

National Clearinghouse on Child Abuse and Neglect
(800) 394-3366  ◌  (703) 385-7565

National Committee to Prevent Child Abuse  ◌  (312) 663-3520

Rape, Abuse and Incest National Network (RAINN)
(800) 656-HOPE (656-4673)  ◌  www.rainn.org

## Overview of Child Abuse

*Crisis Intervention:* Perception of abandonment by the family, worry about reuniting, fear of blame from the family, need for healing of physical injuries

*Short-Term Counseling:* Uncertainty if abuser will be part of the family, fears, nightmares, bedwetting, sees self as criminal (if child was removed and abuser stayed in the home)

*Long-Term Counseling:* Being able to return home, when/if abuser will return home, has abuser changed, how does family feel about the child since disclosure, fear of retaliation

*Secondary Victimizations:* Worry about siblings being abused, removal from a familiar environment, loss of friends, stress associated with court interviews and procedures, stigma of foster care placement, adjusting to new school and home, possibility of new abuse at foster home

*Social/Public Services Needed:* Child protective services, crisis intervention counselor; guardian ad litem; prosecutor/attorney for child; defense attorney for abuser; offender treatment; family counseling; sibling counseling; if offender is arrested, family may need financial assistance; housing and job placement services; spouse counseling; school guidance counselor; short-term counseling for child, family, siblings, offender; play or developmental play therapy; prevention skills; long-term counseling for child, family, siblings, offender; assertiveness training for child and siblings

## Childhood Sexual Abuse

○ Victims of childhood sexual abuse are 27.7 times more likely to be arrested for prostitution as adults than are nonvictims. (Widom 1995)

○ Convicted rape/sexual assault offenders serving time report two-thirds of their victims were under the age of 18, and 58 percent said their victims were age 12 or younger. (U.S. Department of Justice 1997)

○ In 90 percent of child rapes in children less than 12 years old, the child knew the offender. (U.S. Department of Justice 1997)

○ One of every seven victims of sexual assault reported to law-enforcement agencies was under the age of six. (U.S. Department of Justice 1997)

### VICTIM'S STORY                                          *MICAH*

*Micah was four years old when he was brought to counseling by his mother and grandmother. They had concerns that he was sexually acting out with his eighteen-month-old brother and some playmates. Micah's suspected abuser was his stepfather, Richard.*

*Micah began by insisting he had never been touched. Later he admitted he had been, but could not tell. Then he began to talk about his knowledge of oral sex and other behaviors. When Richard became aware Micah was being taken to counseling, Micah's story changed. He alleged he was playing outside his home when a man walked past and touched his penis —outside his clothing—three times in a row. Each time he told the story, it was more or less elaborate, depending on Micah's desire to discuss it.*

*A year later, Micah was placed in a children's play group. By that time, he was living with his grandparents. At any mention of the word "family," he would get on his hands and knees and buck like a bronco. Although his feelings took some time to access, it was clear that removing him from the unstable environment with his mother and placing him with grandparents was a good move toward his eventual recovery.*

*Micah remained in counseling off and on throughout his childhood— returning to work on issues related to delayed social and emotional development. By the time he was an older teen, he had successfully completed counseling and seemed to have integrated his sexual abuse experiences and healed significantly.*

## BACKGROUND INFORMATION

The most common form of childhood sexual abuse is incest, which has been defined as the "sexual abuse of a child by a relative or other person in a position of trust and authority over the child" (National Center for Victims of Crime and Crime Victims Research and Treatment Center 1992). Incest can be committed by persons with a direct blood or caregiving relationship to the victim, such as grandparents or aunts and uncles or a parent's lover, live-in nanny, or housekeeper. In addition, as indicated by the dictionary definition of incest, it can be committed by siblings or cousins. And, of course, a child can be sexually abused by friends as well as strangers. In this chapter, we look at the consequences and treatment of childhood sexual abuse (primarily incest), and in the following chapter on rape and sexual assault, we look further at the long-term effects and treatment of adult victims of incest.

Many victims of childhood sexual abuse suffer long-term mental-health consequences. Children who are sexually abused often exhibit physical, behavioral, and emotional symptoms. This is crucially important for adults to understand in order to make sure that early intervention occurs. The physical problems that accompany sexual abuse, as well as the emotional and behavioral changes in the child, are often discernable if one knows for what one is looking. In fact, behavioral changes often precede physical symptoms as first indicators of sexual abuse (American Humane Association Children's Division 1993). To this end, adult education is crucial in intervening in childhood sexual abuse cases.

Consistent research has shown that children who experience sexual abuse have symptoms that range from chronic depression to low self-esteem, from sexual dysfunction to dissociative identity disorder. Raped children have shown higher life-time prevalence rates of psychological problems, compared with nonvictim groups, and are at significantly higher risk for depression, anxiety, PTSD, sexual dysfunction, and relationship problems than are other groups (Briere 1996; Hulme 2000; Jumper 1995; McCauley et al. 1997). As mentioned in Chapter 2, consulting a list of trauma-related disorders can help counselors identify the types of disorders that are likely to occur as a result of untreated physical and sexual child abuse.

The developmental tasks of childhood are based on successful completion of tasks at previous stages (Cicchetti and Lynch 1995). Sexual abuse disrupts these developmental milestones. The disruption of critical developmental tasks has the potential to cause profound negative long-term effects (Hulme 2004), including a constellation of adult symptoms that in various combinations typify the psychological disorders of borderline personality disorder, dissociative identity disorder, substance abuse, somatization, and eating disorders (Cole and Putnam 1992). These effects are described in greater detail in Chapter 12 as examples of adult symptoms of sexual trauma that were untreated during childhood.

Other disruptions include damage to physical and psychological self-integrity, self-regulatory skills for affect and impulse control, and the capacity for age-appropriate relationships (Cole and Putnam 1992). Powerlessness experienced in child abuse can result in a reduced internal locus of control and a lowered sense of competency and efficacy that often continues into adulthood (Putnam and Trickett 1993; Trickett and Putnam 1993). In addition, children who are abused or neglected are more likely to become criminal offenders as adults than are children who have not been victimized.

## INDICATORS OF SEXUAL ABUSE

Behavioral indicators of sexual abuse are red flags for intervention. Although some of the indicators listed below could be linked to other life circumstances, this constellation of symptoms warrants further investigation:

○ Sexually precocious, seductive, or sexual acting out

○ Abnormal knowledge about sex or sex acts

○ Radical mood swings

○ Sense of impending danger

○ Changes in eating habits

○ Boredom with same-age peers or activities

○ Nightmares or sleep disturbances

○ Change in school performance, including radical improvement in grades (overachieving)

○ Depression

○ Substance abuse

○ Damaged goods syndrome

○ Hostile behavior

○ Fear of adults or adolescents

○ Fear of being photographed

○ Anxiety toward authority figures

○ Refusal to disrobe in gym class

○ Pseudo-maturity

○ Overcompliancy

○ Aggressiveness

○ Babyish or clinging behavior

○ Bedwetting

○ Attention-getting behavior, beyond normal

○ Recruiting other peers into involvement with adults

○ Suicidal tendencies

○ Inability to trust

○ Hints regarding sexual abuse

○ Self mutilation or other self injury

○ Hyperactivity, inability to concentrate

In addition, counselors should be alert to the physical markers of sexual abuse in children:

○ Sexually transmitted diseases

○ Bruising or bleeding on any area of body, particularly sexual areas

○ Frequent stomach or digestive pain

○ Somatic illnesses

○ Urinary tract and yeast infections

○ Difficulty urinating

○ Colon problems

○ Significant weight loss or gain

○ Purging

○ Foul odor from sexual organs

○ Discharge from sexual organs

○ Lubricant residues around vagina and rectum

○ Persistent sore throats

○ Strong gagging reflex

○ Exhaustion

(Brown 1991; Hammerschlag 1996)

## CRISIS INTERVENTION

Acquiring disclosure from sexually abused children is of great concern to counselors, Department of Social Service workers, prosecutors, victim advocates, and expert testimony providers. Entire cases, and thus the child's future, can be made or broken on how the information is elicited. Unfortunately, the issue of how information was derived often receives more attention than what the child actually discloses.

Interviewing young children can present many difficulties, especially in the case of sexual abuse. The child may not be able to comprehend the abuse, have difficulty defining the abusive behaviors to adults, and have trouble processing related emotions. Questioning the child directly or indirectly can result in memories being pushed further into the subconscious as an act of repression. In addition, how you as a counselor elicit information from a child can be seen as contamination of the case, should it go to court.

To address these issues, protocols have been developed to elicit information, indicating what you can and cannot do, what can be said and what cannot, and who is in the best position to interview the child to assure protocols are followed. Elaborate training is now offered about how to interview children and how to provide counseling that will not contaminate a case. This training should be mandatory for counselors who work with children.

Interviewing should focus on the child's beliefs, assumptions, and attitudes about the abuse, along with observing the symptomatology the child displays. Areas of questioning include the following:

- How the sexual abuse was initiated
- Who was responsible
- Any role the child may have had in its occurrence or continuance
- How the child feels about herself
- How the child feels about the offender and her family

Assessment and testing are important in cases of childhood sexual abuse. Because PTSD often manifests differently in children than in adults, some specialists recommend that you use a broad spectrum instrument or supplemental tests and inventories that target other types of responses besides those related to PTSD. In some cases, it may be advisable to have the child tested by a clinical child psychologist who has experience with a broad range of instruments and tools.

Following disclosure of abuse, the same procedures apply to counseling sexually abused children that were covered in the discussion of physical abuse. The state must be notified, as required by mandatory reporting laws. After the state has investigated and interviewed the child, family, and others involved in the case, the state may request or suggest the use of a rape exam, if applicable, for the child. Although all efforts should be made to spare the child this kind of invasive procedure, if physical evidence will make the difference between a prosecutable case and a non-prosecutable case, it may be requested. Physical evidence is especially critical when the child is too young or has poor verbal skills. For children, the pelvic and anal exam can be as traumatic as the initial sexual abuse because it feels like and emotionally represents the assault itself. More counseling is called for following an exam of this nature.

In addition to the aspects of crisis intervention and stabilization discussed for victims of physical abuse, additional factors may apply for victims of childhood sexual abuse. For instance, during the crisis, it is not unusual for children to feel they are "damaged goods." This feeling reflects the societal and familial perception of the child's abuse and transfers to the child's own self perception of being weak, vulnerable, used, and often partially to blame for what happened. In older children, the damaged goods syndrome includes concerns about pregnancy, sexually transmitted diseases, or even AIDS. Older children may act out what they have been made to feel: a "whore," a "slut," or "no longer a good boy or girl." Some children become apathetic toward their emerging sexuality. This is reflected in their choices about when and with whom to have sex.

The guilt in children who have been sexually abused differs slightly from that of victims of physical abuse. Because of the level of participation involved in sexual abuse, children feel more guilty about not fighting harder, not fighting at all, or participating, even under severe duress. Guilt can be heightened if the abuser leads the child to believe she encouraged it, invited it, or seemed to enjoy it because she did not fight enough. If victims become sexually aroused during the abuse, they may feel guilt, confusion, and anger toward their bodies for betraying them.

You can reduce a child's fear and anxiety by decreasing arousal responses to cues and by teaching the child how to neutralize feelings about the fear and the cue that brought the fear back. Providing assertiveness training and teaching stress-management and anger-management techniques also help. Allowing older children a safe environment in which to talk about their fears and the specifics of abuse will lessen the effect the memories have on them. Younger children may need help with safety procedures before bedtime to test if any abusers are present. This could include looking under the bed, helping to lock the doors, reading a story that makes them feel safe or empowered, and rehearsing safety or prevention skills or plans.

### Client Concerns

- ○ Removal from home and abuser
- ○ Guilt, fear
- ○ Fear of disclosure
- ○ Perceived abandonment, loss of friends and family
- ○ Finding safe persons
- ○ Rape exam
- ○ Testifying in court
- ○ Healing of physical and sexual injuries

### Secondary Victimizations

- ○ Stigma from sexual abuse
- ○ Adjusting to new environment (if moved into the foster-care system)
- ○ Insensitive treatment by the court system
- ○ Constant interviews

### Social Services Needed for the Whole Family System

- ○ Child protective services
- ○ Rape/medical exam
- ○ Guardian ad litem (for child victim)
- ○ Crisis intervention counselor
- ○ Prosecutor or attorney (for child victim)
- ○ Defense attorney (if abuser is family member)
- ○ If abuser is removed from home, family may need financial assistance
- ○ Family counseling
- ○ Sibling, spouse, offender counseling
- ○ School guidance counselor

## SHORT-TERM COUNSELING

Beginning short-term counseling can be difficult when family members, parents, and the sexually abused child are struggling with trust issues, role confusion, and blurred boundaries. Finding key safe persons for the child and building rapport and trust are key elements at the outset of treatment. Although it would be natural for the parents to fill this role, if one parent is the abuser and the other is in denial, too stressed, or has PTSD, you may need to turn to extended family members instead (e.g., an older sibling, cousin, aunt, or uncle).

The child's safe person can serve as a bridging tool in the following ways:

○ Preparing the child for counseling

○ Exhibit stability

○ Support the child throughout counseling

○ Come to the actual counseling sessions with the child

○ Help the child express feelings and content (if needed)

○ Protect the child from the abuser or unsafe family home life

During short-term counseling, you will notice some deficits in the child. Sexually abused children are often isolated from others; they may be instructed to not enter into relationships with others as ways of protecting the abuser from a child's disclosure. Poor social skills are the likely outcome. The child may seem awkward in attempts to relate to other children and may even be listless and disinterested. Underneath are issues of helplessness, powerlessness, and lack of control.

Trust issues can arise both in the counseling setting and when trying to resolve family issues. If the abuser was a parent or family member, the child will have lost trust in that person. Trust will also be lost toward a parent who failed to stop the abuse. Some children will naturally begin to distrust all adults if the abuser was an adult. Additionally, the outcome of reporting will also affect trust. Was the disclosure made to an adult who ignored it or who did not intervene? Was the case turned over to law enforcement and the criminal-justice system, only to have nothing done? Such issues can seriously undermine a child's trust in not only individual adults but also social systems. If the child's level of trust is very low, significant time may be needed to rebuild it. Often the slowest part of treatment is building trust and rapport.

While some sexually abused children have low social skills and are immature for their age, others display pseudo-maturity. Despite outward signs of pseudo-maturity, however, the children are still dependent and have not completed some basic developmental tasks for their age. Children who are sexually abused are thrust very quickly into ways of coping that do not allow them to be children for long. Development can be delayed in areas related to affect as well as cognition. Older children may have to take on roles of pseudo-adults, such as taking care of younger children, cleaning and cooking, and generally anticipating and fulfilling other people's needs. Because sexual abuse strips children of control and mastery, therapy needs to focus on helping them choose options that empower them and enhance the mastery of skills. Appropriate strategies include assertiveness training, communication skills, prevention skills, and building self-esteem.

Counselors should be aware that parents frequently minimize the effects of trauma on their children (Sternberg et al. 1993); they may under-report internalizing behaviors (e.g., the child's fears or anxieties), while over-reporting externalizing behaviors (Perrin, Smith, and Yule 2000). Therefore, working with the parents (or the nonoffending parent) to enable them to more accurately understand and respond to the child's traumatic response is very helpful. Training parents in behavior management can increase the parents' recognition of trauma-related avoidance behaviors and other relevant dynamics. The better parents understand the experience of traumatized children, the more they can become allies for the counselor and provide pertinent information that will move the therapy ahead.

### Client Concerns

- Inability to trust others
- Removal from home or removal of offender
- Guilt, shame, stigma
- Disclosure
- Loss of family and friends
- Healing from physical and sexual injuries
- Misunderstanding of what is happening to them emotionally

○ "Damaged goods" syndrome

○ Helplessness, lack of control

### Secondary Victimizations

○ Court system, interviews

○ Media coverage that may identify the child as a victim

○ Stigma of sexual abuse

○ Trouble in school with grades or acting out

### Social Services Needed for the Whole Family System

○ Child protective services

○ Guardian ad litem (for child victim)

○ Short-term counselor

○ Prosecutor or attorney (for child victim)

○ Defense attorney (if abuser is family member)

○ Financial assistance (if abuser is removed from home)

○ Housing and other social services (if needed)

○ Family counseling

○ Spouse, sibling, offender counseling

○ School guidance counselor

## LONG-TERM COUNSELING

Treating sexually abused children differs from treating adult survivors of sexual abuse. Different issues must be considered for male child victims and female child victims. Assessing the trauma to determine the most appropriate direction for counseling can be accomplished with the resources described in Chapter 3, on assessments. Methods other than cognitive therapies are often necessary when working with children.

Because childhood trauma can lead to adult psychopathy (Fairbank et al. 1993; Keane et al. 1994), the goal of intensive therapy for child abuse is to ward off future pathology. Long-term counseling can deal with such issues as anger, rage, and hostility. A child may try to cope with the anxiety produced by the traumatic experience either through approach strategies (e.g., aggressive behavior, inappropriate sexual behavior) or in ways that signal avoidance and denial (e.g., guilt, shame, running away). Gathering information from adult sources about the child's behaviors (i.e., whether approach or avoidance) will help guide your treatment strategies.

Anger is almost always a treatment issue. Young juvenile offenders who have been victimized exhibit a great deal of anger. They need to learn how to direct anger at the appropriate person and issues so that it is not deflected and turned inward or misdirected and used on innocent others. Early intervention can go a long way toward deactivating the anger and rage that turns children into juvenile offenders or becomes debilitating when they reach adulthood.

The child's anger toward the non-offending adult is equally important to address. Adult women abused as children often spend considerable time working through ambivalent feelings toward a nonabusing caregiver who, they feel certain, knew or had a hunch something was happening and did not intervene.

If you are working with the family unit, family therapy and approaches to codependency and addiction can be incorporated. Groups can be utilized as a resource for offenders, spouses, siblings, and child victims. Creative therapies (e.g., music, art, play, movement, and journaling) are ways to help non-cognitive, non-expressive children give voice to their pain and inner conflicts.

Sexually abused children are often seen in counseling throughout their childhoods and adolescence, even if only intermittently. Counseling typically is required during important developmental periods. The counselor should leave the door open for more counseling, as the need arises. It is also important for parents to understand that a particular set of counseling sessions may not conclude the child's long-term treatment.

### Client Concerns

- Reuniting with the family (if the child has been removed)
- Wondering whether the offender has really been rehabilitated
- Fear of abuse from others
- Blame

### Secondary Victimizations

- Stigma of sexual abuse
- Loss of familiar environment
- Trouble with schoolwork, failing school
- Acting out aggression or sexuality
- Repeated court hearings
- Exposure by media coverage and being identified as a sexual abuse victim

### Social Services Needed by the Whole Family System

- Child protective services
- Guardian ad litem (for child victim)
- Prosecutor or attorney (for child victim)
- Defense attorney (if offender is a family member)
- Long-term counselor
- Family counseling
- Sibling, spouse, offender counseling
- School guidance counselor
- Counseling to bridge child back into the home

## RECOMMENDED READING

Deblinger, Ester, and Anne Hope Heflin. *Treating Sexually Abused Children and Their Nonoffending Parents: A Cognitive-Behavioral Approach* (Interpersonal Violence: The Practice Series). Thousand Oaks, CA: Sage Publications, 1996.

Friedrich, William N. *Psychological Assessment of Sexually Abused Children and Their Families* (Interpersonal Violence: The Practice Series). Thousand Oaks, CA: Sage Publications, 2001.

Johnson, Kendall. *After the Storm: Healing after Trauma, Tragedy and Terror.* Alameda, CA: Hunter House Publishers, 2006.

Kluft, Richard, ed. *Incest-Related Syndromes of Adult Psychopathy.* Arlington, VA: American Psychiatric Association, 2005.

Kramer, Donald. *Legal Rights of Children.* Colorado Springs, CO: Shepard's/ McGraw-Hill, 1994.

Mather, Cynthia, and Kristian Debye. *How Long Does it Hurt? A Guide to Recovering from Incest and Sexual Abuse for Teenagers, Their Friends, and Their Families.* San Francisco, CA: Jossey-Bass, 2004.

Pence, Donna, and Wilson, Charles. *Team Investigation of Child Sexual Abuse: The Uneasy Alliance.* Thousand Oaks, CA: Sage Publications, 1994.

Rossman, B.B. Robbie, and Mindy Susan Rosenberg. *Multiple Victimization of Children: Conceptual, Development, Research and Treatment Issues.* New York: Haworth Maltreatment & Trauma Press, 1998.

Tobin, Pnina, and Sue Levinson Kessner. *Keeping Kids Safe: A Child Sexual Abuse Prevention Manual.* Alameda, CA: Hunter House Publishers, 2002.

**RESOURCES**

American Humane Association Children's Division
(303) 792-9900

Children's Defense Fund
(800) 233-1200    ○    (202) 628-8787

ChildHelp USA
(800) 4ACHILD (422-4453)

Family Violence and Sexual Assault Institute
(903) 534-5100

National Center for Children Exposed to Violence
www.nccev.org

National Child Traumatic Stress Network
www.nctsnet.org

National Clearinghouse on Child Abuse and Neglect
(800) 394-3366    ○    (703) 385-7565

National Committee to Prevent Child Abuse
(312) 663-3520

Rape, Abuse and Incest National Network (RAINN)
(800) 656-HOPE (656-4673)    ○    www.rainn.org

## Overview of Child Sexual Abuse

*Crisis Intervention:* Child's removal from the family/abuser, guilt and fear, fear of disclosure, perceived abandonment, rape exam, testifying in court, healing of physical and sexual injuries

*Short-Term Counseling:* Inability to trust others, removal from home/offender, guilt, shame, stigma, disclosure, loss of family and friends, misunderstanding of what is happening emotionally, "damaged goods" syndrome, helplessness, out of control

*Long-Term Counseling:* Reunification issues, wondering if offender has been rehabilitated (if applicable), fear of abuse from others, blame

*Secondary Victimizations:* Stigma from sexual abuse, adjusting to new environment (if removed or placed in foster care), insensitive treatment by the court system, constant interviews, media coverage that may identify child as the victim, academic decline, loss of familiar environment, acting out aggressively or sexually

*Social/Public Services Needed by the Whole Family System:* Child protective services; rape or medical exam; guardian ad litem (for child victims); crisis intervention counselor; prosecutor or attorney (for child); defense attorney (if abuse is family member); if abuser is removed, financial assistance may be needed; short-term counselor for child; long-term counselor for child; family counselor; sibling, spouse and/or offender counseling; school guidance counselor; reunification counseling

## Adolescent Violence—
## When Kids Can Be Victims or Offenders

○ In 2001, 1.8 million teens (12 to 19 years old) were victims of violence.

○ 83,000 were raped or sexually assaulted.

○ 47 violent deaths occurred in schools.

○ Violent victimization during adolescence raises the odds of being a perpetrator or a victim of violence in adulthood.

○ Violent victimization in adolescence nearly doubles the odds of drug use in adulthood.

○ Violent victimization in adolescence doubles the odds of getting PTSD.

○ 20 percent of students reported the presence of street gangs at their school. (National Center for Victims of Crime website)

○ In 1997, 1,700 juveniles were implicated in 1,400 murders. (Office of Juvenile Justice Programs website)

## VICTIM'S STORY                                    *BLAKE*

*Blake was only six when his father left. After that, he encountered a series of his mother's deadbeat boyfriends, one after another. Many of them beat him, abused him, and even molested him. His life was filled with challenges, such as poverty, hunger, and lack of supervision (he was a latch-key kid). He was never treated for the abuse he suffered at his mom's boyfriends' hands; in fact, his mother didn't even know about the incidents. By age 12, Blake had renamed himself "Blade," and his anger had become evident. His life was punctuated with small petty crimes, including fighting, truancy, stealing, and breaking and entering. These petty crimes grew into felonies as Blade continued to manifest his anger, often saying, "I'm just getting even with the bastards who hurt me." Car jackings, weapons charges, and drug dealing all landed him time in the juvenile justice system. Gang involvement, assault, and attempted murder were added to his list of charges when he was age 17. By 18, Blade's life had become that of a career criminal.*

*His life reminds us how common it can be for an untreated victim to slip through the cracks and let his anger to turn him into an offender. The juvenile justice system is full of such stories of victims who became offenders.*

## BACKGROUND INFORMATION

Today's youth and teens face shocking amounts of violence. This includes not only violence from earlier childhood neglect, physical abuse, or sexual abuse, but violence that permeates other areas of their dating, school, and social experiences. It is harrowing to think that youth face the following forms of violence so early in life:

○ School bullying

○ Peer assaults or peer-to-peer homicides

○ Sexual exploitation by a teacher, coach, or clergy member

○ Cyberstalking

- Concealed weapons on campus
- Violent drug deals gone bad
- Gang attacks
- Abduction
- Date rape or physical abuse between dating partners
- Hate crimes based on race, ethnicity, or sexual orientation
- School shootings

The school has become a prime location for violence in many young people's lives. The Columbine school shootings are still a vivid memory, and more school shootings take their place among the traumas we will never forget. Ironically, the day I began writing this chapter, the Minnesota School Shooting (March 2005) occurred, reminding me of the violence and trauma youth face on a daily basis and the needs they have for competent counseling and advocacy.

Hamburg, Elliott, and Williams (1998) reported that nearly one-fourth of students nationwide had brought a gun to school. This was the case even though one in four major school districts used metal detectors to reduce the number of weapons brought into schools (Wheeler and Baron 1993). According to Ward, in 1997, one youth was murdered by gun fire every two hours. Students in the ninth through twelfth grades reported being offered, sold, or given illegal drugs in school (Kaufman et al. 2000), and 35 percent of students reported a gang presence in their schools (Howell and Lynch 2000). Moreover, teachers don't always provide a safe place for troubled youth; according to one study, the primary reason for teacher certification revocation was sexual misconduct (Whiteby 1992).

Personal relationships are not safe ground, either. As many as 45 percent of young females and 43 percent of young males in one survey indicated physical abuse occurred among their dating partners (O'Keefe and Trester 1998). Arrests of juveniles for murder increased 85 percent between 1987 and 1991 (National Crime Prevention Council 1995), and multiple offender homicides involving juvenile offenders more than doubled between the mid 1980s and late 1990s (Snyder, Sickmund, and Poe-Yamagata 1997). Clearly, with the growing amount of youth violence and victimization, counselors are likely to encounter juvenile victims.

CRISIS INTERVENTION

Because youth violence covers a broad range of crimes, counselors and advocates should consult the other chapters in this book for treatment issues and client concerns (e.g., rape, homicide, domestic violence, stalking) relevant to this population.

When working with youth violence, you should keep the following in mind:

○ Potentially low desire to report crimes

○ Possible low motivation to enter or stay in counseling

○ Influence by peer perceptions of counseling as "uncool"

Normal teenagers often have a difficult time with communication; this can be exacerbated when a young person is traumatized. Although youth may be unwilling to disclose, their victimization can result in significant issues to be addressed during counseling. Depending on the victimization and reaction to it, a youth may present with the following:

○ Physical ailments (but no mention of the victimization)

○ Withdrawal from peers

○ Apparent indifference to learning

Assessment and testing can guide your intervention. It may be necessary to coordinate testing and other services through the school guidance counselor and alert that person to some of the youth's behavioral and academic issues.

Crisis stabilization is determined not only by your assessments and testing, but also by the teen's clinical response. Intervention for PTSD can include symptom reduction, reducing anxiety or flashbacks, managing intrusive thoughts, and decreasing arousal responses.

As mentioned in the child abuse chapter, mandatory reporting laws exist for child abuse if a teen has experienced it. Other victimizations, however, may fall under client privilege. You should be familiar with which ones you must report and which you cannot report or disclose to the parents without the teen's permission.

Victimizations that happen on a school campus should be reported to the school if the victim is willing. Teens who victimize others can place the school at higher risk of even more serious violence than what has been committed so far. Escalating acts of violence are common on campus and victimizers are often able to recruit others to join in.

Crisis intervention can help teens decide how to report the incident and how to deal with the stigma that may be applied to them because of their disclosure. Concern about increased victimization is understandable.

In addition, victimization places youth at an increased risk for drug and alcohol abuse, which can have a trickle-down effect to other problems in their lives and disrupt learning and development. The drugs and alcohol used to medicate feelings about the victimization also place youth at a greater risk for committing violent acts themselves (National Center for Victims of Crime website). Crisis intervention can focus on preventing substance use and on teaching self-soothing and stress management skills.

### Client Concerns

- Whether to report crime to law enforcement
- Reluctance to report the crime to school
- The need to notify school guidance counselor
- PTSD symptoms (if applicable)
- Campus safety
- Peer pressure about reporting and/or counseling

### Secondary Victimizations

- Loss of friends due to crime and/or reporting
- Stigma of being a snitch if a report is made
- Injuries and treatment
- Academic difficulties
- Increased risk for drug and alcohol abuse

### Social/Public Services Needed

- Protective services (if applicable)
- Guardian ad litem (if applicable)
- Prosecutor

- ○ Crisis intervention counselor

- ○ Medical treatment, if applicable

- ○ School guidance counselor

- ○ Also see services listed in chapters where the specific type of victimization the youth experienced is discussed

## SHORT-TERM COUNSELING

Any issues that remain following crisis intervention, such as fear of disclosure, fear of increased campus violence, PTSD symptoms, and academic problems can continue to be the focus during short-term counseling.

Counselors should be aware that youth who have been victimized at an early age and who are untreated are likely to develop at-risk behaviors. Untreated youth show traumatic stress symptoms and have an impaired capacity to succeed in school and develop healthy relationships (National Center for Victims of Crime website). In some cases, untreated youth violence can lead to a diagnosis of conduct disorder (in children under age 18) and antisocial personality disorder (in adults over age 18). The diagnosis of conduct disorder actually transfers to the diagnosis of antisocial personality disorder if a youth meets the criteria when turning 18. Juveniles who fall into this diagnosis are at a high risk for taking the leap from victim to offender.

The literature indicates that the development of antisocial behavior (i.e., conduct disorder) is the result of the interplay of multiple factors (Dekovic, Janssen, and Van As 2003). The etiology of this diagnosis in youth who have been victimized relates to the following factors:

- ○ Neuro-biological and neuro-physiological impairment, often from previous chronic trauma and psychological exposures (Dekovic et al. 2003)

- ○ Attachment disorder, including such factors as pathological parenting (Frick et al. 1992)

- ○ Parental drug use

- ○ Cognitive functioning deficits (problem solving and verbal ability)

- ○ Family characteristics, such as poor conflict management, monitoring, and supervision

○ Peer influences, such as association with deviant peers, lack of association with pro-social peers, and poor socialization skills

○ School predictors of low academic achievement, such as dropout, low commitment to education, and poor structure within the school

○ Community constructs, such as violence exposure, neighborhood criminal activity, and lack of neighborhood support (Henggeler and Sheidow 2003)

These represent a few of the possible influencing factors (see Chapter 2, "The Psychodynamics of Trauma"). Assessments or testing that can reveal these types of issues will help the counselor when considering short-term counseling goals. Life skills, positive peer associations, resiliency, and coping skills can provide proactive interventions to counteract negative family and environmental influences.

Early childhood and youth violence appear to be part of the equation that leads a youth victim to become a youth offender, as seen in Blake's victim story at the beginning of this segment. This progression highlights the necessity for treatment to avoid adult psychopathology. Many different family-focused interventions aim to reduce problem behavior in youth (Kazdin 1997). Unfortunately, many youth with problem behaviors remain untreated (Koot and Verhulst 1992). Many parents also are reluctant to seek help. Although the parents may manage to cope with their children's problems while still small, when the children reach adolescence, their problems can become more serious (Dekovic and Janssen 2003). These problems can morph into teenage acts of violence. Many of the parents whose teenagers went on school shooting rampages recognized the youth had problems, but did not think they would ever develop into killers.

Early treatment of children who were victimized is often easier and more effective than treating teen offenders who were victimized as children. The treatment of this latter group is complicated not only by their years of untreated victimization and resulting trauma disorder, but also by their criminal-justice involvement, social deviancy, and the problems chronic delinquency and academic failure bring. While the core issues of early victimization are the same for both a victimized child and a teen offender victimized as a child, the layers of additional problems that manifest in a teen offender's life make treatment longer and more difficult than it would have been if treated initially. This, of course, suggests that the earlier we treat victimization, the more likely we are able to prevent teen delinquency or adult psychopathy.

### Client Concerns

- ❍ Peer reactions to the victimization and/or reporting
- ❍ Increase in campus violence (if applicable)
- ❍ Injuries and treatment
- ❍ Reduction in social skills
- ❍ Academic problems
- ❍ Symptom reduction

### Secondary Victimizations

- ❍ Loss of friends due to crime and/or reporting
- ❍ Stigma of being a snitch if a report was made
- ❍ Increased risk of drug and alcohol abuse
- ❍ Stress from court procedures
- ❍ Increased risk of association with deviant youth

### Social/Public Services Needed

- ❍ Protective services (if applicable)
- ❍ Guardian ad litem (if applicable)
- ❍ Prosecutor
- ❍ Short-term counselor
- ❍ Medical treatment (if applicable)
- ❍ School guidance counselor
- ❍ Remedial mediation
- ❍ Teen group for specific victimization
- ❍ Life skills group
- ❍ Positive peer associations through groups or athletics
- ❍ Also see services listed under the chapter for the type of victimization the youth experienced

## LONG-TERM COUNSELING

Not all teens opt for long-term counseling. Counselors should seek to address as many issues as early as possible because of reluctance to continue in long-term counseling.

Issues not resolved in short-term counseling should be rolled over into long-term counseling. Additionally, focusing on offender prevention and positive peer relationships as a long-term deterrent should be included.

Counselors should be aware that youth can be exposed to violence and offending behavior because of their at-risk home life, especially if their caregivers are violent, addicted, or mentally ill. Counseling should seek to uncover the conditions of the teen's home life as well as the family's mental-health history. Resulting antisocial behavior in the youth is the logical consequence of negative family conditions. Problems such as caregiver mental illness, drug abuse, poverty, high stress, and low social support create impediments to treatment for youth from these families. Treatment for the whole family is warranted. Counseling should focus on improving family interactions; developing the family social support system; increasing the youth's pro-social peer relationships, while minimizing contact with anti-social peers; and enhancing school support and interactions (Henggeler and Sheidow 2003). Any other treatment approaches that treat exposure to violence and its associated symptoms should also be incorporated.

### *Client Concerns*

- Whether long-term counseling is warranted
- Peer reactions to the victimization and/or reporting
- Increase in campus violence (if applicable)
- Reduction in social skills
- Academic problems
- Symptom reduction

### *Secondary Victimizations*

- Loss of friends due to crime and/or reporting
- Stigma of being a snitch if a report is made
- Increased risk for drug and alcohol abuse

○ Stress of court procedures

○ Increased risk of association with deviant youth

### Social/Public Services Needed

○ Protective services (if applicable)

○ Guardian ad litem (if applicable)

○ Prosecutor

○ Long-term counselor

○ Family counselor (if warranted)

○ Medical treatment (if applicable)

○ School guidance counselor

○ Remedial mediation

○ Teen group for specific victimization

○ Life skills group

○ Positive peer associations through groups or athletics

○ Also see services listed under the chapter for the type of victimization the youth experienced

## RECOMMENDED READING

Creighton, Allan, with Paul Kivel. *Helping Teens Stop Violence: A Practical Guide for Counselors, Educators, and Parents.* Alameda, CA: Hunter House Publishers, 1992.

Deaton, Wendy. *I Saw It Happen: A Child's Workbook about Witnessing Violence.* Alameda, CA: Hunter House Publishers, 1998.

Flannery, Daniel J., and C. Ronald Huff. *Youth Violence: Prevention, Intervention and Social Policy* (Clinical Practice). Arlington, VA: American Psychiatric Association, 1998.

Friedrich, William N. *Psychological Assessment of Sexually Abused Children and Their Families* (Interpersonal Violence: The Practice Series). Thousand Oaks, CA: Sage Publications, 2001.

Howard, Matthew O., and Jeffrey M. Jenson. *Youth Violence: Current Research and Recent Practice Innovations.* Annapolis Junction, MD: NASW Press, 1999.

Johnson, Kendall. *Trauma in the Lives of Children,* 2nd Edition. Alameda, CA: Hunter House Publishers, 1998.

Kivel, Paul, and Allan Creighton with the Oakland Men's Project. *Making the Peace: A 15-Session Violence Prevention Curriculum for Young People.* Alameda, CA: Hunter House Publishers, 1997.

Kolko, David, and Cynthia Cupit Sweson. *Assessing and Treating Physically Abused Children and Their Families: A Cognitive Behavioral Approach* (Interpersonal Violence: The Practice Series). Thousand Oaks, CA: Sage Publications, 2002.

Kramer, Donald. *Legal Rights of Children.* Colorado Springs, CO: Shepard's/ McGraw-Hill, 1994.

Mather, Cynthia, and Kristian Debye. *How Long Does it Hurt? A Guide to Recovering from Incest and Sexual Abuse for Teenagers, Their Friends, and Their Families.* San Francisco, CA: Jossey-Bass, 2004.

Richman, Jack M., and Mark W. Fraser. *The Context of Youth Violence: Resilience, Risk and Protection.* Westport, CT: Praeger Publishers, 2000.

Rossman, B.B. Robbie, and Mindy Susan Rosenberg. *Multiple Victimization of Children: Conceptual, Development, Research and Treatment Issues.* New York: Haworth Maltreatment & Trauma Press, 1998.

Vasquez, Hugh, M. Nell Myhand, and Allan Creighton, with the Todos Institute. *Making Allies, Making Friends: A Curriculum for Making the Peace in Middle School.* Alameda, CA: Hunter House Publishers, 2003.

## RESOURCES

American Humane Association Children's Division
(303) 792-9900

Children's Defense Fund
(800) 233-1200    ○    (202) 628-8787

ChildHelp USA    ○    (800) 4ACHILD (422-4453)

Family Violence and Sexual Assault Institute    ○    (903) 534-5100

National Center for Children Exposed to Violence
www.nccev.org

National Child Traumatic Stress Network    ○    www.nctsnet.org

National Clearinghouse on Child Abuse and Neglect
(800) 394-3366    ○    (703) 385-7565

National Committee to Prevent Child Abuse
(312) 663-3520

Rape, Abuse and Incest National Network (RAINN)
(800) 656-HOPE (656-4673)   ○   www.rainn.org

## Overview of Adolescent Violence— When Kids Can Be Victims or Offenders

*Crisis Intervention:* Whether to report the crime to law enforcement, reluctance to report it at school (if it happened there), need to notify school guidance counselor (if crime happened at school), injuries and treatment, campus safety, peer pressure related to reporting and counseling

*Short-Term Counseling:* Emotional impact of the violence, reporting issues (both to law enforcement and school officials), PTSD symptoms (if applicable), campus safety, peer pressure related to report and counseling

*Long-Term Counseling:* Whether long-term counseling is warranted, peer reactions to the victimization, reduction in social skills, academic problems, symptom reduction, substance abuse prevention

*Secondary Victimizations:* Loss of friends due to the crime and/or reporting, stigma of being a snitch if a report was made, increased risk of drug and alcohol abuse, stress of court procedures, increased risk of association with deviant youth

*Social/Public Services Needed:* Protective services (if applicable), guardian ad litem (if applicable), prosecutor, crisis intervention counselor, school guidance counselor, teen group for specific victimization, mediation, life skills group, medical treatment (if applicable), positive peer associations through groups or athletics, also see services listed under the chapter for the type of victimization the youth experienced for other possible services

# CHAPTER 10

# Sexual Trauma

## Rape and Sexual Assault

Sexual assault is one of the most feared acts of violence. The aftereffects of this violation leave their mark upon a victim's life for an extended time. A counselor's effective intervention and counseling skills can help the victim resume a more normal life more quickly.

- In 2001, 248,000 people were raped or sexually assaulted in the United States.
- 91 percent of victims of rape or sexual assault are female.
- Nearly one third of rape victims develop rape-related PTSD.
  (National Center for Victims of Crime website)
- One out of every three women will be sexually assaulted in her lifetime.
- 78 percent of rape victims know their attackers.
- One out of seven women are raped by their husbands.
- Rape victims visit doctors twice as often as non-rape victims do.
  (Sexual Assault Information Page of the University of Tennessee, http://www.utc.edu/Departments/womencenter/rapemain.php.)

**VICTIM'S STORY**                                    *COLETTE*

*I never knew there was a term for date rape. Dan and I were friends for years, all the way through college. I went to a party at his house and, yes, I had too much to drink. He told me I could crash on his couch, so I wouldn't endanger myself by driving home.*

*I remember being awakened by his advances and telling him that, no, we were friends, and this was not right. I was still a virgin and wanted to keep it that way. But he kept going ahead, and I kept saying no.*

*The next morning I was mortified. He continues to this day to refer to it as "mutual." But it wasn't. While at a college lecture on date rape, I realized it had a name. I said, "Yes, that's what happened to me." I was raped by a previously good friend.*

## BACKGROUND INFORMATION ON RAPE

Rape is one of the most frequently committed violent crimes, but its incidence is slowly starting to decline due to robust social and legal efforts, including rape-prevention trainings, law-enforcement efforts, and prosecution. Unfortunately, rape also remains highly underreported. The exact number of rapes cannot be known, due to this fact.

There are three primary types of rape:

1. Acquaintance rape is a sexual assault by an individual known to the victim; it is often called date rape.

2. Stranger rape is a sexual assault by an individual unknown to the victim.

3. Marital rape is a sexual assault by a woman's spouse or ex-spouse.

Rape includes penile penetration by another adult or group of adults. The use of instruments without penile penetration is considered rape by instrumentation. Statutory rape is rape perpetrated by someone 18 years of age or older (depending on state law) against a minor (under 18). In many states, administering drugs or alcohol to a victim in order to have intercourse with an unconscious or mentally medicated victim can also be considered rape (Meadows 2001). Rape, for the purposes of this chapter, is differentiated from sexual assault, which does not involve penile penetration, but consists of other types of sexual contact (e.g., fondling, inappropriate sexual touching, and digital penetration). Both forms of sexual victimization are addressed in this chapter.

Not only are rape and sexual assault traumatizing, but victims often experience a societal stigma associated with forms of sexual assault. More-over, victims of rape or sexual assault can be blamed for the assault based on how they looked, what they wore, where the rape or assault took place, or what alcoholic beverages or drugs they consumed that evening. What ends up on trial is not only the sexual assault by the rapist, but also the victim's morals, lifestyle, and dress, which often make it difficult to obtain a convic-tion (National Center for Victims of Crime website). For example, victims of acquaintance rape can be blamed for not having had better judgment. In martial rape, the victim's relationship with her spouse almost implies that rape could not occur. In the end, victims must not only face their own viola-tions, but also the attitudes, prejudices, and assumptions of others. These injuries become secondary victimizations that are also painful to the victim.

Additionally, rape and sexual assault victims face other issues that can affect the prosecutable nature of their cases, such as alcohol or drug usage by the victim at the time of the rape. One study found 50 percent of females involved in acquaintance rapes on college campuses had been drinking (Bohmer and Parrot 1993). Although this should not negate the fact that a rape occurred, it has become the sole focus of many trials' proceedings. Rape victims who do not go immediately for a rape exam find similar diffi-culties in prosecuting their cases if DNA evidence was not gathered. In ac-quaintance rape or assault, the fact that the victim might have once had a sexual relationship with the attacker can make it difficult to determine when that part of the relationship started and ended. Yet, cases are argued on those bases.

When victim-blaming issues become the focus of a trial, the system that is supposed to help and support the victim ends up injuring the vic-tim. The accusations brought up during the trial can be as painful emo-tionally as was the rape or assault. The system's injurious behaviors can end up being lumped together with the overall rape or assault in the victim's memory. Counselors have to help the victim deal with violations felt dur-ing their court experience.

## RAPE THEORIES

Rape can cause both short-term and long-term stress reactions. Over the years, these reactions have been named and renamed. Researchers are coming up with more and more theories regarding rape, and many of these theories are being drawn from new knowledge acquired in the areas of trauma and related reactions and disorders. Rape trauma syndrome (RTS) was one of the first descriptors put forth by Burgess and Holmstrom in the 1970s. They identified three phases of rape:

1. Impact

2. Recoil

3. Recovery

 (Burgess and Holmstrom 1974b)

More recent literature has expanded on this foundational research/ writing to better understand the dynamics of rape (see Recommended Reading at the end of the chapter). Rape-related post traumatic stress disorder (RR-PTSD) was developed as an alternative model of rape symptom identification. This model proposed four of the major symptoms seen in PTSD, but that were specific to rape:

○ Re-experiencing the trauma

○ Social withdrawal

○ Avoidance behaviors and actions

○ Increased physiological arousal characteristics

 (National Victims Center and Crime Victims Research and Treatment Center 1995)

Although both RTS and RR-PTSD cover many of the same types of reactions, RR-PTSD most closely parallels the symptoms of PTSD described in Chapter 2. Therefore, we will use this model as a basis for the discussion in this chapter concerning rape.

The *Rape in America* study noted that 31 percent of rape victims go on to develop RR-PTSD. Keep in mind as you read the following sections, however, that the RR-PTSD symptoms discussed under crisis intervention and short- and long-term counseling can appear at any time during the counseling process. They are discussed here as probable scenarios for that particular phase of the counseling process.

CRISIS INTERVENTION

Counselors have often attested to their own emotional difficulty working with rape victims immediately following the trauma. Because rape is a significantly traumatizing event, even if the victim presents with a flat affect, the counselor can feel the underlying surges of deep trauma. The report *Rape In America*, which has been widely cited by the National Victims of Crime and the Crime Victim's Research and Treatment Center, noted that rape victims were

- 13.4 times more likely to have two or more major alcohol incidents
- 26 times more likely to have two or more serious drug abuse problems
- 3 times more likely to develop major depression
- 4.1 times more likely to contemplate suicide

This rise in risk rates should alert counselors to the devastation that rape causes.

Immediately following a rape, you should pay attention to the following crisis intervention needs. First, the victim needs to be in a safe place. If the victim was attacked in her own home, her first instinct may be to leave. This may put her in further danger if she wanders the streets while feeling disoriented. If the attack occurred away from home, it may be harder for her to find safety, especially if she was taken to an area she wasn't familiar with. Additionally, the rapist may have taken her car, clothing, keys, or cell phone.

If you are contacted immediately following the rape, make sure someone spends the night with the victim. Under no circumstances should she be left alone. If possible, arrange for someone to stay with her over the next few days or weeks, not only for her safety, but also so that she does not become isolated.

Second, you should consider whether or not the victim should call the police. As much as law-enforcement intervention may be a legitimate goal, the victim should not be forced to call the police. You should inform the victim that filing a report will help in catching and convicting the rapist. She should also be told that notifying the police does not obligate her to press charges or go through with criminal proceedings. She can stop the process at any point. This helps the victim regain a sense of control over her current disrupted life. If the victim chooses not to file a report, she should not feel guilty for choosing not to file. In acquaintance and marital rapes, it is particularly difficult for victims to report people they know.

Third, you should consider whether the victim needs medical attention. It is advisable for victims to be evaluated by medical personnel immediately following the rape. Even though the victim may not feel injured, she may be so traumatized she is not able to recognize injuries, especially internal ones. For prosecution, it is important to gather DNA evidence. While this is terribly intrusive, it is a necessary step. While gathering DNA, testing can also be conducted for STDs, HIV, and pregnancy. Most states provide free HIV testing for victims. In case the rapist is captured, the state can force him to submit to HIV testing and provide the results to the victim.

The victim's test results can be held, and she can decide later whether to prosecute. Victims are often overwhelmed during this time and cannot plan ahead, so medical evidence may seem of little importance. You should suggest that the victim undergo these procedures in case she decides to prosecute in the future.

Medical evidence in the form of DNA is often enough to successfully prosecute a case. Medical evidence is not limited to seminal fluid, but can also include documentation of lacerations and bruises, pubic hair, clothing fibers, and skin beneath a victim's fingernails. She can request that a female doctor handle any medical procedures, when possible. Of course, a victim should never be forced to submit to the medical procedures, no matter how disoriented she is. If she goes home without being tested and does not shower, she could come back the next day and still be tested.

Finally, crisis intervention should focus on processing the traumatic experience. The victim's need to begin to talk about and process the rape is paramount. You should provide a private and secure place for the victim interview. Allow the victim to bring someone with her who can stay in the room (if the victim desires) while she talks with you. The victim interview can take place immediately following the rape, or it can happen days, weeks, or even months later. During the interview, allow the victim to tell you what is significant to her about the event. This will give you clues about where she may be stuck in the traumatic experience. The elements the victim chooses to focus upon may seem illogical; she may focus on some small detail or something prior to the rape.

Normal emotional feelings during the crisis include self-blame and guilt. Victims need to hear repeatedly that they did not cause or contribute to the assault. Victims often feel guilty about not fighting back or about not fighting back strongly enough. You can reinforce the idea that what ever she did was successful because she survived. Because she had good judgment, she is still alive today. Victims often fear telling their friends, family, or significant other about the rape. Offer to be with the victim when she tells whomever she is concerned about telling. Giving instructions to that person in advance about what to expect and what to say and not say can help the victim and her family in the long run. Educating the victim and her family about the procedures for DNA collection, medical testing, and law-enforcement prosecution will help them anticipate the next stages.

According to RR-PTSD theory, one of the symptoms of rape trauma is the re-experiencing of the original trauma. During this time, rape victims may have "uncontrollable, intrusive thoughts about the rape." Many rape victims also have "realistic nightmares about the actual rape" and may re-live the event "through flashbacks and feel the experience as if it were happening now." Victims may avoid any situations that "symbolize the trauma and avoid talking about the event or any situation that could be a reminder" (National Center for Victims of Crime website).

Victims who come for crisis intervention often do so because of the overwhelming effects of re-experiencing the trauma. Crisis intervention, while focusing on the various issues discussed above, must also help the victim find symptom relief. Depending how long after the rape you encounter the victim, her presenting symptoms may differ. You should begin by assessing her symptoms.

Teaching the victim to manage intrusive memories will go a long way toward reducing anxiety and PTSD symptoms, but be aware that the re-experiencing of the trauma symptoms may last well into the early phase of long-term counseling, depending on how quickly the victim is able to process the traumatic memory. For more information about how to teach a client to manage intrusive memories, check the literature on PTSD or anxiety reduction techniques.

### Client Concerns

- Wondering if the rape should be reported
- Wondering whether to have a medical exam
- Pregnancy
- HIV

- ○ STDs
- ○ Fear of the rapist's return
- ○ Fear friends or family will learn of the incident and judge her
- ○ Fear of being alone
- ○ Concern about impending procedures, if the rape is reported
- ○ Need to process and vent anger
- ○ Desire to stop intrusive memories and flashbacks

### Secondary Victimizations

- ○ Medical costs
- ○ Time off from work
- ○ Replacement of car, clothes, credit cards, or whatever may have been taken or damaged during the rape incident
- ○ Media insensitivity or finding her story in the news
- ○ Insensitive law-enforcement officers or medical personnel
- ○ Rapist may be caught and released on bond
- ○ Being subjected to a polygraph test or psychiatric evaluation
- ○ Blame by others
- ○ Fear of being fired from a job because of the stigma of sexual assault

### Social/Public Services Needed

- ○ Crisis-intervention counselor
- ○ Medical or rape exam; education about HIV and STDs
- ○ Victim assistance through law-enforcement agencies
- ○ State crime compensation
- ○ Prosecutor or attorney

## SHORT-TERM COUNSELING

Most rape victims are seen in short- and even long-term counseling. However, some victims refuse crisis-intervention services, others drop out immediately following crisis intervention, and yet others discontinue counseling after a brief introduction to short-term counseling. Those who drop out before short- and long-term counseling are often seen in counseling years later with what seem to them to be unrelated counseling issues. Untreated rape trauma can become a counseling issue for victims years later.

By the time victims enter short-term counseling, many have often moved through the denial stage and are symptomatic with the kinds of reactions noted in the RR-PTSD model. The symptoms of intrusive memories and of social withdrawal from activities and people tend to be the most problematic for victims. Social withdraw is described as "psychic numbing" and the feeling of being "emotionally dead." The victim may not experience any feelings or her feelings may be limited to a very narrow range. Victims often have a "greatly diminished interest in living" and lose interest in their jobs, normally enjoyed activities, spirituality, sexuality, and relationships with family and friends. This withdrawal should not, however, be confused with suicide ideation (National Center for Victims of Crime website).

This kind of social withdrawal takes a toll on personal relationships. The victim's job may be affected by her dwindling interest in the details of her work, coupled with an inability to concentrate due to intrusive memories. Detachment often occurs in close personal relationships and adversely affects the victim's marriage or dating relationship. Meeting with the victim's husband or significant other is helpful in addressing these kinds of reactions. Detachment can also occur toward her children, and may manifest as a lack of responsiveness to the joy of children. Counseling can help the victim become aware of her own detachment and begin to deal with the impending damage to those closest to her.

Avoidance behaviors and actions may be quite observable during counseling. Victims have a "general tendency to avoid any thoughts, feelings, or cues that could represent the most traumatizing elements of the rape." The victim may avoid driving by the place where the violation occurred or, if she knows the rapist, she may avoid going near places where he lives, works, or hangs out. She may stop using the perfume she wore the night of the attack, or even avoid the part of her bedroom where the perfume is kept because that reminds her of what happened. Her mind has to work overtime to try to keep the frequent intrusive flashbacks at bay, as well as to avoid behaviors and actions that serve as reminders of the rape. These avoidance behaviors can begin during the crisis stage and peak during short-term counseling, but they can also extend into long-term counseling.

*Client Concerns*

- How the judicial process will work, how she will handle it, and whether justice will be served
- How the rape will change her relationship with her husband or significant other
- Losing her job because of time missed at court, counseling, or other rape-related appointments or because she is unable to concentrate or perform well
- Loss of privacy
- Safety
- Retribution
- Fear of further or new victimizations
- Loss of sexuality because of forced sexual violation
- Desire to stop social withdrawal from friends and family
- Desire to stop intrusive memories and flashbacks
- Desire to stop avoidance behaviors surrounding rape symbols

*Secondary Victimizations*

- Legal costs
- Cost of counseling
- Time lost from work or loss of job
- Change in residence
- Divorce or loss of relationship
- Rapist being acquitted or found not guilty
- Being asked to corroborate or plea bargain
- Lack of information about the status of the case
- Pregnancy
- STDs, HIV/AIDS
- Stigma
- Suicide attempts

*Social/Public Services Needed*

○ Victim assistance from law-enforcement agencies

○ Short-term counselor

○ Group counseling

○ State crime compensation

○ Medical care or health department, if applicable

○ Attorney or prosecutor

## LONG-TERM COUNSELING

The need for long-term counseling should be assessed based on the client's prior victimization history, how well she resolved previous victimizations, and her ego strength. Particularly in cases of rape, if the victim has not undergone crisis-intervention treatment or some processing of the event, she may require treatment later in life. Typically, women who come to counseling years after a rape finally recognize that the event did affect them and continues to affect their daily living.

Long-term counseling can address the RR-PTSD symptoms that were not resolved during short-term counseling. Victims seen in long-term counseling may continue to re-experience the trauma symptoms, as well as exhibit social withdrawal and avoidance behaviors and actions. You should be aware of the capacity for PTSD symptoms to continue for long periods of time. In some cases, the effects of PTSD prove to be permanent. If the victim's symptoms are resistant to treatment, long-term counseling should focus on symptom management and alleviation.

The RR-PTSD symptom of increased physiological arousal can be particularly distressful to victims (and those who witness it in the victim). The victim may experience an exaggerated startle response when she hears a noise or someone approaches her from behind. She may be hyperalert to her environment, noting every sound and sight around her. She may also develop sleep disturbances, both in falling asleep and in staying asleep. These heightened physiological reactions can physically tire the victim. If untreated, these symptoms can manifest later as such medical conditions as adrenal fatigue, chronic fatigue, and auto-immune disorders brought on by the increased physiological reactions.

Rape victims need to know that some RR-PTSD symptoms are likely to reappear over time. A victim may leave counseling and feel her symptoms are well managed, only to come back to counseling when the symptoms resurface. This can occur due to another victimization that reactivates the PTSD. For example, if the victim's children reach the age the victim was when she was raped, her PTSD can be triggered and cause her to reengage in counseling. Thus, counseling should focus on treating symptoms as they appear and reappear, rather than expecting complete recovery.

Some symptoms may respond well to counseling, while others are more likely to become reactivated. Help the victim to understand that it is okay to come back to counseling for symptom management whenever necessary. Understanding RR-PTSD symptomatology can also aid you in choosing alternative therapies that may be helpful for a particular client. These include the use of rape or PTSD support groups, referral to a doctor for anti-anxiety medication, art therapy, and (depending on the victim's comfort level with touch) massage therapy.

Recovery occurs when victims begin to integrate the rape experience into their life perspective and no longer see the crime as the only focus of their life. Feelings of anger and fear diminish, giving emotional energy to invest in other areas of life. The victim's mental state becomes more balanced. Although victims may still talk about the assault, they do so with greater composure. They recognize that the world is not as safe as they once thought and continue to take steps to ensure their own and their children's safety. They may see how to prevent a future attack, but they no longer blame themselves for the previous attack(s). Rather than deciding to mistrust everyone, they selectively choose people they can trust. Recovery can be delayed if the victim does not have an effective plan of action to follow, such as that provided during counseling. The victim's position is strengthened if she knows she is heading in the right direction, even if it may take time to get there.

Although the following suggestions may seem simplistic, they can help stabilize a rape victim throughout the counseling process. Because some of these steps are basic, more paraprofessionals are now being employed in this process. Nonetheless, the steps are viable throughout the three stages of counseling.

1. Help victims accept that the rape will affect their life, not ultimately making it worse (although it currently feels that way), but making it forever changed. Help them accept that relationships and the ways they perceive life, others, and themselves will also change.

2. Assist victims in structuring their days to avoid long-term depression. Make a list of things they want to get done for the day and suggest they do these things one at a time. Advise them to celebrate small successes. Teach them to expect that not every day will be smooth. Reassure them tomorrow may be better.

3. Educate victims about how to nurture themselves and self-soothe. Help them make a list of things that feel good to them and encourage them to go back to the list on bad days. Help them learn to say no to others' demands when they can't possibly meet them. Help them to set strong boundaries and work through their codependency.

4. Remind victims to take care of themselves physically (eat; exercise; take vitamins and don't abuse food, alcohol, drugs); socially (go out with friends who understand their condition, not isolate themselves); emotionally (counseling, support group, 12-step program, self-defense classes); spiritually (pray, take a religious class, read books of encouragement); and educationally (read books on rape, recovery, self-growth).

5. Remind victims to fight negative thinking. Remind them of what they did right and that the rape was not their fault. Help them focus on their strengths and direct their energies to positive outcomes (lobbying for victims' rights or rape-prevention programs). Show them how to reach out to others who are not as far along in recovery as they are.

6. Teach them how to express their feelings. Discourage repressing or denying. Encourage them to call their counselor, group member, friend, or write in their journal. Show them how to draw their fear, dance their anger, sculpt their healing. Allow them to yell, cry, and ask questions.

7. Tell victims to accept that no one has all the answers. Stress that victims maintain a strong support group. Remind them that isolating themselves makes it harder to heal. Instruct them to rely on a couple of people and later expand their support network.

8. Most of all, remind victims to give themselves time to heal. Guide them to respect themselves for choosing to heal. Not all choose to begin the work of healing (Brown 1991).

### Client Concerns

○ Safety of self

○ Safety of children and significant others

○ Fear of HIV/AIDS and STDs

○ Mistrust of men in general, her husband or significant other, dating

○ Frustration with impaired sexuality or impaired emotional intimacy

○ Loss of self-esteem, self-respect, and level of functioning

○ Perceptual distortions

○ Marriage or dating problems, attempts to reenter dating or sexual relationships

○ Rapist being released and looking for her

○ Being re-victimized

○ Desire to reduce intrusive memories and flashbacks

○ Desire to reduce social withdrawal

○ Desire to reduce avoidance behaviors

○ Desire to reduce physiological arousal behaviors

### Secondary Victimizations

○ Divorce or breakup

○ Cost of home safety equipment

○ Cost of self-defense classes

○ Cost of counseling

○ Change of job

○ Lack of information about legal process

### Social/Public Services Needed

○ Long-term counselor

○ Group counseling

○ State crime compensation

○ Attorney or prosecutor

○ Self-defense classes

## RECOMMENDED READING

Lee, Sharice. *The Survivors Guide.* Thousand Oaks, CA: Sage Publications, 1995.

Wiehe, Vernon, and Ann Richards. *Intimate Betrayal: Understanding and Responding to the Trauma of Acquaintance Rape.* Thousand Oaks, CA: Sage Publications, 1995.

## RESOURCES

National Sexual Violence Resource Center
(877) 739-3895   ⟳   www.nsvc.org

National AIDS Clearinghouse   ⟳   (800) 458-5231

National Crime Victims Research and Treatment Center
(843) 792-2945   ⟳   www.musc.edu/cvc/

Rape, Abuse and Incest National Network (RAINN)
(800) 656-HOPE (656-4673)   ⟳   www.rainn.org

National Organization for Victim Assistance   ⟳   www.trynova.org

National Sexual Violence Resource Center   ⟳   www.nsvc.org

## Overview of Rape and Sexual Assault

*Crisis-Intervention Issues:* Intrusive memories and flashbacks, numbness, rape exam, PTSD symptoms, medical attention, processing the experience, reducing guilt and shame

*Short-Term Counseling Issues:* Criminal-justice system, pregnancy, STDs and HIV, disclosure to family members, issues of fear and safety, attempts at repressing memories, PTSD symptoms, social withdrawal, low self-esteem, employment problems

*Long-Term Counseling Issues:* Sexual problems, fear issues, distrust of males, interpersonal relationship problems, safety, PTSD symptoms, physiological reactions, sleep disorders

*Secondary Victimization:* Medical costs, time off work, replacement of articles stolen or damaged, fear of rapist being released, legal costs, loss of job, divorce and break up, cost of security devices, loss of sexual desire, counseling costs

*Social/Legal Services:* Medical exam; rape exam; DNA testing; victim advocate; state crime compensation; crisis-intervention counseling; short- and long-term counseling; job placement if job is lost; legal aid or attorney or prosecutor; housing and, if needing to relocate, temporary shelter

## Considerations for Special Rape Populations

Some specific groups of sexual assault and rape victims warrant a counselor's special knowledge and attention. These include male victims, the elderly, and the mentally ill. The following sections should help in determining the unique needs and issues that can help when you are assisting these types of victims after an assault:

### RAPE/SEXUAL ASSAULT OF MALE VICTIMS

The rape of males was more widely recognized in ancient times. For instance, in Greek mythology, examples abound of male abductions and sexual assaults by other males. The rape of a defeated male enemy was a special right of the victorious warrior and a sign of total defeat. A male who was sexually penetrated forcefully had lost his manhood and could no longer be a warrior or a ruler. Gang rape was seen as an extreme form of punishment (Donaldson 1990).

Today, male rape is an often overlooked victimization, even though male rape victims have been found to make up 5 percent to 10 percent of the sexual assault population (Pino and Meier 1999) and 34 percent of college men have reported they have been involved in a coercive sexual situation since age sixteen.

Rape is an act of aggression, regardless of the gender or age of the victim or assailant. It is neither about sexual desire nor sexual deprivation, but is motivated by power and control. The majority of rapists are not homosexual (Donaldson 1990; Whealin 2005), yet males face the stigmatization that only gay men are raped. Although gay men are often targeted and raped because of their sexual orientation, "straight" men are also raped. (For more information on gender-based violence, see Chapter 6.)

Male rape victims underreport their victimizations, in many cases because of myths about male rape. Some do not report the crime out of fear they will be disbelieved (i.e., men do not get raped). Male rape victims also avoid seeking treatment due to victim blaming and to myths about male rape. They may not be able to find treatment focused on male rape because there aren't enough male rape victims in their area to have a separate program (Donnelly and Kenyon 1996). In the clinical arena, a lack of substantial information and research about male rape exists. The scant information that does exist is not kept up-to-date the way information about female rape is. This places treatment of male victims at a distinct disadvantage.

Despite the lack of research and the tendency of underreporting, a startling 65 percent of male rape victims develop PTSD. This is nearly twice the rate of PTSD men develop after life-threatening combat (Kessler et al. 1995). Male symptoms of PTSD are very similar to those of female rape victim (Rogers 1997; Whealin 2005), although confusion about sexual orientation is more likely to occur with male rape victims than with female victims because most male rapes are same-gender rapes, whereas women's are not. Male rape victims are also more likely to have physical injuries from an assault, be victimized by more than one assailant, and seek medical treatment for secondary injuries without reporting the rape, than are female victims (Isely and Gehrenbeck-Shin 1997).

Most male rape victims who seek counseling do so based on a different incident and disclose the rape only later during the course of counseling (McCann and Pearlman 1990). Those who seek counseling as a direct result of rape often struggle with shame and the belief that men should be able to ward off sexual assaults (Whealin 2005). It is an affront to their "maleness" to be subjected to such a powerless and humiliating experience, which has been described as "emasculating by domination" (Dorais 2002). If they internalize this message, men may feel they collaborated with the offender and actually desired the assault. This may lead them to question their preferred sexual orientation and even their sexuality (McCann and Pearlman 1990), especially if there was any physiological stimulation. Men need to be educated that sexual arousal is a normal physiological response.

Some of the maladaptations in exerting power or dominance may result from disruption of a man's power schemas (McCann and Pearlman 1990). When men experience these maladaptations, they can go to great lengths to prove their masculinity; for example, by engaging in daredevil stunts, sexual promiscuity (Whealin 2005), violent behavior, law breaking, military exploits (Lew 1988), body building, excessive focus on physical strength, or homophobia (Dorais 2002).

Male rape victims face a lack of support by other men. According to one survey, men tended to blame other male rape victims for their own rape (Whatley and Riggio 1993) and expected men to resist more. Very little support is given to men who indicated they did not resist.

The experience of rape may affect gay and straight men differently. Rape counselors have reported that gay men have difficulties in their sexual and emotional relationships with other men and think the assault occurred because they were gay. Straight men often begin to question their sexual identify and are more disturbed by the sexual aspects of the assault than the violence involved (Brochman 1991).

Male rape victims should be encouraged to seek medical treatment, whether or not they are going to prosecute. Physical symptoms, especially disease, can take weeks or months to manifest. Male rape victims can receive the following injuries:

- Rectal and anal tearing and abrasions that may require attention and put the victim at risk for bacterial infection
- Potential HIV exposure
- Exposure to other STDs (National Center for Victims of Crime website)
- Encopresis (bowel incontinence) (Whealin 2005)

Male victims need to know that, if they report the rape to police, an immediate medical exam will be necessary to collect physical evidence for the investigation or prosecution. Victims who are unsure whether they will prosecute should have the physical evidence collected in case they do decide to prosecute.

You should expect the same types of RR-PTSD symptoms in male rape victims that you see in female victims. Check with your local rape crisis center for services geared to male victims. They may even have male rape counselors available.

## RAPE/SEXUAL ASSAULT OF ELDERLY VICTIMS

Sexual abuse of the elderly is the least perceived, acknowledged, detected, and reported type of elder mistreatment (Teaster and Roberton 2003). This leaves a wide gap in prevention, intervention, and treatment for sexually abused elders. The small amount of data available on this subject should alert counselors that abuse of the elderly should be studied more carefully.

Sexual assault of the elderly is easy for a rapist to successfully complete. Intimidation by physical force is all that is necessary to subdue victims in most of the cases (Muram, Miller, and Cutler 1992). The elderly are especially vulnerable to injury. One study found older women (55 years and older) sustained more genital injuries than did women eighteen to forty-five years old. Any kind of injury places the elderly at risk for infection and even death. In fact, another study reported that 50 percent of elderly sexual assault victims died within twelve months of their assault (Burgess, Dowdel, and Prentky 2000).

Women who are targeted most frequently are those with limited cognitive functioning who reside in nursing homes and those whose orientation, ambulation, or ability to manage their finances was compromised (Burgess et al. 2000). Nursing home residents can also be traumatized if they witness a sexual assault.

Prosecuting can prove to be difficult for elderly victims if they have cognitive disorders that affect recognition or memory. One study reported that 56 percent of elderly sexual abuse cases resulted in criminal conviction, but only 25 percent of the offenders received prison sentences (Payne and Civokic 1996). This sends a clear message that assaults on the elderly carry smaller penalties than do assaults on younger victims.

The fact that most victims (ages seventy through eighty-nine) were residing in nursing facilities during their sexual assault should alert the nursing home community to this high risk factor. The most prevalent forms of abuse were kissing, fondling and unwelcomed sexual interest. Most of the perpetrators were nursing home residents age sixty or older (Muram et al. 1992). According to Burgess and colleagues (2000), "A lack of sensitivity by nursing homes staff to the gravity of the assaults on the residents" accounts for lack of prevention and intervention.

Reporting sexual abuse is frightening for most elderly victims because they must continue to face their abusers within the nursing home environment. In addition, they may fear they will be disbelieved due to dementia or other medical conditions. Thus, an elder victim easily becomes trapped in an abusive environment.

Myths and stereotypes abound with regard to elder sexual abuse. Thinking older people are "not sexual" or "can't sexually perform" leaves elders without someone to patrol their sexual safety. Recognition, reporting, and treatment remain challenges for elderly sexual assault victims.

Counselors need to take into consideration any medical or cognitive impairments that might inhibit reporting or hamper communication during counseling.

## RAPE/SEXUAL ASSAULT OF MENTALLY ILL VICTIMS

As in the case of male and elderly sexual assault victims, little information is available about sexual assaults on the mentally ill. One reason for the lack of research on this population is that victims with more extensive pathology are less likely to use emergency mental-health services than victims with less pathology (Lehman and Linn 1984). Another reason is that severely mentally ill persons often are homeless, and gathering statistical information on transient populations is difficult. Other severely mentally ill persons are institutionalized, which also makes it hard to estimate how many are sexually assaulted each year or what kind of care they receive.

The transient status of many sexually assaulted mentally ill victims makes it a challenge to provide sexual assault treatment services for them. In addition, the homeless mentally ill are at increased risk of sexual assault simply due to their level of exposure on the street. The mentally ill who are institutionalized may be assaulted by employees or other residents. Like the elderly who are in long-term care, the mentally ill may never report the crime due to fear of being disbelieved or fear of further victimization while institutionalized.

Women with schizophrenia or bipolar disorders have been found to be at a higher risk of rape than are other populations (Davres-Bornoz et al. 1995). In fact, the worse their mental illness (or substance abuse), the more types of victimization they are likely to have experienced. This should be a red flag to counselors treating mentally ill women. If you are counseling a woman with one of these types of diagnosis, exploring her victimization history is warranted.

Certain disorders characterized by flattened or inappropriate affect and emotional expressions can result in situations in which the victim responds "oddly" to victimization. You may find such a client hard to "read" if her presentation of RR-PTSD symptoms is atypical. Victims who are psychotic may or may not be giving appropriate rape-related information. Mentally retarded victims may have cognitive restrictions that prevent them from understanding what happened to them, or they may have a limited ability to communicate what did happen. Severely mentally disordered individuals may lack self-protection skills and be unable to read situations that place them at risk.

Crisis-intervention service providers may fear treating severely mentally ill individuals who show up for services. Although some counselors assume the mentally ill are likely to be violent and thus to be abusers, the mentally ill are actually more likely to be victims than perpetrators (Campbell, Stefan, and Loder 1994). Mentally ill victims are more vulnerable to physical assault than are members of the general public (Marley and Buila 2001). In addition, their mental illness often prevents them from reaching out for assistance when a rape or other victimization occurs. Repeated victimizations can lead to increased alienation (DeNiro 1995), and the alienation can lead to further isolation, loneliness, and a decline in overall functioning. The lower their level of functioning, the less likely mentally ill victims are to seek services. Stress can also set off depression, mania, and psychosis, which can also hinder victims from reaching out for counseling. These factors can also limit the ability of a counselor to decipher what the victim is trying to say.

The most prevalent reason the mentally ill did not seek treatment, according to one study, was their perception of a stigma associated with being considered mentally ill; one quarter of the fifty million persons experiencing mental illness did not seek treatment based on stigma (Brown and Bradley 2002). Mental illness has been noted as one of the most stigmatized conditions in our society (Corrigan and Penn 1999). Negative attitudes about mental illness include labeling, attributions, and misinformation, especially regarding violence (Link and Phelan 1999). The stigma of mental illness encourages fear, mistrust and violence against people with mental illness (Brown and Bradley 2002). These unique barriers present challenges about which counselors working with the sexually assaulted mentally ill should be aware.

### RECOMMENDED READING

*Archives of Gerontology and Geriatrics* (professional journal)

*The Clinical Gerontologist* (professional journal)

*The Gerontologist* (professional journal)

Groth, Nicholas A., and B. A. Birnbaum. *Men Who Rape: The Psychology of the Offender.* New York: Plenum, 1979.

Harris, Maxine, and Christine L. Landis. *Sexual Abuse in the Lives of Women Diagnosed with Serious Mental Illness* (New Directions in Therapeutic Interventions). Amsterdam, The Netherlands: Harwood Academic Publishers, 1997.

*Journal of American Geriatrics Society, Age and Ageing* (professional journal)

*The Journal of Applied Gerontology* (professional journal)

*Journal of Elder Abuse and Neglect* (professional journal)

*Journal of Women's Health and Gender-Based Medicine* (professional journal)

Mezey, Gillian C., and Michael B. King. *Male Victims of Sexual Assault.* New York: Oxford University Press, 2000.

McMullen, Richie. *Male Rape: Breaking the Silence on the Last Taboo.* London, England: GMP Publishers Ltd., 1990.

National Research Council. *Elder Mistreatment: Abuse, Neglect and Exploitation in an Aging American.* Washington, D.C.: National Academies Press, 2003.

Quinn, Mary Joy, and Susan K. Tomita. *Elder Abuse and Neglect: Causes, Diagnosis, and Intervention Strategies.* Woodstock, CT: Spring Publishing Company, 1997.

Sandell, Diane S. *Ending Elder Abuse: A Family Guide.* Fort Bragg, CA: QED Press, 2000.

Scarce, Michael. *Male on Male Rape: The Hidden Toll of Stigma and Shame.* Cambridge, MA: Perseus Books, 1997.

Sgroi, Suzanne M. *Male Victims of Same-Sex Abuse: Addressing Their Sexual Response.* Towson, MD: Sidran Press, 2002.

Sgroi, Suzanne M. *Vulnerable Populations: Sexual Abuse Treatment for Children, Adult Survivors, Offenders, and Persons with Mental Retardation.* New York: Lexington Books, 1989.

Sonkin, Daniel Jay, and Lenore E.A. Walker. *Wounded Boys, Heroic Men: A Man's Guide to Recovering from Child Abuse.* Cincinnati, OH: Adams Media Corporation, 1998.

Thompson, James W., and William R. Breakey. *Mentally Ill and Homeless: Special Programs for Special Needs* (Chronic Mental Illness Series). Amsterdam, The Netherlands: Harwood Academic Publishers, 1998.

William, Christopher. *Invisible Victims: Crimes and Abuse Against People with Learning Disabilities.* London: Jessica Kingsley Publishers, 1995.

## RESOURCES

National Sexual Violence Resource Center
(877) 739-3895    ⊃    www.nsvc.org

Men's Resource Center    ⊃    (503) 235-3433

National AIDS Clearinghouse    ⊃    (800) 458-5231

National Crime Victims Research and Treatment Center
(843) 792-2945    ⊃    www.musc.edu/cvc/

Rape, Abuse and Incest National Network (RAINN)
(800) 656-HOPE (656-4673)    ⊃    www.rainn.org

Male Survivors    ⊃    www.malesurvivor.org

Male Childhood Abuse    ⊃    www.menweb.org/sexabupg.htm

Male Abuse    ⊃    www.nextstepcounseling.org

National Organization for Victim Assistance
www.trynova.org

National Center on Elder Abuse    ⊃    www.elderabusecenter.org

National Committee for Prevention of Elder Abuse
www.ncpea.org

National Sexual Violence Resource Center
www.nsvc.org

## Adult Survivors of Sexual Abuse by Incest

It is hard to fathom how many survivors, both male and female, have been marred by intrafamilial sexual abuse. These victims, who suffered at the hands of their own families, need specialized care in order to heal.

⊃ 46 percent of rape victims are raped by family members.

> (National Center for Victims of Crime, Crime Victims Research and Treatment Center 1992)

### VICTIM'S STORY                                        *MARIE*

*My father molested me throughout my whole childhood. He made nearly nightly visits to my bed, which started with fondling and built to intercourse. I think my mom suspected but did nothing. I hate them both.*

*As an adult, my life is so screwed up—my emotions, my sex life, every-thing. I just don't know if I will ever be good relationship material. I am so damaged.*

## BACKGROUND INFORMATION

In Chapter 9, incest was defined as "the sexual abuse of a child by a relative or other person in a position of trust and authority over the child" (Vanderbilt 1992), and we looked at incest as it occurs in children. Adult survivors of incest are, unfortunately, not as rare as we would like to think. Incest knows no distinctions of gender, socioeconomic status, race, or religious affiliation. It occurs in all types of families and causes a wide continuum of psychological effects, many of which are serious and have long-term effects.

Counselors who opt to work in the field of incest must come to terms with some of the darkest details of human behavior. If you work with this population, you must consider the toll it will take on you as a professional. Engaging in counseling yourself and or seeking clinical supervision will help with the process of defusing counter-transference issues, which are very common among counselors treating incest. Not only are the dark details difficult to hear, but it is staggering to see how many disorders can result from incest. This often pushes counselors to the edge of their tolerance level for hearing about such violence. Many counselors only treat a few incest survivors, or they only treat them for short periods of time and then discontinue all together, or they take breaks during which they do not see these kinds of survivors. You will have to find the right pacing for your practice. Be aware that practitioners who treat many incest survivors work with fewer overall clients and spend a portion of their income on their own counseling and clinical supervision. Financially, there is often a price to pay for working with this population.

## FORMS OF SEXUAL ABUSE

The following are forms of sexual abuse related to incest:

- ○ Fondling of sexual parts or being made to fondle others' sexual parts
- ○ Being penetrated orally, anally, or vaginally by any instrument or penis

○ Being made to watch or to perform sex acts with animals

○ Being made to watch or to perform sex acts with children

○ Digital (finger) penetration in the vagina or rectum or being made to penetrate another's vagina or rectum

○ Being made to listen to age-inappropriate dialogue containing sexual jargon or pertaining to sexual acts

○ Being made to read or talk about age-inappropriate subjects containing sexual jargon or pertaining to sexual acts

○ Being made to watch or look at age-inappropriate literature, tapes, or people acting in sexual ways

○ Being photographed in ways that make one uncomfortable

○ Being subjected to oral sex or being forced to perform oral sex with others

○ Being looked at or leered at in ways that make one uncomfortable, or being subjected to inappropriate remarks about one's developing body
(Brown 1991)

Counselors provide therapy to adult survivors of incest years after the initial trauma. Due to the psychobiological effects of PTSD, many survivors continue to relive the incestuous events through flashbacks, intrusive memories, and other physiological reactions that keep the trauma reoccurring (see Chapter 2, "The Psychobiology of PTSD"). The incest survivor may act as if the trauma occurred more recently than it actually did. Some survivors have repressed (Blume 1990) or amnesic memories (Briere and Conte 1993; Gold, Hawes, and Hohnecker 1994); as a result, their cognitive minds do not remember the abuse, but their repressed memories still trigger physiological reactions. This may cause them to have PTSD symptoms without any knowledge about why PTSD might be occurring. Others have small flashes of disjointed memories that are sufficient to prompt them to wonder if abuse occurred. Still others remember most of what happened to them.

Regardless of their actual memories, the symptoms victims have are remarkably similar in presentation and severity, and form a constellation of symptoms referred to as "post sexual abuse syndrome" (Briere 1996). These symptoms can include the following:

○ Depression and anxiety (Beitchman, Zucker, Hood, DaCosta, and Cassavia 1992)

○ Low self-esteem, feeling soiled, helpless, powerless

○ Social adjustment problems (DiLillio 2001) and social isolation (Gibson and Hartshome 1996)

○ Re-victimization (DiLillio 2001)

○ Somatic symptoms and frequent surgery

○ Drug abuse, eating disorders, and other addictions, impulse disorders, compulsive behaviors, and self-destructive behaviors

○ Dissociation and other disorders related to dissociation (Nash, Hulsey, Sexton, Harralson, and Lambert 1993)

○ Chronic feelings of betrayal, impostor syndrome, lack of trust

○ Pathological object relations (Omduff 2000) and disordered attachment (Saunders and Edelson 1999)

○ PTSD in various stages, delayed or chronic, including signs of memory leakage causing flashbacks and numbing, night terrors, and phobias

○ Chronic interpersonal difficulty with family, parents, friends, at places of employment, and with sexual relationships (DiLillio 2001)

○ Sexual problems (Beitchman et al. 1992; Wonderlich et al. 2001)

○ Numerous previous unsuccessful counseling attempts

○ Previously diagnosed borderline personality disorder or has borderline behaviors or features or other Axis II diagnoses (Wonderlich et al. 2001), mutilation or suicide attempts or gestures

In addition to this wide array of psychiatric symptoms, medical disorders are often associated with this population of survivors, as indicated by the symptom of frequent somatic illnesses and surgeries. Medical professionals have begun to recognize the correlation between early childhood trauma and medical problems in later life. Medical disorders seen in survivors include but are not limited to the following:

○ Digestive disorders

○ Chronic migraines

○ Endometriosis and/or early hysterectomy

○ Autoimmune diseases

○ Sexual dysfunction

○ Stress-related disorders

○ Temporomandibular joint (TMJ) syndrome

○ Undiagnosed chronic pain

○ Obesity

Not all persons who present with these types of medical disorders are survivors of incest. But these disorders can be red flags to explore if abuse started in childhood and is related to incest. If you are working in the field of trauma, you should always take a medical history as part of the intake and assessment. If the victim discloses these types of medical disorders, you should discuss their possible etiology.

## POSSIBLE TREATMENT APPROACHES

Incest is a difficult trauma to treat in adult survivors. The relating disorders can be pervasive and complicated. Counselors often feel their work is like pulling a loose string and watching the whole garment unravel. Once they hear the stories and sense the underlying symptoms and disorders, it is baffling to know where to start with these victims. Counselors with some theoretical and experiential knowledge and active chair time in treating emotional developmental delays, grief issues, and PTSD or other trauma disorders will have a foundational understanding from which to treat these survivors. Counselors new to victimology should not normally take on incest cases until they have gained more experience working with trauma victims.

Literature about incest therapy written in the 1980s provides guidelines about how theory can direct the treatment approach with adult survivors of incest. Approaches cited in the literature include "feminist, traumatic stress, developmental, and loss theories" (Courtois 1988). These approaches were selected because they address the following victim's deficits:

○ Feminist therapy re-empowers the victim, for whom abuse has been disempowering.

○ Traumatic-stress therapy treats the trauma, while recognizing the experience of victimization.

○ Developmental therapy is geared toward the gaps that develop in the victim's personality during the abuse stage.

○ Loss therapy focuses on grieving all things lost (e.g., childhood, stable upbringing, adequate parenting, virginity).

Each survivor must be approached individually and her trauma deficits assessed to determine what approach(es) best fits them.

## CRISIS INTERVENTION

As previously mentioned, adults may come to counseling with varying degrees of knowledge about their abuse. It is important to know the signs of undisclosed incest in case the client cannot or does not disclose it (see the list of symptoms above for postsexual abuse syndrome). Additionally, consult the disorders listed in Chapter 2 (see page 12), which are particularly noteworthy in incest.

Incest that began in childhood can often result in Axis II personality disorders, so using an assessment that gives an Axis II diagnosis is important. Personality disorders warrant a particular approach in counseling and can often complicate the treatment. It is beyond the scope of this book to address Axis II treatment approaches; however, a counselor is wise to have training and supervision when working with these complex clients. A class or workshop in Axis II treatment and or psychopathology would be valuable.

The approaches to incest treatment developed in the 1980s and 1990s are still applicable today and represent the essential features of a well-rounded approach to incest therapy. The foundational literature notes the following as goals of treatment. While both short- and long-term counseling will be needed to accomplish these goals with the victim, you can begin to focus on the following issues during crisis intervention:

○ Developing a commitment to treatment and establishing the therapeutic alliance

○ Acknowledging and accepting the occurrence of incest

○ Recounting the events of incest

○ Recognizing the feelings of isolation and stigma

○ Recognizing, labeling, and expression of feelings

○ Resolution of responsibility and survival issues

○ Grieving

○ Cognitive restructuring of distorted beliefs and stress responses

○ Self-determination and behavioral changes

○ Education and skill building

(Courtois 1988)

During the crisis-intervention stage, you can expect to face a variety of needs on the part of the victim. First assess the victim's safety. Is the victim in an environment that is free from the potential of re-victimization and free from contact with the abuser? Counseling cannot begin until the victim's daily safety is secured.

Survivors often come to counseling because they are having a breakthrough memory leakage that is causing abreactions (emotional and physical reactions to traumatic memory), and they are being flooded with memories. Victims are often dissociative and overstimulated and need crisis intervention to de-activate their flood of memories. Victims need relief from their immediate symptoms and should not be asked to do any memory work at this time. If the victim is not currently abreacting, continue to teach stress management and relaxation as a preventive method and work toward building ego strength.

You should help the victim to reduce stress reactions and symptoms and to increase coping. The victim can be shown how to remove triggers that are inducing abreactions and flooding, such as avoiding any interaction with the abuser, getting rid of photographs of the abuser or items the abuser gave her, not reading books about abuse, and not watching movies with high sex content. Provide appropriate resources for the victim and help her search out resources for herself, such as support people, support groups, counseling programs, 12-step groups, and religious groups.

Crisis stabilization can take from several weeks to several months to achieve. Retrieving repressed memories or working with new memories should not be considered until the victim is actively stable in her daily activities of living and has learned to manage overwhelming floods of affect, which memory work is sure to bring.

### Client Concerns

○ Desire to stop or to be able to handle abreactions and flooding of memories

○ Fear of "making up" memories of incest; disbelief in her own memories

○ Unable to manage dissociation

○ Fear of the inability to manage new memories or symptoms

○ Fear of interactions with unsupportive family members or abuser

○ Fear of confronting the abuser

○ Fear of a reduction in functioning level

○ Concern over stigma of incest

### Secondary Victimizations

○ Inability to maintain close relationships

○ Divorce or break up

○ Medical costs for somatic illnesses

○ Counseling costs

○ Loss of employment due to low functioning

○ Drug, alcohol, or other addiction rehabilitation

○ Inability to care for children due to low functioning

○ Lost childhood

○ Unhappy adulthood

○ Re-victimization in other areas of life

### Social/Public Services Needed

○ Crisis-intervention counselor

○ Psychiatrist (if medication is needed)

○ Drug and alcohol addiction rehabilitation or groups

○ Attorney or prosecutor (if applicable)

## SHORT-TERM COUNSELING

Incest survivors typically require long-term counseling. Short-term counseling can be seen as an extension of crisis intervention if symptoms have not been managed adequately. Short-term counseling also provides a transition during which long-term counseling issues can be assessed.

Most often, incest survivor's immediate needs are containing the abreactive flooding of memories. Once the survivor learns how to manage the abreactions, short-term counseling can focus on more cognitive and behavioral therapies, such as education about abuse, depression, and elevated levels of stress. You can also work with the cognitive distortions that are a normal by-product of incest, including erroneous beliefs and dichotomies the client has about herself, the abuser, or the abuse. Memory work about past abuse experiences often begins during short-term counseling—but only when the client has successfully learned how to manage her abreactions.

Past abuse memories can be so overwhelming that clients usually need to be taught techniques that allow them to process the memories without overpowering affect. You may need to learn these techniques from workshops or other clinicians. As a client works on memory retrieval, abreactions are likely to begin again. Slowing down the memory retrieval and working on abreaction stabilization will be necessary. Finding the client's unique pacing for this type of work is crucial. Much of short-term counseling will involve starting memory retrieval and slowing it down again in order to stabilize. You may work hard on memories one week and stabilize for the next week or two. This kind of starting and stopping is common. You should also check with your clients frequently during this time about drug, alcohol, eating, or any other compulsive behaviors that may be used as defensive coping while undergoing counseling.

Once the client has learned to manage abreactions, an incest therapy group can be helpful (Price, Hilsenroth, Petretic-Jackson, and Bonge 2001). Clients are able to gather support, hear similar stories, and learn new coping strategies. A group has also been noted to decrease psychiatric symptoms, increase social adjustment, increase healthy interpersonal functioning, and decrease distress and depression (Callahan, Price, and Hilsenroth 2004), as well as increase self-esteem (de Jong and Gorey 1996). However, group therapy is only recommended for clients who have learned to manage overwhelming affect, because hearing other survivor's stories can produce these symptoms.

Additionally, it is widely debated whether clients with multiple diagnoses, personality disorders (especially borderline personality disorder), or both can tolerate the intensity of the group experience. It is contraindicated in some cases (Cloitre and Koehen 2001). For instance, in lieu of incest therapy group, clients with a borderline diagnosis are often referred to dialectic behavioral therapy (DBT), which is a cognitive approach to managing affect. You should investigate the best possible group experience for a client based on the types of disorders diagnosed for that client and information you have gathered in assessments.

### Client Concerns

- Stigma and shame
- Inability to maintain close relationships
- Trust
- Emotional intimacy
- Inability to nurture children
- Distorted self-image or sexual identification
- Lack of sexual desire
- Managing abreactions
- Uncontrollable rage
- Confidentiality

### Secondary Victimizations

- Divorce or break up
- Medical costs for somatic illnesses
- Counseling costs
- Drug, alcohol, or other addiction rehabilitation
- Lost childhood
- Unhappy adulthood

### Social/Public Services Needed

- Short-term counselor
- Incest therapy group

○ Addiction therapy group (if applicable)

○ Eating disorder program (if applicable)

○ Financial assistance while undergoing therapy if unable to work

○ Attorney (if prosecution is desired)

○ Psychiatrist (if medication is needed)

○ Job rehabilitation or career counseling

### LONG-TERM COUNSELING

Some adult survivors are sporadic with respect to their participation in on-going counseling. They may seem committed, only to end up leaving short-term counseling for periods of time. Although clients are usually in a hurry to "get it all over with" and to do memory processing, their lack of coping skills to manage abreactions often drives them out of counseling. However, when they experience a crisis, they return for more counseling. Because this pattern is often related to unmanaged abreactions and lack of coping skills, initial counseling should teach clients how to prepare for these waves of intense emotion.

Much of your long-term counseling may be based on this kind of in-and-out when it comes to treatment. If a client has personality disorders, the challenge of keeping her in counseling over the long term will be even greater. For clients who are committed to counseling and who have learned some effective coping skills and abreaction management skills, long-term counseling can focus on the following issues:

○ Trauma processing

○ Transferring active trauma to past memory

○ Termination of counseling
   (Burgess, Hartman, and Kelley 1990)

#### Trauma Processing

Trauma processing involves four aspects:

1. Sensory: learning techniques to control the arousal of memories

2. Perceptual: negative and positive cue identification related to what sets off either memories or arousal responses

3. Cognitive: learning to reframe dysfunctional and distorted beliefs
4. Interpersonal: rebuilding and restoring old relationships and making new supportive ones

(Burgess, Hartman, and Kelley 1990)

### Transferring Active Trauma to Past Memory

As the client's memories are retrieved, experienced, and processed during therapy, the memories become emotionally de-charged. This is a process of neutralizing. Once the memories are de-charged, they can be moved from active memory to past memory. At that point, many of the client's symptoms begin to subside.

### Termination

After the client's symptoms have been consistently managed for some time, and her memories have been processed and de-charged, it is time to talk about termination. For some survivors, this work may occur after one to three years of work, depending on comorbidities. You can begin to discuss termination when goals have been reached and as the client's daily activities are consistently without intrusive symptoms.

At this time, the client begins to have a future-oriented view of life. She can see herself in activities in the future and has some anticipation of future events. She is able to set positive goals for herself and sees herself as more than a victim. She sees herself as a survivor—or better, as a thriver.

For termination to be effective, the decision to terminate should be mutual. This unfortunately does not always occur. Some survivors leave therapy when they feel better or stabilized, but this feeling of stability may be short-lived. Thus, their perceptions about when to terminate may not be the same as yours. Expressing your concerns if you feel they are not ready to terminate is acceptable. However, if they do terminate, respect their choice to do so and leave an open door should they decide to reenter counseling when their stability wanes.

Final termination should be worked toward as an expressed goal and addressed early in treatment so that both of you and the client will recognize when that point has been reached. Asking the client to write out her conception of the goals to be accomplished before termination can be a useful reference if premature termination is attempted. Pathology may also be an issue in premature termination because clients with personality dis-orders often struggle with consistency in many areas of their lives.

### Client Concerns

○ Restabilization of self, world view, and relationships
○ Return of sexual desire
○ Strengthening of interpersonal relationships
○ Strengthening and establishing spiritual beliefs
○ Abuse and family confrontations
○ Future victimizations
○ Ability to protect her children adequately
○ Self-esteem and value
○ Trust
○ Career choices and options
○ Lifestyle issues

### Secondary Victimizations

○ Cost of counseling
○ Addiction rehabilitation
○ Loss of childhood
○ Loss of adult happiness
○ Loss of virginity (if applicable)

### Social/Public Services Needed

○ Long-term counselor
○ Incest therapy group (if applicable, based on comorbidity)
○ Career counseling
○ Eating disorder group (if applicable)
○ Addiction group
○ Attorney (if prosecution is desired)
○ Financial aid (if therapy renders client unable to work)
○ Other community services to meet current needs

## RECOMMENDED READING

Berceli, David. *Trauma Releasing Exercises: A Revolutionary New Method for Stress/Trauma Recovery.* North Charleston, SC: Booksurge Publishing, 2005.

Courtois, Christine A. *Healing the Incest Wound: Adult Survivors in Therapy.* New York: Norton Publishers, 1988.

Donaldson, Mary Ann. *Group Treatment of Adult Incest Survivors* (Interpersonal Violence: The Practice Series). New York: Norton Publishers, 1994.

Kluft, Richard, ed. *Incest Related Syndromes of Adult Psychopathy.* Arlington, VA: American Psychiatric Association, 2005.

Paddison, Patricia L. *Treatment of Adult Survivors of Incest.* Arlington, VA: American Psychiatric Association, 1993.

## RESOURCES

Survivors of Incest Anonymous World Service Office
www.siawso.org

Incest Survivors Anonymous (ISA)
(562) 428-5599

Rape, Abuse and Incest National Network (RAINN)
(800) 656-HOPE (656-4673)    ○    www.rainn.org

National Crime Victims Research and Treatment Center
(843) 792-2945    ○    www.musc.edu/cvc/

National Organization for Victim Assistance
(703) 535-NOVA (535-6682)    ○    www.trynova.org

National Center for PTSD
(802) 296-6300    ○    www.ncptsd.va.gov

International Society for Traumatic Stress Studies
(847) 480-9028    ○    www.istss.org

PTSD Alliance
(877) 507-PTSD (507-7873)    ○    www.ptsdalliance.org

Trauma Info Pages
www.trauma-pages.com

The Sidran Foundation
www.sidran.org

The National Center for Victims of Crime
(202) 467-8700    ○    www.ncvc.org

## Overview of Sexual Abuse by Incest

*Crisis-Intervention:* Abreaction of new memories, reducing abreactions, depression, PTSD, relationship problems, addictions, somatic illnesses, self-mutilation, memory leakage, increasing coping, safety, stress management, strengthening resources

*Short-Term Counseling Issues:* Establishing trust alliance, acknowledging incest, recounting incest, stigma, expression of feelings

*Long-Term Counseling Issues:* Resolution of responsibility, survival issues, grieving, cognitive restructuring of distorted beliefs, behavioral changes, education and skill building, trauma processing, transferring trauma to past memory, termination

*Secondary Victimizations:* Inability to maintain close relationships, counseling costs, medical costs for somatic illnesses, lost employment, addictions, ostracization by family members

*Social/Legal Services:* Medical attention for somatic illnesses, attorney if prosecuting, rehab training if new job skills are needed, crisis intervention, short- and long-term counseling, family counseling, addictions and/or compulsion programs, housing if leaving abuser, temporary shelter

# CHAPTER 11

# Homicide

AN ESPECIALLY FEARED victimization due to its permanence, homicide in all forms rattles the public's sense of safety. Often, our sense of safety in the world is influenced by what we see on the nightly news and how many murders we do or do not hear about. Surviving family members bring powerful imagery of death to the counseling chair.

○ More than 20,000 murders occur annually in the United States.

○ In 2001, males comprised 76 percent of all murder victims, females 23 percent.

○ In 2001, firearms were used in 63.4 percent of all murders.

○ One third of all murder victims and half of all offenders are under the age of 25.

○ African-American males are six times more likely to be murder victims and seven times more likely to commit homicides.

○ Arguments are the most frequently cited circumstance before a murder.

(U.S. Department of Justice, Office of Justice Programs, Bureau of Justice Statistics website)

**VICTIM'S STORY**                                    *SANDY*

*All I remember is being called in the middle of the night that my dad was murdered. I don't know why, but I went to the place where he was murdered. There was his life blood—splashed over cars and filling street gutters. What affected me most was his hand prints in his blood on a parked car where he struggled to stand up after the stabbing. His hand prints slid down the side of the car to the spot where he eventually died. That is the haunting memory I can't get out of my head. Those bloody hand prints—his blood, his life—his death on that car.*

## Background Information

The nightly news is filled with stories of all types of murders. As a nation, we have almost become numb to the stories that blare from our TV sets as we fix dinner. With so many variations in how one can be murdered, these stories become part of the fabric of our nightly overview of the state of our union. Murder is part of America, and more than 20,000 such crimes occur each year (U.S. Department of Justice, Office of Justice Programs, Bureau of Justice Statistics website).

### TYPES OF MURDER

For those who may not have had a personal experience with this form of victimization, the specific types and variations of murder (or homicide) may be unfamiliar. These include mass or multiple murders, serial murders, single incident murder, vehicular homicide, and manslaughter or accidental homicide.

*Mass or Multiple Murders:* Mass murders are committed by the same person(s), involve more than one victim, and are committed during one incident. These murders are a "blitz" style and are referred to as "massacres." Examples include the Columbine School shootings, the 9/11 event, and the Oklahoma City bombing. Numerous people were killed in each of those events.

*Serial Murders:* Serial murders are committed by the same person(s), involve more than one victim, but are not committed at the same time. Ted Bundy and BTK were serial murderers who killed numerous people over a period of time. Generally, serial murders follow patterns that are similar in style, technique, and victim orientation.

*Single Incident Murder:* These murders are the kind most frequently mentioned on the nightly news. They involve crimes of passion, rapes and robberies, and one-on-one killings. Examples include the murders of Laci Peterson and Lori Hacking. They can be random or pre-meditated.

*Vehicular Homicide:* This type of homicide occurs as the result of negligent or reckless driving, or driving while intoxicated or drugged. This type of homicide is now considered intentional in most states, based on the belief that a car is a weapon that can kill a person through the driver's usage or neglect to drive it safely and while unimpaired.

*Manslaughter or Accidental Homicide:* This type or murder is committed without malice. It may be accidental in nature. If the courts cannot prove a murder was committed with malice, the sentence is reduced from first- or second-degree homicide to manslaughter.

## HOMICIDE SURVIVORS

The FBI (1999) defined murder as "the willful killing of one human being by another," but a homicide survivor defined it as "the blackest hell accompanied by a pain so intense that even breathing becomes an unendurable labor." The direct victims of homicide are not among us. They died at the hands of someone else. But homicide survivors are the surviving family members and friends of those who were murdered. Typically, these survivors number about ten per family. Survivors are also referred to as "co-victims" (Spungen 1998) because they are left behind to deal with the criminal courts, media, medical examiner, and law-enforcement agencies. In this way, the pain of the survivor constitutes a secondary victimization that can continue for years.

Homicide survivors' losses have specific qualities. Beyond the obvious loss of life, they are disturbed by memories of the event and the how the loss of life occurred. Imagery of the violence their loved one experienced in his or her last minutes haunts the survivor. Survivors worry about the amount of pain the victim felt prior to death (Redmond 1989). To this end, many survivors want to know the grizzly details of the murder: how much blood, what kinds of wounds, how much pain, what kind of murder weapon. This is often puzzling and disconcerting to counselors who don't understand the need for this information.

The lost relationship with the murder victim is also paramount. This loss includes the dreams or expectations for a future life with the victim. Death ends any possibility of resolving past disagreements with the victim, which can linger among the traumatic memories the survivor experiences. The survivor also feels the loss of personal control, independence, and faith, as well as work lost while attending the trial (Asaro 2001).

Surviving family members often blame themselves for their inability to save the victim. Persistent thoughts about how they could have prevented the murder can stall their ability to work through the grief process. Survivor guilt is common.

Loss due to the trauma of homicide can bleed over into the family system. Family structures weaken (Asaro 2001); what was once a support system and resource can become a source of friction and turmoil. Many support and family relationships are lost because of the insurmountable grief each family member experiences without feeling the ability to reach out to one another for mutual comfort or support. Self-survival becomes paramount as the family system unravels.

Because murder is often judged to be about the victim's character and is not simply regarded as an act of violence, outside social support for survivors may be lacking. Financial loss is almost guaranteed when family members lose work time for legal proceedings, have to cover the final medical expenses of the victim, pay counseling fees to manage their PTSD, buy medications for anxiety and depression, and take care of other out-of-pocket expenses.

One of the most devastating losses for survivors is the shattered concept of personal safety and the loss of the belief that the world is safe and sane (Asaro 2001). The survivors' locus of control is radically shifted as their worldview is mutilated by images of violent death.

Homicide survivors sometimes have reactions to the murder that startle counselors. These include the survivors' own murderous impulses and frightening levels of rage. Previous anger in the relationship between the victim and survivor is one possible cause for underlying rage (Rando 1993). A desire for revenge and revenge fantasies are also common (Redmond 1989). These impulses may conflict with the survivor's sense of right and wrong, religious training, or morality, thus producing even more distress. While the survivor can be frightened by feeling out of control, the counselor is likely to be worried about the victim's safety and intent.

Survivors also have reactions related to cognitive dissonance (Redmond 1989; Figley 1985) or about the inability to process such overwhelming concepts and trauma. A survivor can get stuck in the questions "Why did this happen?" or "How did this happen?" to the point that the counselor becomes concerned about the client's ability to recognize and accept the reality of the loss in order to bring closure to it.

Homicide ranks as one of the most traumatic experiences someone can endure. The degree of psychological impact can easily inhibit the survivor's ability to successfully work through the tasks of grieving (Asaro 2001). The individual may not have sufficient internal resources to cope with the trauma (Rando 1993). This combination of high trauma, together with inadequate coping resources, led to the newly proposed DSM diagnosis of "traumatic grief."

Homicide survivors are at an elevated risk for developing comorbid conditions, such as depression, other anxiety disorders, and drug or alcohol dependence. Depending on a survivor's previous mental health and coping strategies, the individual also may be at risk for developing PTSD with associated comorbidity and complicated mourning (Asaro 2001).

## SITUATIONAL FACTORS AFFECTING HOMICIDE SURVIVORS

Situational factors that involve the specifics of the murder, as well as the specific coping strategies of the survivor, can hinder the survivor's recovery.

Witnessing the murder or seeing the aftermath leaves lasting impressions and can increase PTSD reactions. Those who witness a murder usually feel more self-blame and fantasize they could have saved the victim. They may fear retaliation and not want to testify. While this is a common reaction, it can add to a survivor's internal conflict by making it more difficult to overcome guilt about not having been able to prevent the murder.

The survivor's relationship to the assailant is often a factor in trauma. Murders that are intrafamilial add complications related to loyalty, the process of prosecution, and family system dynamics. One mother whose son murdered her new husband asked me, "Which side of the table do I sit on? The prosecution or the defense? I know he did it. He needs to be punished. But he's my son, and I love him. And I don't want the death penalty. But I can't guarantee that, can I? I lost my husband, now I am losing my son."

Survivors' reactions can vary depending on the type of murder that was committed (e.g., vehicular homicide, murder accompanied by sexual assault, murder accompanied by torture, murder preceded by kidnapping, or murder in which the body is violated or mutilated after death). Attributes of the murderer can also affect survivors' traumatic reactions:

○ Was there more than one murderer?

○ Does the assailant have children?

○ What are the assailant's age (juvenile, adult, elderly), race, religious orientation, and marital status?

Likewise, attributes of the victim can affect the survivor:

○ How old was the victim (infant, child, adult, elderly)?

○ What was the victim's sexual preference, race, and marital status?

○ Did he or she have children or other dependents?

○ What significant events occurred in the victim's life prior to the murder (engaged, won an award, or maybe already victimized)?

The geographic distance between where the murder occurred and where the survivor lives can have an impact. For instance, a close proximity may cause the survivor to fear he or she will also be victimized. A long distance between the two may cause the survivor to feel a lack of closure because he or she has not seen the location of the murder or may not have the finances to go to the funeral. Distance may also affect crime compensation if more than one state is involved.

## SPECIAL CONSIDERATIONS IN SECONDARY VICTIMIZATION

Homicide and the violence of murder brings special considerations to the issue of secondary victimization. In Chapter 2 we discussed how "systems" often negatively affect a grieving or wounded victim. The category of homicide brings with it the possibility of intense secondary victimization. Murder is always highly emotional, media-visible, and criminally complicated. This often leads to the entanglement of the various systems that are trying to help the surviving family members, and can produce mixed or painful results.

In the case of homicide, systems often inflict secondary injuries that magnify the original trauma. These are known as "injurious systems" and include the media, criminal-justice system, law-enforcement system, probate/estate system, medical system, and mental-health system. Many homicide survivors recognize these types of systems as the cause of their secondary victimizations. These systems can complicate the grieving process and add trauma to existing PTSD because survivors believe these systems exist to assist them. They struggle with the concept of a safe and sane world, only to find the systems are also causing them pain. Treating secondary victimization is especially necessary in the case of homicide.

## Media

The media's right to know overrides the survivor's right to privacy and the right to grieve alone. Murder is often the highlight of newspapers, TV news coverage, daytime television shows, and rag mags. Media can be intrusive at the times when a survivor is in most need of privacy. This can include the moment of death notification, the funeral, emerging from a trial, and during a verdict. The survivor may find his or her name or the victim's name plastered on the front page, pictures of the murder scene on TV, or shots of the body bag. The murder victim may be described by the media in disparaging terms, suggesting the victim's character caused the murder.

## Criminal-Justice System

Most survivors are shocked to find out murder is a "crime against the state," not a crime against their family. Because of this, it is treated as a "depersonalized" crime, and the interactions between the prosecuting court system and family can be limited. The family is often seen as secondary because the state is considered the primary survivor. This can decrease the amount of sensitivity shown to the surviving family; for example, information may be given out without thought to the impact on the family members when they hear the details.

In some states, the family is barred from the court proceedings during a trial and allowed in only for the sentencing phase. Some family members are barred because the defense informs the court they will be used as witnesses, but they are never called. Or, family members may be barred if they show any emotional response to any content in the proceedings. The criminal's family, however, is allowed stay in the courtroom and show emotion.

Some improvements have occurred over the years. For example, most courts now allow a victim-impact statement, in which the family can define its loss in personalized terms. Nevertheless, inadequate notification is still often given for trials, hearings, releases, bond hearings, trial postponements, and date changes for these hearings.

Most murder trials do not even begin for at least nine months after the incident and are postponed an average of three to six times. Once the trial begins, the family members see the murderer walking past them and have to listen to the verbal attacks of the defense counselor about the victim's character and favorable descriptions of the murderer by character witnesses. They may hear their victim's case plea-bargained to a minimal sentence. The murderer usually files an appeal if convicted, and the process can take up to nine years, putting survivors through further emotional turmoil and criminal-justice exposure. Once the murderer is paroled, the family lives in fear.

### Law-Enforcement System

Insensitive death notification is a primary complaint of survivors. The death itself or other details about the crime are often relayed in the notification without any recognition of the traumatized family's feelings. A request for more information or details is often overlooked by law enforcement, whose job is to gather evidence and find a killer. The details the family desires may be withheld "pending investigation," and the victim's personal property can be held as evidence for years. Victim advocates who work through law-enforcement agencies are often the best resource for homicide survivors. They will work closely with families to get the information they need and to guide them through the court processes.

### Probate/Estate System

A murder automatically causes a person's estate to be put into probate. Moving through the probate system often requires definite information about the cause of death, which can take time to establish. The actual estate settlement may not occur until more than two years after the murder. During that time, families have to bear the burden of the final hospital bill and funeral, cremation, or burial costs. Grieving families can be targets for financial exploitation by attorneys, doctors, and other service providers.

### Medical System

The survivors and family may be treated insensitively by doctors, hospitals, emergency medical technicians, fire rescue workers, or other medical staff. In some cases, hospitals bill for services to the victim that were never rendered (e.g., anesthesiologist or operating room charges, after the coroner pronounced the victim "dead on arrival"), yet the survivors do not have the emotional strength to fight the bill. Other families object to information disclosed in autopsy reports (e.g., AIDS diagnosis or drug use by the victim, which implies character defects) that the defense later uses to sue the victim. Funeral directors may be insensitive and fail to close the casket of a victim who was severely mutilated.

### Mental-Health System

The fact that many counselors are not trained or are poorly trained to work with issues of homicide leaves many families at a distinct disadvantage. Some homicide survivors have been hospitalized and others have been over-medicated by untrained counselors who reacted to the survivors' revenge fantasies. Other survivors were given shock treatments in an effort to get them to forget the murder. If we ever hope to move past this barbaric revictimization of homicide survivors, counselors must receive specialized training.

## Crisis Intervention

Crisis intervention begins with assessment of the surviving family members. Chapter 3 includes numerous tools from which to choose. The Clinician Administered PTSD Scale is an assessment with particular relevance for homicide survivors. In addition, you might want to find a grief assessment instrument to go along with the PTSD scale. Some experts recommend that assessment continue throughout the counseling process (Rando 1993). Some available instruments allow you to measure the effectiveness of treatment in reducing PTSD symptoms, thus allowing for truly continual assessment. Likewise, some grief instruments can be used as a pre- and posttest.

The goals of crisis intervention are to resolve the immediate crisis and teach the survivor effective coping strategies for dealing with future difficulties. Achievement of these goals hinges on the following survivor characteristics:

○ Perception of the murder

○ Prior coping skills

○ Presence of social support
   (Aguilera 1990)

PTSD is diagnosed in many homicide survivors. Noteworthy symptoms in homicide survivors include persistent re-experiencing of the murder event, hyperarousal, avoidance behaviors (Amick-McMullan, Kilpatrick, and Resnick 1991; Parkes 1993; Rynearson and McCreery 1993), denial and numbing (Murphy et al. 1999). Survivors who come to counseling can present with a range of conditions, from the avoidant to the highly stimulated. At the beginning of crisis intervention, some survivors feel the need to tell and retell their stories, perhaps in the minutest and bloodiest details. This is an attempt to come to terms with the reality that the victim is dead, while processing what actually happened (i.e., the murder). Revenge fantasies can spring up and rage can be unbridled. Other survivors may be close to a catatonic state.

Survivors come to counseling for help with the overwhelming affect, but also because they do not know how to function within a fractured family system. A murder can blow apart an already dysfunctional family system, and cause a less dysfunctional system to unravel. Family members may react differently to the same murder. Some may refuse to be part of the court process, whereas others need and want to be present. Some may openly grieve, while others remain stoic. Some may need to talk repeatedly about the murder event, but others refuse to acknowledge it. These varied types of coping styles can wreak havoc within a grieving family system, especially if one family member judges another for having different reactions, feelings, or needs (Brown 1991).

Survivors can also be overwhelmed by the sheer number of systems with which they must deal. Sources of system overload include reporters, prosecutors and defense attorneys, state agencies, the hospital, morgue and funeral home, police or sheriff's department, and homicide and crime scene investigators. Dealing with all of these at a time when survivors are still in shock, denial, or feeling numb forces them to push grieving aside, and thus contributes to the possibility of delayed, chronic, exacerbated, or complicated grief.

If family members do not have a victim advocate working with them, you should help them obtain one. In the case of homicide, a victim advocate would be an employee of the local police or sheriff's department whose sole purpose is to assist victims though the various systems. Such an advocate can save you, as a counselor, considerable time spent in arranging social service placements. The advocate also can keep you and the family posted about the status of the case within the criminal-justice system, guide the family through the maze of law-enforcement and criminal processes, and make community referrals for assistance.

Counselors often play a functional role during the crisis-intervention stage by helping survivors through the events they must face. You may need to help the family members plan the funeral, attended the funeral with them, and help them process it afterwards. Families who attend funerals move through grief more quickly than do those who avoid the funeral. However, a survivor's choices about whether or not to attend must be respected.

Counselors can serve as educational tools for survivors during crisis intervention. They provide information about the survivor's rights concerning media representatives, interviews, photographs, and so on. You need to assist surviving families with filing crime compensation forms or social security benefit forms, or help them find comprehensive clean-up services if the victim was murdered at home. (Survivors should never clean up the murder scene, because that can cause further traumatization. Specialized services are available for this.)

During crisis intervention, the victim's overwhelming grief and PTSD symptomatology must both be addressed, but the counselor may be unsure about which to address first. Ultimately, PTSD symptoms need to be reduced so underlying grief issues can be addressed; however, in practice, grief and stress symptoms may need to be treated separately or simultaneously (Rando 1997). You can accomplish this by allowing the survivor some time in the session to grieve, cry, and talk about the victim, while using the rest of the session to reduce such PTSD symptoms as anxiety, sleeplessness, flashbacks, or whatever the survivor identifies as problematic. You should also think about the best possible future approaches for PTSD treatment for this survivor.

The crisis stage of a homicide survivor can feel overwhelming to the counselor due to the intense nature of the act of violence. Counselors who work with high-violence trauma cases develop their own traumatic imagery, which can trigger counter-transference or cause secondary post traumatic stress in the counselor, often referred to as "vicarious trauma" (McCann and Pearlman 1990). You should stay in supervision throughout the treatment of a homicide survivor and pay particular attention to your own self-care practices during this time.

### Client Concerns

- ○ Was the murder preventable?
- ○ Has the murderer been apprehended?
- ○ Will the murderer go to trial?
- ○ Dealing with the media
- ○ Dealing with the investigation
- ○ Return of family possessions taken as evidence during the investigation
- ○ Funeral arrangements
- ○ Family problems
- ○ Explaining the death to children
- ○ Inability to work

### Secondary Victimizations

- ○ Loss of income
- ○ Paying funeral expenses, medical expenses
- ○ Counseling costs
- ○ Insensitive media, criminal-justice system, law enforcement

### Social/Public Services Needed

- ○ Victim advocate
- ○ Trained crisis counselor
- ○ Homicide detective or private investigator
- ○ Prosecuting attorney
- ○ State crime compensation (financial aid)
- ○ Life insurance company
- ○ Homicide clean-up crew (if appropriate)
- ○ Clergy (if appropriately trained in homicide)

## Short-Term Counseling

Your assessments should provide information about the existence of PTSD or other comorbid factors. Because survivors often have overlapping symptoms of grieving and PTSD, you have to balance your approach to incorporate several treatment elements.

Complications can occur when a survivor does not move through the normal process of grieving. This can result from the survivor's perception of the suddenness, deliberateness, and preventability of the murder (Rando 1993). Add probable posttraumatic stress and other comorbid conditions, and you have an equation that looks like this:

> **TRAUMATIC EVENT**
> − **ADEQUATE COPING RESOURCES**
> + **COMPLICATED GRIEVING**
> + **POSTTRAUMATIC STRESS DISORDER**
> + **COMORBID CONDITIONS**
> = **SIGNIFICANTLY TRAUMATIZED SURVIVOR**

Some indicators of failure to move through the normal grieving process include murderous impulses; phobic-like fears; intense survivor guilt; irrational other-oriented blame; violation of primary beliefs and values concerning safety, worldview, or human behavior; severe emotional withdrawal; and cognitive distortions. Other research has noted that the following three particular syndromes are typical in complicated mourning:

- Problems expressing the loss (absent, delayed, or inhibited mourning)
- Skewed aspects (distorted or conflicted mourning)
- Problems with closure (chronic mourning)
  (Rando 1993)

The goals of short-term counseling should focus on reducing symptoms and minimizing secondary losses (Rando 1993). Counseling must address the defense mechanisms a survivor uses to keep affect at bay. In addition, homicide survivors may need to be treated for depersonalization; hallucinations, both visual and auditory; dissociation; and an intensified focus on the violent murder event. If the anxiety generated by traumatic memories is too strong, the victim may develop posttraumatic amnesia and lose access to event-related memories (Rando 1997).

A multimodal treatment approach is often helpful for survivors. This can include individual counseling, group therapy, family therapy, medication, and peer support groups.

## INDIVIDUAL COUNSELING

Individual counseling approaches allow the survivor to personally deal with issues related to the trauma and loss outside the context of the loss to the family. The focus can be personalized to the relationship between victim and survivor. Individual counseling allows for a focus on symptom reduction related to PTSD and comorbid conditions. In fact, the process of working through grief and the process of PTSD symptom reduction can be similar for homicide survivors (Rando 1993).

Although some counselors may not have be overtly aware of how a person's worldview affects mental health, this issue is important in the individual counseling of homicide survivors. Because the homicide survivor's worldview is connected with feeling safe, fear for the future, and reactivating hyperarousal (aspects seen in both grief and PTSD), restructuring of the survivor's worldview is paramount. You should assist the survivor to develop a worldview that incorporates the experience of the victimization (Janoff-Bulman 1985). While this focus may begin in short-term counseling, it is likely to extend into long-term counseling. The goals of restructuring the survivor's worldview are to find meaning in the event; face personal vulnerability; re-experience the world as a comprehensible and understand place; and view oneself once again in a positive way, without blame, rage, or fear. Incorporating all these elements into a new internal structure can be a time-consuming process for the survivor.

## PHARMACOLOGICAL

Survivors who have PTSD or PTSD features and other comorbid conditions frequently require medication. Untreated PTSD often results in substance abuse, so medication should be considered (Brady et al. 2000).

Clients should consult with a psychiatrist about the kinds of medications used to treat PTSD.

## FAMILY THERAPY

The counselor should assist the family members in providing social support for each other. The goals of family therapy include assisting the family members to complete any unfinished business between them and the murder victim, and to reorganize the remaining family roles and relationships (Horwitz 1997). These goals are best accomplished by using resources within the family structure; therefore, some knowledge of family systems is necessary.

## GROUP THERAPY OR PEER SUPPORT

At some point in treatment, group or peer support may be intensely helpful for a survivor. The benefits of group or peer support are well known. However, homicide survivor groups need to be victimization-specific. Survivors should not be placed in other types of groups, because members of those groups who have not experienced a homicide may find their stories overwhelming. As a result, members of the group may withdraw from the survivor, thus increasing social isolation. Victim advocates often know about available homicide support groups. Twelve-week focal psychotherapy groups have been established in some areas (Redmond 1989).

Peer support groups are often run by other homicide survivors who are further along in the process of healing and recovery. A survivor must have regained some ego strength and reduced PTSD symptoms in order to actively participate in such as group. You should assess whether participation in the group increases hyperarousal or other PTSD symptoms. Increased symptoms may be an indicator the survivor is not yet ready for a group experience. A survivor should not begin group therapy until that person has worked through the shock and numbness typical of the initial phases of grief.

## SPIRITUAL COUNSELING

Survivors struggle to understand how a benevolent God would allow murder. Even survivors who do not attend church or services regularly may struggle with faith and spiritual issues within the context of their worldview. People of faith can have dramatic setbacks as a result of insensitive statements made by untrained clergy or other people of the faith. "God's Will," "Just World," and "Sin in Their Life" theories have devastated some survivors and disconnected them from potential sources of support. Some clergy have been trained in homicide and can provide comfort, support, and aid in providing closure for the survivor. Refer the survivor to a trained clergy member or do not make any referral for spiritual counseling.

## OTHER APPROACHES

Because of the intensity of a survivor's traumatic reactions, many therapeutic approaches have been attempted. These include eye movement desensitization and reprocessing (EMDR), thought field therapy, traumatic incident reduction, guided imagery, and neurolinguistic programming. The efficiency of these therapies with homicide survivors is widely debated, so you should investigate thoroughly before using any of them.

### Client Concerns

- Still obsessed with the murder and if it were preventable
- When the trial will start or murderer will be apprehended
- Inability to work, complications with work
- Is the grief process progressing as it should/will I always feel this way?
- Phobias and fears about safety
- Survivor guilt
- Murderous impulses and rage
- Wondering where God was

### Secondary Victimizations

- Loss of income
- Counseling costs
- Insensitive media and law enforcement
- Delayed trial dates
- Withdrawal of social support by friends and family
- Clergy asks to forgive the killer or offers insensitive counsel

*Social/Public Services Needed*

○ Victim advocate

○ Short-term counselor

○ Family therapy counselor

○ Group counselor or peer support group

○ Homicide detective or private investigator

○ Prosecuting attorney

○ State crime compensation

○ Clergy (if trained in counseling homicide survivors)

## Long-Term Counseling

While reactions following a murder are similar to those for other acts of violence, murder reactions are longer and more intense. Symptom relief can take up to five years, and resolution up to ten (Brown 1991). The most difficult time for survivors is from six months after the murder through two years posthomicide. This is due to a variety of factors cited below:

○ The grief process is progressing, but with it comes the intense pain of mourning.

○ The reality of the murder has set in, but previous coping mechanisms have not held up in the face of the trauma.

○ People in the survivor's support system may suggest it is time to "be over it by now."

○ Previous friends may avoid the survivor because of the intensity of emotion and imagery related to the murder.

○ The trial has begun, and with it come many continuances, hearings, and setbacks.

○ The survivor's physical health may be failing; somatic illnesses may occur frequently.

○ Unless the counselor has helped the family system, it may have shut down by this time.

○ Marriages are struggling.

○ Financial problems occur because the survivor is unable to work or is frequently absent.

○ The survivor may be undergoing a spiritual crisis and may feel anger toward God.

○ Holidays, death anniversaries, and the birthday of the murder victim continue to amplify the difficulties experienced by the survivor.

Self-blame is prevalent among survivors, even when they could not possibly have prevented or been responsible for the murder. It may be painful for you to watch the person agonize over perceived personal responsibility for the murder. Do not challenge the victim's self-blaming process prematurely. When the survivor is able to fully process the attendant meaning and emotion, these schemas will change and the person will be able to move closer to acceptance (McCann and Pearlman 1990).

Individual counseling may be sporadic if the survivor comes for counseling for a few weeks and then feels no need for further help or cannot face the intensity of the feelings therapy elicits. The starting and stopping of counseling is common. But survivors should be encouraged to stay in individual counseling during this time. If they have begun group or peer counseling, they may have gained much-needed new support persons and coping mechanisms.

PTSD symptoms can increase or relapse during the trial. This is one reason to encourage survivors to remain in counseling. The principles used previously in individual and group counseling can be used again to help them reconnect with what they have learned and experienced. Support from group members during and after the trial can greatly reduce isolation. Group member support may be preferred over therapeutic support. When survivors are able to talk about feelings and reactions, they are able to embrace a greater compassion and sensitivity to the feelings and needs of others (Tedeschi and Calhoun 1996).

You can gauge the success of long-term counseling in terms of forward movement in the grief process and symptom reduction and stabilization of PTSD. The resolution in these two areas indicates the survivor is moving toward closure and that long-term counseling will soon terminate.

Resolution of grief symptoms is characterized by the following client behaviors and abilities:

○ Acknowledging the loss and its meaning, expressing feelings about the loss

○ Identifying and grieving any additional losses

○ Describing the circumstances of the death

○ Verbalizing transformation in the emotional attachment to the deceased, moving the relationship from present to memory

○ Reviewing the positive and negative aspects of the relationship with the deceased

○ Verbalizing shock/numbness, stress, anger, anxiety, sadness, despair, hostility, idealization, depression, and psychological reorganization

(Rando 1993)

The concept of post traumatic growth can be an indicator of the survivor's movement toward resolution (Calhoun, Cann, Tedeschi, and McMillian 2000). This is akin to the philosophy of existentialism, according to which survivors can find meaning and purpose in the face of suffering. In fact, one study found that those who were able to not only process the trauma but find meaning in the traumatic event were more likely to report posttraumatic growth (Calhoun et al. 2000). A survivor's ability to find meaning in the traumatic event may be evidence of reconstruction of the assumptive world destroyed by the traumatic event (Janoff-Bulman 1985).

Survivors demonstrating post traumatic growth will perceive themselves in a more positive manner, have a changed sense of relationship with others, and have a changed philosophy of life. Changes in self-perception can include a sense of self-reliance and confidence derived from living through the trauma. Emotional strength comes from knowing they survived the most difficult experiences they are likely to ever face (Tedeschi and Calhoun 1996).

Lastly, survivors begin to change their life priorities. They begin to appreciate life and not take others for granted. This is similar to the phase of the grief process during which others are reintegrated into the individual's life flow (Tedeschi and Calhoun 1996). Nevertheless, not all who experience trauma demonstrate posttraumatic growth as a result of counseling (Calhoun and Tedeschi 1999). Some carry the ravages of PTSD symptoms into their lives for years to come.

### Client Concerns

- Need for increased coping skills
- Need for varying types of social and legal support
- Help dealing with the media, trial procedures, other systems
- Family system falling apart
- Physical health problems
- Spiritual problems
- Approaching holiday, death anniversary, or birthday dates

### Secondary Victimizations

- Loss of income
- Loss of physical health
- Counseling costs
- Court delays
- Intruding media
- Loss of family support or lost relationships

### Social/Public Services Needed

- Victim advocate
- Long-term counselor
- Group or peer support counseling
- Prosecuting attorney
- Clergy
- Vocational rehabilitation if a new job is needed

## RECOMMENDED READING

Buscholz, Judie A. *Homicide Survivors: Misunderstood Grievers (Death, Value and Meaning)*. Amityville, NY: Baywood Publishing Company, 2002.

Figley, C. R., B. E. Bride, and N. Mazza. *Death and Trauma: The Traumatology of Grieving*. Washington, DC: Francis & Taylor, 1996.

Figley, C.R. *Trauma and Its Wake: The Study and Treatment of PTSD*. New York: Brunner/Mazel, 1985.

Goetting, Ann. *Homicide in Families and Other Special Populations.* Woodstock, CT: Springer Publishing Company, 1995.

Hospice Foundation of America. *Living with Grief: After Sudden Loss, Suicide, Homicide, Accident, Heart Attack and Strokes.* Washington, D.C.: Hospice Foundation of America, 1996.

Matakis, Aphrodite. *Survivor Guilt.* Oakland, CA: New Harbinger Publications, 1999.

Rando, Teresa A. *Treatment of Complicated Mourning.* Champaign, IL: Research Press, 1993.

Spungen, Deborah. *Homicide: The Hidden Victims: A Resource for Professionals* (Interpersonal Violence: The Practice Series). Thousand Oaks, CA: Sage Publications, 1998.

Tedeschi, R. G., and R. G. Calhoun. *Trauma and Transformation: Growing in the Aftermath of Suffering.* Thousand Oaks, CA: Sage Publications, 1995.

## RESOURCES

Grief Recovery Institute
(818) 907-9600 ○ www.grief-recovery.com

National Crime Victims Research and Treatment Center
(843) 792-2945 ○ www.musc.edu/cvc/

National Organization for Victim Assistance
(703) 535-NOVA (535-6682) ○ www.trynova.org

National Center for Victims of Crime
(202) 467-8700 ○ www.ncvc.org

National Organization of Parents of Murdered Children
& Other Homicide Survivors
(513) 721-5683 ○ www.pomc.org

Mothers Against Drunk Driving
(800) 438-6233 ○ www.madd.org

PTSD
(207) 236-8858 ○ www.giftfromwithin.org

Crime Victims
(301) 898-1009 ○ www.witnessjustice.org

National Center for PTSD
(802) 296-6300 ○ www.ncptsd.va.gov

## Overview of Homicide

*Crisis Intervention:* Shock, numbness, PTSD, dealing with funeral arrangements, estate management, media, handling crime investigators, family interpersonal relationships, site clean-up services

*Short-Term Counseling:* Family interpersonal relationships, beginning of grieving process, criminal-justice system and treatment, fear and safety, survivor guilt

*Long-Term Counseling:* Fear, anger, rage, family relationships, continuation of criminal-justice problems, grieving process, job dysfunction, addictions and compulsions

*Secondary Victimizations:* Loss of income (if primary income producer), final medical costs for victim, time off work, murderer may be released on bond, case may not go to trial, insensitivity of criminal-justice system, lack of information given by crime investigators, slow payment by insurance company, funeral expenses, counseling costs, intense media coverage

*Social/Public Services:* State crime compensation, victim advocate, legal aid, short- and long-term counseling, private investigator, trial attendants

# CHAPTER 12

# Societal Trauma

THE IMAGES ARE WHAT we cannot get out of our minds: destroyed buildings; grieving, frantic mothers looking for their children; terrorized people running in all directions; and the aftermath of rubble, hunger, and unmet needs. Societal victimization affects us all, including emergency workers. It touches us at the core of our sense of safety, making us worry about the future, our children, and the safety and sanity of the world. Someone has to help those who survive traumas that occur at a societal level. Often, it is mental-health workers and counselors who are called on to respond.

○ In 1999, 168 adults and children were killed by a bombing in Oklahoma City.

○ In 2001, anthrax was used to terrorize postal workers, elected officials, and the general public.

○ The tsunami in the Indian Ocean on December 26, 2004, killed approximately 275,000 people; other natural disasters have killed thousands more.

○ The September 11th attacks produced 2,986 casualties; 28,000 surviving family members of these victims; 2,400 people who were physically injured; 111,000 direct witnesses, and millions of people who saw it repeatedly on TV. (National Center for Victims Research and Treatment Center website)

**VICTIM'S STORY**                                    *LEE*

*I lost my house in a tornado when I was a child. We fled, but my father stayed and was nearly killed. We were homeless after that, and it took us years to even get furniture. Some people were very kind and generous, and others were awful. Some looted our houses. Other girls at school made fun of my charity clothes because I was wearing their dresses that were handed down to me.*

*I think I am stronger for having lived through this. But it changed our financial lives and position forever. We never really did bounce back.*

## Background Information

Societal trauma is increasingly recognized as an assault on our psychological functioning. As the potential types of disasters increase, the by-products of fear, PTSD, and other stress reactions mount. Societal trauma can encompass the following types of incidents:

○ Natural disasters, including earthquakes, tsunamis, tornadoes, wildfires, landslides, and hurricanes

○ Technological disasters, including plane crashes, gas refinery explosion, structural collapses

○ War, including war-related trauma experienced by soldiers and relief workers

○ Silent disasters, including nuclear accidents (e.g., Chernobyl, Three Mile Island)

○ Terrorism, including biological, chemical, or nuclear attacks
   (Kilpatrick 2001)

The most prevalent anticipatory reaction to various types of societal trauma is terror. Whether we fear Mother Nature or a human-made attack, we are a society on edge. Terrorism instills fear and helplessness in people and holds society or government "hostage" by raising the level of fear about potential destruction or harm (American Psychological Association 2002).

After such events occur, people must try to cope with the acute stress and trauma. These reactions are increased when the traumatic acts are random, unprovoked, or intentionally focused on innocent and defenseless citizens (American Psychological Association 2002). Although the initial responses to natural and human-made disasters may be similar (Burkle 1996), the effects of human malevolence are more prolonged than those related to natural causes (NSW Institute of Psychiatry and Center for Mental Health 2000). The extent of casualties, fear, inability to escape, mass destruction, loss, and dislocation are influencing factors in pathological outcomes for both natural and human-made disasters.

The fear society feels about human-made disasters has been referred to as "epidemic hysteria" or "mass sociogenic illness," which is characterized by widespread symptoms of illness involving excitation and loss of functioning (Weir 2005). For example, a noxious smell in a school turns into fear of chemical warfare or bioterrorism, and people begin to get sick even though it is a harmless odor. In 1990, during the Gulf War, after the first missile launch on Israel by Iraq, people were staggering and having breathing problems, despite the fact that no chemical attack had occurred (Bartholomew and Wessley 2002).

While stress reactions to a societal trauma may initially seem extreme, not all persons exposed develop chronic problems. Many people recover fully from even moderate stress reactions within six to sixteen months. How long people are affected depends on the nature of the event and the strengths of each individual. Resilience plays a large role in preventing chronic problems. In addition, a sense of altruism, helping and comforting others, and gratefulness for surviving the disaster can combat the onset of more dire psychological problems (NSW Institute of Psychiatry and Center for Mental Health 2000).

Each type of societal trauma carries its own unique impact that counselors need to consider. For instance, bioterrorism causes psychological trauma both because of uncertainty about the extent of exposure to toxic agents and because of uncertainty about how long those health effects would take to develop (National Crime Victims Research and Treatment Center). Unlike natural disasters or mass murders, no clear beginning and end are associated with the disaster exposure.

When many people are affected by the event, community members also have a greater chance of knowing or being related to a seriously injured or dead person. In small communities, the chances of knowing a victim are even greater. Any time a trauma occurs, a high percentage of assistance usually comes from the community. But in the case of mass disasters, less assistance may come from community members because they too are traumatized by the event. Disaster relief teams are available at a moment's notice from all over the United States and the world, so people outside of a traumatized area can come to work in the affected area. However, these events also take a toll on the existing professionals, officials, and service workers who are exposed to the same level of trauma.

Any mass disaster is widely reported in the media through in-depth stories and film footage of images that can be traumatizing. As a result of their exposure to the disaster through the media, "vicarious trauma" can occur in individuals who were not even a part of the mass disaster. For example, many people who were not in Manhattan on 9/11 developed a form of secondary PTSD from overexposure to traumatic images. The diagnosis criteria for PTSD includes those who witness traumatic events, so millions were at risk of developing PTSD or reactivating previous PTSD based on their exposure to the 9/11 imagery.

And indeed, this happened. In September 2001, I was working at a medical hospital in North Carolina and noticed the mass dissociation happening with the staff. Most people said they went home and watched hours of news coverage every night, even though little was presented that was new. They had seen the plane crash into the towers a hundred times. Stunned and glassy-eyed, the hospital struggled to provide a "fresh team" of workers. In an attempt to manage this secondary PTSD, I sent an e-mail to the employees warning about overexposure. My phone began to ring off the hook with employees telling me that was exactly what happened to them—they were feeling all the signs of PTSD without the direct experience.

How much more frequently is this happening today now that there are so many mass disasters being televised, providing new stressors for society to feed on? There are hours of film footage of the tsunami, or weeks of news reports on wildfires ravaging people and homes, or up-close-and-personal pictures of dead bodies, body bags, or people literally suffocated in a mud slide. Hurricane Katrina produced weeks of footage of people trapped on roofs and unmet food and water needs.

Disasters—or at least the media coverage of them—seem to be occurring closer together. Just as we are trying to process one terrorist attack, we are faced with the photos of a natural disaster. The United States is slowly becoming a nation of vicariously traumatized citizens—voluntarily traumatized in many cases because we don't turn off the media to spare our psyches. This is creating stress reactions that, as a counselor, you are likely to see following disasters, even ones that did not happen locally or even in this country.

Just how many survivors will go on to develop PTSD following societal trauma? According to National Center for PTSD, symptoms of PTSD are much more likely to occur with human-made than natural disasters (see the table below).

*Percentage of PTSD Symptoms from Different Types of Societal Traumas*

| Natural disasters | 4–5% |
|---|---|
| Bombing | 34% |
| Plane crash into hotel | 29% |
| Mass shooting | 28% |

(National Center for PTSD website)

Factors associated with aggravating a stress reaction and increasing a survivor's risk of developing negative outcomes include the following:

○ Lack of emotional and social support

○ Presence of other stressors (e.g., fatigue, cold, hunger, fear, uncertainty, loss, dislocation, and other psychologically stressful experiences)

○ Difficulties at the scene

○ Lack of information about the nature of and reasons for the event

○ Lack of or interference with self-management during the crisis

○ Treatment given in an authoritarian or impersonal manner

○ Lack of follow-up support in the weeks after the exposure

(NSW Institute of Psychiatry and Center for Mental Health 2000)

## Crisis Intervention

Disaster teams will probably deal with the most immediate needs of disaster victims. If you are on a disaster or crisis response team, you have already been trained in crisis intervention. If you are not a trained in disaster response, your intervention with victims of societal trauma is likely to occur after the immediate fact. This could range from days to months or years after the victims' exposure. Victims could also come for counseling as a result of vicarious exposure. Therefore, your approach must include more than just psychological debriefing.

In the past, debriefing was offered to disaster victims immediately following the event. Debriefing was developed to assist first responders, such as fire and police, not survivors of disasters or their relatives. Debriefing was never intended as a substitute for therapy (National Center for PTSD website). How this approach got carried over to societal traumas is unsure. Nevertheless, this one-time debriefing session has been widely used in disaster counseling and consists of the victim describing the traumatic event (e.g., thoughts, feelings, and facts). Counselors then reassure victims their responses are normal, prepare them for future emotional reactions, and tell them how to deal with those reactions. The victims are referred for more help.

However, debate is ongoing with respect to whether this is the correct approach to use with disaster victims. The results of studies about psychological debriefing are mixed and do not support the efficacy of a one-session intervention shortly after the trauma in decreasing psychological disturbances (Bisson, Jenkins, and Bannister 1997). Societal trauma often produces severe effects, and studies have reported that victims often have long-term PTSD and other mental-health problems as a result. These findings suggest that many victims receive either insufficient or ineffective mental-health treatment (National Crime Victims Research and Treatment Center).

Insufficient treatment could result from a session of psychological debriefing in which the victim feels the debriefing session is all the treatment needed. In many mass traumatic events, individuals who were not injured or killed feel they are better off than others and therefore should not be so upset or affected. They may not seek help because others who were more directly affected need the help more. This can complicate their PTSD.

The belief that seeking mental-health assistance makes someone "weak" can also prevent victims from accepting help that is offered at the time of the incident or seeking help on their own. Societal traumas that occur on a large scale may drive individuals to seek informal support from family and friends as they hash and rehash the events. However, this probably will not be sufficient to prevent long-term psychological distress (Sprang 2000).

Agencies that provide disaster response are not set up for extensive follow-up with victims whom they see briefly or for whom they provide one-session psychological debriefing. Many of these victims may fall between the cracks and fail to receive the ongoing mental-health care they need. Whether they were directly harmed by the event or witnessed it, these individuals may approach counseling days, months, or years after the crisis. A new stressor or victimization could reactivate any untreated PTSD resulting from a previous societal trauma. You should determine if the victim did receive psychological debriefing and if the person had additional trauma-specific individual or group counseling following the debriefing. Assessment will clarify whether the PTSD was treated and will gauge its severity.

Complicated mourning can be an issue in disasters and presents as intense separation distress or anxiety. The victim may become highly aroused while scanning the environment for a lost friend or relative, particularly if that person has not been found to be dead or the body has not been identified. These searching behaviors can lead to anger and irrational behavior (National Center for PTSD website). You should discuss with the victim if any of these types of behaviors occurred following the disaster. This can alert you to the possibility of complicated bereavement.

As in the case of homicide, the victim may have witnessed death, dismemberment, or other traumatic images, either personally or vicariously. Approaches similar to those used with homicide survivors can also be used with societal trauma (see Chapter 12). Reviewing Chapter 2, about PTSD and treatment approaches, will be helpful. As is the case of PTSD, fear, safety issues, hyperarousal, and flashbacks may require symptom management. If loved ones were killed in the event, grieving and survivor guilt are likely to be issues, as well. The victim's worldview will need to be considered in the overall treatment approach.

You should also inquire into the positive elements that helped the survivor cope during the disaster. Protective factors that mitigated possible negative effects can be incorporated into counseling. These factors include the following:

- ○ Social support the survivor received
- ○ Survivors with high levels of income and education have less overall psychological distress than do survivors with low levels of income and education
- ○ Successful mastery of past disasters and traumatic events
- ○ Limitation or reduction in exposure to any previously aggravating factors
- ○ Care, concern, and understanding on the part of disaster services personnel
- ○ Provision of regular and appropriate information concerning the emergency and the reasons for the actions taken
  (National Center for PTSD website)

In the case of vicarious trauma, psychoeducation is important. Victims need to be trained about overexposure, secondary PTSD, hyperarousal, and the importance of self-care.

### Client Concerns

- ○ In vicarious trauma, may have no idea why symptoms are occurring
- ○ Is the world safe? Will this event occur again?
- ○ Loss of family and friends or other forms of support
- ○ Grieving the loss of a loved one, sense of safety, or other losses
- ○ Survivor guilt
- ○ Flashbacks and hyperarousal
- ○ Sleep disorders
- ○ Ability to function
- ○ Need to assign blame
- ○ If human related, the need for justice
- ○ Overall symptom management

○ How to rebuild, what agencies need contacting, who will help them

○ Basic needs: shelter, food, safety, water

### Secondary Victimizations

○ Loss of income due to emotional impairment

○ Counseling costs

○ Overexposure by media

○ No follow-up by disaster response teams

○ Lack of financial compensation from state or federal agencies

### Social/Public Services Needed

○ Crisis-intervention counselor

○ Services associated with trauma (Red Cross, other compensational agencies via state or federal government, or private insurance companies)

○ Housing, food, water, emergency services

○ Clergy (if trained)

○ Unemployment compensation (if unable to work)

○ Vocational rehabilitation counseling (if applicable)

## Short-Term Counseling

Victims may present with a varying degrees of symptomatology. Paying particular attention to avoidance and numbing symptoms may allow you to identify those at risk for PTSD and other comorbid disorders (Difede et al. 1997). Depending on the particular societal trauma the victim has experienced, grieving may be one of their symptoms. This includes the possibility of grief that was disrupted and has become complicated mourning.

Victims who had a possible chemical exposure may be focused on health issues and a fear of future health problems. This can manifest in both stress reactions and somatic disorders. Victims of natural disasters face systems that are slow in responding or re-providing services (e.g., insurance companies, people to clean up, builders to re-build homes, power companies to reestablish power). These victims may remain homeless for extended periods of time and may take a year or longer to re-establish their homesteads. Permanent changes to their community are inevitable if landmarks have been damaged or the appearance of the town altered.

In the case of mass disasters, the community may have been depleted of resources and it may take months or years to resume normal life patterns. Service providers are just as likely as other members of the community to have PTSD. These victims may have continual exposure to the initial disaster because they live and work in the region. Because PTSD is affected by length of exposure, intensity, and other stressful factors, these victims are of particular concern.

Short-term counseling can be affected by the victim's readiness. The inability to previously approach counseling or to stay in counseling may have been related to trying to cope with practical problems caused by the experience (e.g., finding housing, pursuing insurance claims, undergoing physical tests and treatment). Or, the victim may not have felt ready to face the emotional damage caused by the trauma. Some victims may think their short-term emotional reactions will eventually pass, only to discover this did not happen (National Center for PTSD website). Such victims may approach counseling tentatively because they did not expect to need it and may even resent needing it.

Psychoeducational approaches are helpful. Although the value of psychological debriefing in one-session approaches has been debated, short-term counseling sessions that involve teaching the victim about normal reactions to trauma; improving and strengthening coping; self-care; symptom management techniques; stress management; and understanding vulnerability to depression, anxiety, and substance use are considered acceptable. Referrals to other community resources for aid, and even to group therapy that is focused upon victims of this disaster, can be helpful.

You need to be alert for exacerbation of trauma-related problems during anniversaries of the events (National Center for PTSD website). For hurricane victims, this could be each year during the beginning of the hurricane season. Other milestones related to the event (e.g., last removal of debris, or a terrorist who is finally captured) can be stressful. Although these may even be viewed as positive milestones to the general public, they can be stressful for the victims.

### Client Concerns

○ Fear and safety issues

○ Loss of family and friends or other forms of support

○ Grieving the loss of a loved one, sense of safety, material losses

○ Survivor guilt

○ Flashbacks and hyperarousal

○ Sleep disorders

○ Ability to function

○ Overall symptom management

○ How to rebuild, what agencies need contacting, who can and will help

○ Basic needs: shelter, food, safety, water

○ Spiritual conflicts

### Secondary Victimizations

○ Loss of income due to emotional impairment

○ Counseling costs

○ Overexposure by media

○ No follow-up by disaster response teams

○ Lack of financial compensation by state or federal agencies

○ Loss of home, community, health

### Social/Public Services Needed

○ Crisis-intervention counselor

○ Services associated with trauma (Red Cross, other compensational agencies via state or federal government, or private insurance companies)

○ Housing, food, water, emergency services

○ Clergy (if trained)

○ Unemployment compensation (if unable to work)

○ Vocational rehabilitation counseling (if applicable)

## Long-Term Counseling

Those who have long-term effects from a societal trauma warrant long-term follow up and possibly treatment. However, many large-scale disaster relief efforts are not set up for comprehensive follow up. Relief agencies come and provide emergency services for the first few days, weeks, or months, but outside mental-health workers and other service providers eventually go home. Long-term care, although recognized as necessary, has been a challenge for many disaster programs.

Long-term counseling is especially relevant for disaster victims because PTSD sometimes has a delayed onset. Thus, coordination between emergency service providers and those who follow up later can be difficult. Some victims are displaced and have no forwarding address or phone, and thus, they are basically homeless. To locate them months later and assess PTSD can be difficult.

Factors for consideration in long-term counseling are associated with the following risk factors.

○ Level of trauma exposure (e.g., seeing death, dying, or mutilation)

○ Physical injuries from the disaster

○ Level of loss (e.g., home, other family members, possessions)
  (National Center for PTSD website)

Especially important are acute levels of traumatic stress symptoms, which predict later chronicity. For instance, three-fourths of mass disaster victims who show signs of acute stress disorder will develop chronic PTSD by the six-month mark (Bryant and Harvey 2000). Residual PTSD symptoms, comorbidity, and complicated mourning should also guide the focus of counseling.

Support groups that are disaster-specific can continue to increase socialization, reduce isolation, teach healthy coping, reduce stress, and share learned community resources for aid. (See Chapter 2 for more treatment information.)

### Client Concerns

○ Fear and safety issues

○ Loss of family and friends or other forms of support

- Grieving the loss of a loved one, sense of safety, material losses
- Survivor guilt
- Flashbacks and hyperarousal
- Sleep disorders
- Ability to function
- Overall symptom management
- How to rebuild, what agencies need contacting, who can and will help
- Basic needs: shelter, food, safety, water
- Spiritual conflicts

### Secondary Victimizations
- Loss of income due to emotional impairment
- Counseling costs
- Overexposure by media
- No follow-up by disaster response teams
- Societal trauma not financially compensated by state or federal agencies
- Loss of home, community, health

### Social/Public Services Needed
- Crisis-intervention counselor
- Services associated with trauma (Red Cross, other compensational agencies via state or federal government, or private insurance companies)
- Housing, food, water, emergency services
- Clergy (if trained)
- Unemployment compensation (if unable to work)
- Vocational rehabilitation counseling (if applicable)

## RECOMMENDED READING

Johnson, Kendall. *After the Storm: Healing after Trauma, Tragedy and Terror.* Alameda, CA: Hunter House Publishers, 2006.

Kalayjian, Anie S., and Joseph Jaeger. *Disaster and Mass Trauma: Global Perspectives on Post-Disaster Mental Health Management.* Long Branch, NJ: Vista Publications, 1995.

Van der Kolk, B. A., A. C. McFarlane, and L. Weisaeth. *Traumatic Stress: The Effects of Overwhelming Experience on Mind, Body, and Society.* New York: Guilford Press, 1996.

Wilson, J. P., and B. Raphael. *International Handbook of Traumatic Stress Syndromes.* New York: Plenum, 1993.

## RESOURCES

Federal Emergency Management Agency
(800) 745-0243   ○   www.fema.gov   ○   www.disasterhelp.gov

International Society for Traumatic Stress Studies
(847) 480-9028   ○   www.istss.org

National Center for Victims of Crime
(202) 467-8700   ○   www.ncvc.org

National Center for Post-Traumatic Stress Disorder
(802) 296-6300   ○   www.ncptsd.va.gov

National Crime Victims Research and Treatment Center
(843) 792-2945   ○   www.muse.edu/cvc/

National Institute of Mental Health
(866) 615-6464   ○   www.nimh.nih.gov

PTSD Alliance
(877) 507-PTSD (507-7873)   ○   www.ptsdalliance.org

Terrorism Research Center
(877) 635-0816   ○   www.terrorism.com

Research Education in Disaster Mental Health
(802) 296-5132   ○   www.redmh.org

## Overview of Societal Trauma

*Crisis Intervention:* Safety and fear issues, fear of event occurring again, grieving losses of loved ones, home, possessions, survivor guilt, flashbacks, sleep problems, lowered functioning level, what agencies to contact for assistance, basic needs of food, water and shelter

*Short-Term Counseling:* Fear and safety issues; survivor guilt; overall symptom management; hyperarousal; lowered functioning level; basic needs of food, water, and shelter; sleep problems; spiritual conflicts; onset of complicated grieving

*Long-Term Counseling:* Safety as a worldview construct; complicated grieving; long-term PTSD (if applicable); material losses of home, community, and friends

*Secondary Victimizations:* Loss of income due to emotional impairment, counseling costs, overexposure by media, loss of family and friends, lack of follow-up by disaster teams, trauma may not be financially compensated for by state or federal government agencies

*Social/Legal Services:* Trauma counselor; services associated with the trauma (e.g., Red Cross, other compensational agencies through the state or federal government, and private insurance companies); housing, food, water, and emergency services; clergy; unemployment compensation (if unable to work); vocational rehabilitation counseling (if applicable)

# CHAPTER 13

# Conclusion: In the Face of Trauma

AS HUMAN BEINGS FIRST and victim service providers second, counselors must come to terms with the issue of violence in our daily world. As humans, violence affects us on a deeply personal basis. Living in a world that seems to be all about crime, violence, and destruction rattles our sense of individual safety. We worry about what violence will be like in the future, and how it will affect the lives of our children. Day in and day out, we see victims in our offices whose lives and psyches were destroyed by the deliberate act of others or by acts of nature. This, too, reminds us that violence is part of our community, city, and world.

Something inside of us cries out for resolution, restitution, or removal of this pain from our world. We face our own fears in the faces of our clients. We search our systems in an attempt to find solace there. The introduction of more victim services, longer jail time, more law enforcement, tougher rehabilitation demands, and new programs for victims leads us to believe serenity is possible, and the world may be stabilizing. We scan the legislation to see if the scales of justice show any signs of balancing. We listen for sensitive systems that are will "fight the good fight" of fairness for victims. We search for hope wherever we can. As victim-service providers, we bring that hope to the victim. This is one of the greatest gifts we can give clients with whom we work. It is our hope for their future and our optimism for their recovery that help victims continue on in the face of dire adversity. We are hope providers.

In addition to being hope providers, we can also have great influence in the field of victimology. I remain optimistic about the future of victim services. Through us, as hope providers, great potential exists to positively influence victim services. As we reach out to victims and continue to grow in our own education we can

○ offer individual counseling to more adult and child victims

○ develop group therapy programs for specific types of victimizations

○ increase our capacity for effective case management and social work

○ influence legislation on behalf of victims' rights

○ let our voices impart the victim's view within the criminal-justice system

○ support law-enforcement education about victim needs by teaching community leaders and service providers

○ train peer counselors to run support groups

○ teach clergy how to work effectively with crime victims

○ assist hospitals in developing inpatient and outpatient programs for victims of violence

○ document and support research efforts in the field of trauma disorders and victimology

Depending upon our respective interests and fields of study, we can all do something to continue to grow in our roles as hope providers. What lies ahead of us in victim services is only limited by our investment in the field. Thank you for the work you are doing and for the work that lies ahead of you in your service role with victims. Your work is vitally important to the mental health of this nation and for each victim's life that you touch. It is hope providers who will create the health and happiness of tomorrow.

# References

## Introduction

National Center for Victims of Crime website, http://www.ncvc.org.

U.S. Department of Justice. Office of Justice Program, Bureau of Justice Statistics, 2001 (booklet).

## Chapter 2: The Psychodynamics of Trauma

Bisson, J., A. McFarlane, and S. Rose. 2000. Psychological debriefing. In *Effective treatment for PTSD: Practice guidelines from the International Society for Traumatic Stress Studies,* ed. E. B. Foa, T. M. Keane, and M. J. Friedman, 39–59. New York: The Guilford Press.

Brady, K. T., T. K. Killeen, T. Brewerton, and S. Lucerini. 2000. Comorbidity of psychiatric disorders and posttraumatic stress disorder. *Journal of Clinical Psychiatry* 2000, 61(7) : 22–32.

Briere, J. N. 1992. *Child abuse trauma: Theory and treatment of the last effects.* Newbury Park; CA: Sage Publications.

Burgess, A. W., C. R. Harman, and S. J. Kelley. 1990. *Assessing child abuse: The TRIADS checklist.* An instructional handout sheet from a conference by Forensics Mental Health, Tampa, FL.

Cardena, E., J. Maldonado, O. Van der Hart, and D. Spiegel. 2000. Hypnosis. In *Effective treatment for PTSD: Practice guidelines from the International Society for Traumatic Stress Studies,* ed. E. B. Foa, T. M. Keane, and M. J. Friedman, 39–59. New York: Guilford Press.

Chemtob, C., D. Tolin, P. Van der Kolk, and R. Pitman. 2000. Eye movement and desensitization and reprocessing. In *Effective treatment for PTSD: Practice guidelines from the International Society for Traumatic Stress Studies,* ed. E. B. Foa, T. M. Keane, and M. J. Friedman, 39–59. New York: Guilford Press.

Cole, P. M., and F. W. Putnam. 1992. Effects of incest on self and social functioning: A developmental psychopathological perspective. *Journal of Consulting & Clinical Psychology* 60:174–184.

Courtois, C., and S. Bloom. 2000. Inpatient treatment. In *Effective treatment for PTSD: Practice guidelines from the International Society for Traumatic Stress Studies,* ed. E. B. Foa, T. M. Keane, and M. J. Friedman, 39–59. New York: Guilford Press.

Foa, E. B., T. M. Keane, and M. J. Friedman. 2000. Effective treatment for PTSD: Practice guidelines from the International Society for Traumatic Stress Studies. New York: Guilford Press.

Friedman, M., J. Davidson, T. Mellman, and S. Southwick. 2000. Pharmacotherapy. In *Effective treatment for PTSD: Practice guidelines from the International Society for Traumatic Stress Studies,* ed. E. B. Foa, T. M. Keane, and M. J. Friedman, 39–59. New York: Guilford Press.

Grief Research website, http://www.grief.org.au.

Hulme, P. A. 2000. Symptomatology and health care utilization of women primary care patients who experienced childhood sexual abuse. *Child Abuse & Neglect* 24:1471–1484.

Jumper, S. A. 1995. A meta-analysis of the relationship of childhood sexual abuse to adult psycho adjustment. *Child Abuse & Neglect* 19(6): 715–728.

Kessler, R. C., A. Sonnega, E. J. Bromet, M. Hughes, and C. B. Nelson. 1995. Post traumatic stress disorder in the National Comorbidity Survey. *Archives of General Psychiatry* 52(12): 1048–1060.

Kudler, H., A. Blank, and J. Krupnick. 2000. Psychodynamic theory. In *Effective treatment for PTSD: Practice guidelines from the International Society for Traumatic Stress Studies,* ed. E. B. Foa, T. M. Keane, and M. J. Friedman, 39–59. New York: Guilford Press.

McCann, I. L., and L. A. Pearlman. 1990. *Psychological trauma and the adult survivor —Theory, therapy and transformation.* New York: Brunner/Mazel.

McCauley, J., D. G. Kern, K. Kolodner, L. Dill, A. F. Schroeden, H. K. DeChant, J. Ryden, L. R. Derogatis, and E. B. Bass. 1997. Clinical characteristics of women with a history of childhood abuse. *Journal of the American Medical Association* 277: 1362–1368.

McConnell, J. V. 1986. Understanding human behavior. New York: Holt, Rinehart & Winston.

Niles, D. P. 1990. Post traumatic stress disorder vs. post traumatic stress reaction. American Mental Health Counselors Association, *The Advocate* 13:9.

Putnam, F. W. 1985. Dissociation as a response to extreme trauma. In *Childhood antecedents of multiple personality,* ed. R. P. Kluft, 106. Washington, D.C.: American Psychiatric Association.

Putnam, F. W., and P. K. Trickett. 1993. Child sexual abuse: A model of chronic trauma. *Psychiatry* 56:82–95.

Rando, T. A. 1993. *Treatment of complicated mourning.* Champaign, IL: Research Press.

Raphael, B. 1997. The interaction of trauma and grief. In *Psychological Trauma: A Developmental Approach,* ed. D. Black, M. Newman, J. Harris-Hendricks, and G. Mezey, 31–43. London: Baskell.

Raphael, B., and C. Minkov. 1999. Abnormal grief. *Psychiatry* 12:99–102.

Rothbaum, B., E. Meadows, P. Resnick, and D. Foy. 2000. Cognitive-behavioral treatment. In *Effective treatment for PTSD: Practice guidelines from the International Society for Traumatic Stress Studies,* ed. E. B. Foa, T. M. Keane, and M. J. Friedman, 39–59. New York: The Guilford Press.

Schiraldi, G. R. 2000. *The post traumatic stress disorder sourcebook: A guide to healing, recovering and growth.* Los Angeles: CA: Lowell House

Summit, R. C. 1983. The childhood sexual abuse accommodation syndrome. *Child Abuse & Neglect* 7:177–193.

Walker, L. 1991. Post traumatic stress disorder in women: Diagnosis and treatment of battered women syndrome. *Psychotherapy* 25(1): 21–29.

Worden, W. J. 1991. *Grief counseling and grief therapy.* New York: Springer.

Yale Department of Psychiatry website, http://www.info.med.yale.edu/psych/.

## Chapter 3: The Assessment

Blake, Dudley. 1993. Psychological assessment and PTSD: Not just for researchers. *NCP Clinical Quarterly* 3(1).

Briere, J. 1997. *Psychological assessment of adult posttraumatic states.* Washington D.C.: American Psychological Association, 1997.

Burgess, A.W., C. R. Harman, and S. J. Kelley. 1990. Assessing child abuse: The TRI-ADS checklist. An instructional handout sheet from a conference by Forensics Mental Health, Tampa, FL.

McCann, I. L., and L. A. Pearlman. 1990. *Psychological trauma and the adult survivor —Theory, therapy and transformation.* New York: Brunner/Mazel.

## Chapter 4: Stalking and Cyberstalking

### STALKING

Collins, M. J., and M. B. Wilkas. 2001. Stalking trauma syndrome and the traumatized victim. In *Stalking crimes and victim protection: Prevention, intervention, threat assessment and case management,* ed. J. A. Davis, 317–334. Boca Raton, FL: CRC Press.

Kamphuis, J. H., P. M. G. Emmelkamp. 2001. Traumatic distress among support seeking female victims of stalking. *American Journal of Psychiatry* 158(5): 795–798.

Littel, P. 1999. *Addressing the needs of stalking victims.* Focus Group Report. Washington, D.C., Office for Victims of Crime, U.S. Department of Justice.

Meadows, Robert J. 2001. *Understanding violence & victimization,* 2nd Edition. Upper Saddle River, NJ: Prentice Hall Publishers.

National Center for Victims of Crime, Stalking Resource Center website, http://www.ncvc.org.

Spence-Diehl, Emily. 2004. Intensive case management for victims of stalking: A pilot test evaluation. *Brief Treatment and Crisis Intervention* 4(4): 323–341.

Tjaden, P., and N. Thoennes. 1998. *Stalking in America: Findings from the National Violence Against Women Survey.* Washington, DC: U.S. Department of Justice, National Institute of Justice, NIJ Pub 1998.

### CYBERSTALKING

George Mason University Sexual Assault Services website content, 1999, http://www.gmu.edu/facstaff/sexual/.

National Center for Victims of Crime, Stalking Resource Center website, http://www.ncvc.org.

United States Department of Justice. *Cyberstalking: A new challenge for law enforcement and industry.* Office of the Attorney General: Washington, D.C., 1999.

## Chapter 5: Property Crime and Robbery

Cook, Philip. 1991. The technology of personal violence. In *Crime and justice: A review of research* (Volume 14), ed. Michael Tonry. Chicago, IL: University of Chicago Press.

Federal Bureau of Investigation. 1996. *Crime in the United States, 1995.* Washington, D.C.: U.S. Department of Justice.

Greenberg, M. S., and S. R. Beach. 2004. Property crime victims' decision to notify the police: Social, cognitive, and affective determinants. *Law and Human Behavior* 28(2): 177–186.

Miller, T., M. Cohen, and B. Wiersema. 1996. *Victim costs and consequences: A new look.* National Institute of Justice Research Report. Washington, D.C.: National Institute of Justice, U.S. Department of Justice.

National Center for Victims of Crime website, http://www.ncvc.org.

Reiss, A, and J. Roth, eds. 1993. *Understanding and preventing violence.* Washington, DC: National Academy Press.

Roth, J. 1994. *Firearms and violence.* National Institute of Justice Research. Washington, D.C.: National Institute of Justice, U.S. Department of Justice.

U.S. Department of Justice. Office of Justice Programs, Bureau of Justice Statistics 2001.

Waller, I. 1985. Crime victims: Needs, services and reforms. Paper presented at the 4th International Symposium on Victimology, Department of Criminology, Ottawa.

## Chapter 6: Hate Crimes
## (Various Victim Types and Categories)

### INTRODUCTION

Atkinson, D. R., G. Morten, and D. W. Sue. 1998. *Counseling American minorities.* Boston, MA: McGraw-Hill.

Bell, Jeannine. 2002. *Policing hatred: Law enforcement, civil rights and hate crime.* New York: New York University Press.

Blazak, Randy. 2001. White boys to terrorist men: Target recruitment of Nazi skinheads. *American Behavioral Scientist* 44:982–1000.

Federal Bureau of Investigation. 1999. *Hate crimes date reporting guidelines.* Washington, D.C.: U.S. Department of Justice.

Levin, B. 1992–1993. Bias crimes: A theoretical and practical overview. *Stanford Law & Policy Review 1992–1993* 4:165–169.

Levin, B., and J. McDevitt. 1993. *Hate crimes: The rising tide of bigotry and bloodshed.* New York: Plenum Press.

McMahon, B. T., S. L. West, A. N. Lewis, A. J. Armstrong, and J. P. Conway. 2004. Hate crimes and disability in America *Rehabilitation Counseling Bulletin* 47(2): 66.

National Center for Victims of Crime website, http://www.ncvc.org.

Perry, Barbara. 2000. Button down terror: The metamorphosis of the hate movement. *Sociological Focus*, 33:113–131.

Southern Poverty Law Center. 2001. Active hate groups in the U.S. in 2000. *Intelligence Report*, http://www.splcenter.org/intel/intelreport/article.jsp.

Walker, I., and H. J. Smith. 2002. *Relative deprivation: Specification, development and integration.* Cambridge, U.K.: Cambridge University Press.

ETHNIC/RACIAL VIOLENCE

American-Arab Anti-Discrimination Committee 1996. 1995 report on anti-Arab racism: Hate crimes, discrimination and defamation of Arab-Americans. Washington, D.C.

Atkinson, D. R., G. Morten, and D. W. Sue. 1998. *Counseling American minorities.* Boston, MA: McGraw-Hill.

Berk, R. A. 1990. Thinking about hate-motivated crimes. *Journal of Interpersonal Violence* 5(3): 334–349.

Bishop, E., and J. Slowikowski. 1995. *Hate crime: Fact sheet.* Washington, D.C., National Institute of Justice.

Blee, Kathleen. 2002. *Inside organized racism: Women in the hate movement.* Berkeley, CA: University of California Press.

Buchanan, S. H. 1979. Haitian women in New York City. *Migration Today* 7:19–25, 39.

Denkers, A. 1999. Factors affecting support after criminal victimization. *Journal of Social Psychology* 139:191–201.

Ehrlich, H. J. 1990. The ecology of anti-gay violence. *The Journal of Interpersonal Violence,* 5(3): 359–365.

Federal Bureau of Investigation 1996. *U.S. Department of Justice, Criminal Justice Information Services Division: Hate Crimes Statistics, 1996.* Uniform Crime Reports: Washington, D.C.

Frazier, P. A. 1990. Victim attributes and post rape trauma. *Journal of Personality and Social Psychology,* 59:298–304.

Levin, B. 1993. Bias crimes: A theoretical and practical overview. *Stanford Law & Policy Review* 4 (1993): 165.

Hughes, H. S. 2004. Lessons of Rwanda. *Photo District News* (Eastern Ed.) 24(6): 42.

Laguerre, M. S. 1984. *American odyssey: Haitians in New York City.* Ithaca, NY: Cornell University Press.

McDevitt, J. 1989. *The study of the character of civil rights crimes in Massachusetts.* Paper presented at the American Society of Criminology, Washington, D.C.

National Center for Victims of Crime website, http://www.ncvc.org.

Nguyen, L. 1992. Hatred learned from parents and TV. *The Sun.* Baltimore, MD, December 15, 1992, page 2B.

Seligman, L. 1977. Haitians: A neglected minority. *Personnel and Guidance Journal* 55(7): 409–411.

Sue, S. 1998. In search of cultural competence in psychotherapy and counseling. *American Psychologist* 53:440–448.

Sue, S. 1999. Science, ethnicity, and bias: Where did we go wrong? *American Psychologist* 54:1070.

Third Annual Report of the National Asian Pacific American Legal Consortium. Audit of Violence Against Asian Pacific Americans (1995). Washington, D.C.

## GENDER/HATE VIOLENCE

Adam, B. D. 1987. *The rise of a gay and lesbian movement.* Boston, MA: Twayne.

Anderson, M. G. 1993. People are getting hurt. February 23, 1993, *Commonwealth.*

Benshoff, J. J., and T. P. Janikowski. 2000. *The rehabilitation model of substance abuse counseling.* Belmont, CA: Brooks/Cole.

Berk, R. A. 1990. Thinking about hate-motivated crimes. *Journal of Interpersonal Violence* 5(3): 334–349.

Cheng, Z. 2002. Issues to consider when counseling gay people with alcohol dependence. *Journal of Applied Rehabilitation Counseling* 33(3): 10–17.

Federal Bureau of Investigation. 2000. *Crime in the United States, 1999.* Washington, D.C.: U.S. Department of Justice.

Franklin, K. 2000. Anti-gay behaviors by young adults: Prevalence, patterns, and motivations in a non-criminal population. *Journal of Interpersonal Violence* 15:339–362.

Garnets, L., G. Herek, and B. Levy. 1990. Violence and victimization of lesbians and gay men: Mental health consequences. *Journal of Interpersonal Violence* 5(3): 366–383.

Garnets, L., G. M. Herek, and B. Levy. 1992. *Violence and victimization of lesbians and gay men: Mental health consequences.* Newbury Park, CA: Sage.

Herek, G. 1990. The context of anti-gay violence: Notes on cultural and psychological heterosexism. *Journal of Interpersonal Violence* 5(3): 316–333.

Herek, G. M., J. R. Gillis, and J. C. Cogan. 1999. Psychological sequelae of hate crime victimization among lesbians, gays, and bi-sexuals. *Journal of Consulting & Clinical Psychology* 67:944–951.

Herek, G. M., J. R. Gillis, J. C. Cogan, and E. K. Glunt. 1997. Hate crime victimization among lesbian, gay and bi-sexual adults: Prevalence, psychological correlates and methodological issues. *Journal of Interpersonal Violence* 12:195–215.

Levin, J., and J. McDevitt. 1993. *Hate crimes: The rising tide of bigotry and bloodshed.* New York: Plenum.

Plant, R. 1986. *The pink triangle.* New York: Holt.

## Chapter 7: Domestic Violence

Body Shop. 1998. *The many faces of domestic violence and it's impact on the workplace.* New York: Savvy Management.

Domestic Abuse Prevention Project. "The Power and Control Wheel." 202 East Superior St., Duluth MN 55802, (218) 722-2781, http://www.duluth-model.org.

Gerard, Pat. 1991. *Counseling victims of violence,* First Ed. Alexandria, VA: American Counseling Association.

Greenfield, L. A., M. R. Rand, D. Craven, P. A. Klaus, C. A. Perkins, C. Ringel, G. War-chol, C. Maston, and J. A. Fox. 1998. *Violence by intimates: Analysis of data on crimes by current or former spouses, boyfriends, and girlfriends.* Washington, D.C.: Bureau of Justice Statistics, U.S. Department of Justice.

Martin, G. L. 1987. Counseling for family violence and abuse. In *Resources for Christian counseling,* ed. G. Collins, 54–56, 136–157. Waco, TX: Word.

Martin, S., K. Clark, S. Lynch, L. Kupper, and D. Cilenti. 1999. Violence in the lives of pregnant teenage women: Associations with multiple substance use. *American Journal of Drug & Alcohol Abuse* 25:425–550.

Meadows, Robt. J. 2001. *Understanding violence and victimization,* 2nd Ed. Upper Saddle River: NJ: Prentice Hall Publishers.

Molidor, C., R. Tolman, and J. Kober. 2000. Gender and contextual factors in adolescent dating violence. *Prevention Researcher* 7(1): 1–4.

National Center for Victims of Crime website, http://www.ncvc.org.

NSW Domestic Violence Committee. 1991. *Domestic violence information manual.* New South Wales, Australia.

Vaselle-Augenstein, R., and A. Ehrlich. 1993. "Male batterers: Evidence for psychopathology." In *Intimate violence: Interdisciplinary perspectives.* Washington, D.C.: Hemisphere Publishing Corporation.

Walker, L. E. 1979. *The battered woman.* New York: Harper & Row.

## Chapter 8: Elder Abuse

### ELDER ABUSE

Commonwealth of Pennsylvania. Attorney General's Family Violence Task Force: Violence against Elders. September 1988.

Compton, S. A., P. Flanagan, and W. Gregg. 1997. Elder abuse in people with dementia in Northern Ireland: Prevalence and predictors in cases referred to a psychiatry of old age service. *International Journal of Geriatric Psychiatry* 12:632–635.

Dyer, C. B., V. N. Pavlik, K. P. Murphy, and D. J. Hyman. 2002. The high prevalence of depression and dementia in elder abuse or neglect. *Journal of American Geriatric Society* 48: 205–258.

Griffin, Linner Ward, and Oliver J. Williams. 1992. Abuse among African American elderly. *Journal of Family Violence* 7(1): 19–35.

Hardin, E., and A. Khan-Hudson. 2005. Elder abuse—Society's dilemma. *Journal of the National Medical Association* 97(1): 91.

Henton, J., R. Cate, and B. Emery. 1984. The dependent elderly: Targets for abuse. In *Independent Again,* ed. W. H. Quinn and G. A. Hughson, 149–162. Rockville, MD: Aspen.

Lachs, M. S., C. Williams, S. O'Brien, L. Hurst, and R. Horowitz. 1997. Risk factors for reported elder abuse and neglect: A nine year observational cohort study. *Gerontologist* 37:469–474.

Martin, G. L. 1987. Counseling for family violence and abuse. In *Resources for Christian counseling,* ed. G. Collins, 54–56, 136–157. Waco, TX: Word.

Bonnie, Richard J., and Robert B. Wallace. 2002. *Elder abuse: Abuse, neglect & exploitation in an aging America.* Washington, D.C.: National Academy Press, www.newton.nap.edu.

National Center for Victims of Crime website, http://www.ncvc.org.

Pillemer, K. 2004. Elder abuse is caused by the deviance and dependence of abusive caregivers. In *Current controversies on family violence,* ed. D. Loseke, R. Gelles, and M. Cavanaugh. Newbury Park, CA: Sage.

## Chapter 9: Violence Against Children

Ackerman, Robert J., and Dee Graham. 1990. *Too old to cry: Abused teens in today's America.* Blue Ridge Summit, PA: HIS and TAB Books.

American Humane Association Children's Division. 1993. *Child Sexual Abuse: AHA Fact Sheet #4.* Englewood, CO: American Humane Association.

Briere, J. N. 1996. *Child abuse trauma: Theory & treatment of lasting effects.* Newbury Park, CA: Sage Publications.

Brown, Sandra L. 1991. *Counseling victims of violence,* First Ed. Alexandria, VA: American Counseling Association.

Cicchetti, D., and M. Lunch. 1995. Failures in the expectable environment and their impact on individual development: The case of child maltreatment. In *Developmental psychopathology, Vol 2: Risk, disorder and adaptation,* eds. D. Cichetti and D. J. Cohen, 32–71. New York: John Wiley & Sons.

Cole, P. M., and F. W. Putnam. 1992. Effect of incest on self and social functioning: A developmental psychopathological perspective. *Journal of Consulting & Clinical Psychology* 60:174–184.

DeBellis, Michael D. 1999. Developmental traumatology: Neurobiological development in maltreated children with PTSD. *Psychiatric Times* September 1999, Volume XVI, Issue 9.

Fairbank, J. A., W. E. Schlenger, J. M. Caddell, and M. G. Woods. 1993. Posttraumatic stress disorder. In *Comprehensive handbook of psychopathology,* 2nd Ed., eds. P. B. Sutker, and H. E. Adams, 145–165. New York: Plenum.

Finkelhor, David. 1994. Current information on the scope and nature of child sexual abuse. *The Future of Children* 4(2): 31, 46–48.

Foa, E. B., and B. O. Rothbaum. 1998. *Treating the trauma of rape: Cognitive-behavioral treatment for PTSD.* New York: Guilford.

Hammerschlag, Margaret 1996. *Sexually transmitted diseases and child sexual abuse.* Washington, D.C.: Office of Juvenile Justice and Delinquency Prevention, U.S. Department of Justice.

Hulme, P. A. 2000. Symptomatology and health care utilization of women primary care patients who experienced child sexual abuse. *Child Abuse & Neglect* 24:1471–1484.

Hulme, P. A. 2004. Theoretical perspectives on the health problems of adults who experienced childhood sexual abuse. *Issues in Mental Health Nursing* 25:339–361.

Jumper, S. A. 1995. A meta-analysis of the relationships of child sexual abuse to adult psycho adjustment. *Child Abuse & Neglect* 19(6): 715–728.

Keane, T. M., L. M. Fisher, K. E. Krinsley, and B. L. Niles. 1994. Post traumatic stress disorder: In *Handbook of prescriptive treatments for adults,* eds. M. Hersen, and R. T. Ammerman, 237–260. New York: Plenum.

Love, Patricia. 1990. *The emotional incest syndrome.* New York: Bantam Books.

Lyons, J. A. 1987. Post traumatic stress disorder in children and adolescents: A review of the literature. *Journal of Developmental and Behavioral Pediatrics* 8:349–356.

McCauley, J., D. E. Kern, K. Kolodner, L. Dill, A. F. Schroeder, H. K. DeChant, J. Ryden, L. R. Derogatis, and E. G. Bass. 1997. Clinical characteristics of women with a history of childhood abuse. *Journal of the American Medical Association* 277: 1362–1368.

McLeer, S. V., and K. J. Ruggiero. 2000. Short-term correlates of child sexual abuse: Prevalence of psychiatric symptoms. Manuscript submitted for publication.

McNally, R. J. 1991. Assessment of post traumatic stress disorder in children. *Psychological Assessment* 3:531–537.

National Center for Victims of Crime and Crime Victims Research and Treatment Center. 1992. *Rape in America: A report to the nation.* Arlington, VA: National Center for Victims of Crime.

National Center for Victims of Crime website, http://www.ncvc.org.

National Child Abuse and Neglect Data System (NCANDS). 2002. Administration for Children and Families website, http://www.acf.dhhs.gov.

Perrin, S., P. Smith, and W. Yule. 2000. Practitioner review: The assessment and treatment of PTSD in children and adolescents. *Journal of Child Psychology and Psychiatry, and Allied Disciplines* 41:277–289.

Putnam, F. W., and P. K. Trickett. 1993. Child sexual abuse: A model of chronic trauma. *Psychiatry* 56:82–95.

Ruggiero, K. J., T. L. Morris, and J. R. Scotti. 2001. Treatment for children with post traumatic stress disorder: Current status and future directions. *Clinical Psychology: Science and Practice* 8(2): 210.

Rust, J. O., and P. A. Troupe. 1991. Relationships of treatment of child sexual abuse with school achievement and self concept. *Journal of Early Adolescence* 11:420–429.

Scheeronga, M. S., C. H. Zeanah, M. J. Drell, and J. A. Larrieu. 1995. Two approaches to diagnosing PTSD in infancy and early childhood. *Journal of the American Academy of Child and Adolescent Psychiatry* 34:191–200.

Stern, A. E., D. L. Lynch, R. K. Oates, B. I. O'Toole, and G. Cooney. 1995. Self-esteem, depression, behavior and family functioning in sexually abused children. *Journal of Child Psychology and Psychiatry* 36:1077–1089.

Sternberg, K. J., M. E. Lamb, C. Greenbaum, D. Cichetti, S. Dawud, R. M. Cortes, O. Krispin, and F. Lofrey. 1993. Effects of domestic violence on children's behavior problems and depression. *Developmental Psychology* 29:44–52.

Trickett, P. K., and F. W. Putnam. 1993. Impact of child sexual abuse on females: Towards a development psychobiological integration. *Psychological Science* 4:81–87.

United States Department of Justice, Office of Justice Programs, Bureau of Justice Statistics 'Sex Offenders & Their Victims' Report. 1997.

Vogel, J. M., and E. M. Vernberg. 1993. Part 1: Children's psychological responses to disaster. *Journal of Clinical Child Psychology* 22:161–184.

Ward, J. 1999. *Children and guns.* Washington, D.C.: Children's Defense Fund.

Wheeler, E., and A. Baron. 1993. *Violence in our schools, hospitals, and public places: A prevention and management guide.* Ventura, CA: Pathfinder Publishing.

Widom, Cathy Spatz. 1992. *The cycle of violence.* Washington, D.C.: National Institute of Justice, U.S. Department of Justice.

Widom, Cathy Spatz. 1995. *Victims of childhood sexual abuse—Later criminal consequences.* Washington, D.C.: National Institute of Justice, U.S. Department of Justice.

Wikipedia website, http://www.wikipedia.com, accessed December 2005.

Whiteby, E. 1992. Nightmare in our classrooms. *Ladies Home Journal* CIX (1): 74–83.

Yule, W. 1998. Post traumatic stress disorder in children and its treatment. In *Children of trauma: Stressful life events and their effects on children and adolescents,* ed. T. W. Miller, 219–243. Madison, CT: International Universities Press.

## ADOLESCENT VIOLENCE—WHEN KIDS CAN BE VICTIMS OR OFFENDERS

Dekovic, Maja, Jan Janssen, and Nicole Van As. 2003. Family predictors of anti-social behavior in adolescence. *Family Process* 42(2): 223.

Frick, P. J., B. B. Lahey, R. Loeber, M. Stouthamer-Loeber, M. A. G. Christ, and K. Hanson. 1992. Familial risk factors to oppositional defiant disorder and conduct disorder: Parental psychopathology and maternal parenting. *Journal of Consulting and Clinical Psychology* 60:49–55.

Hamburg, B., D. S. Elliot, and K. R. Williams. 1998. *Violence in American schools: A new perspective on youth violence.* New York, NY: Cambridge University Press, 31–54.

Henggeler, Scott W., and Ashli J. Sheidow. 2003. Conduct disorder and delinquency. *Journal of Marital and Family Therapy,* 29(4): 505.

Howell, James C., and James P. J. Lynch. 2000. *Youth gangs in schools.* Washington, D.C.: Office of Juvenile Justice Delinquency Prevention, U.S. Department of Justice.

Kaufman, Phillip, X. Chen, S. Choy, S. A. Ruddy, A. K. Miller, J. K. Fleury, K. A. Chandler, M. R. Rand, P. Klaus, and M. G. Planty. 2000. *Indicators of school crime and safety, 2000.* Washington, D.C.: U.S. Department of Education and Justice.

Kazdin, A. E. 1997. Practitioner review: Psychosocial treatment for conduct disorder in children. *Journal of Child Psychology and Psychiatry* 38:161–178.

Koot, H. M., and F. Verhulst. 1992. Prediction of children's referral to mental health and special education services from early adjustment. *Journal of Child Psychology and Psychiatry* 33:717–729.

National Center for Victims of Crime website, http://www.ncvc.org.

National Crime Prevention Council. 1995. *How communities can bring up youth free from fear and violence.* Washington, D.C.: National Crime Prevention Council.

O'Keefe, M., and L. Trester. 1998. Victims of dating violence among high school students. *Violence Against Women* 4(2): 195–223.

Office of Juvenile Justice Programs website, http://www.ojjdp.ncjrs.org.

Snyder, Howard, Melissa Sickmund, and Eileen Poe-Yamagata. 1997. *Update on violence: Statistics summary.* Washington, D.C.: U.S. Department of Justice, Office of Juvenile Justice and Delinquency Prevention.

## Chapter 10: Sexual Trauma

RAPE AND SEXUAL ASSAULT

Bohmer, Carol, and Andrea Parrot. 1993. *Sexual assault on campus.* New York: Lexington Books.

Brochman, Sue. 1991. Silent victims: Bringing male rape out of the closet. *The Advocate* 582:38–43.

Brown, K., and L. Bradley. 2002. Stigma of mental illness encourages fear, mistrust and violence against people with mental illnesses. *Journal of Mental Health Counseling* 24(1): 81.

Brown, Sandra L. 1991. *Counseling victims of violence,* First Ed. Alexandria, VA: American Counseling Association.

Burgess, A. W., and L. L. Holmstrom. 1974b. Rape trauma syndrome. *American Journal of Psychiatry* 131:981–986.

Burgess, A. W., E. B. Dowdel, and R. A. Prentky. 2000. Sexual abuse of nursing home residents. *Journal of Psychosocial Nursing and Mental Health Services* 36:10–18.

Campbell, J., S. Stefan, and A. Loder. 1994. Putting violence in context. *Hospital and Community Psychiatry* 45:633.

Corrigan, P. W., and D. L. Penn. 1999. Lessons from social psychology on discrediting psychiatric stigma. *Clinical Psychologist: Science and Practice* 7:48–67.

Davres-Bornoz, J., T. Lemperiere, A. Degiovanni, and P. Galliard. 1995. Sexual victimization in women with schizophrenia and bipolar in perceived alienation in individuals with residual-type schizophrenia. *Issues in Mental Health Nursing* 16: 185–200.

DeNiro, D. 1995. Perceived alienation in residual-type schizophrenia. *Issues in Mental Health Nursing* 16:185–200.

Donaldson, Donald. 1990. Rape of males. In *Encyclopedia of homosexuality,* ed. Wayne Dynes. New York: Garland Publications.

Donnelly, D. A., and S. Kenyon. 1996. Honey, we don't do men. Gender stereotypes and the provision of services to sexually assaulted males. *Journal of Interpersonal Violence* 11:441–448.

Dorais, M. 2002. *Don't tell: The sexual abuse of boys.* Montreal: McGill-Queens University Press.

Isely, P. J., and D. Gehrenbeck-Shin. 1997. Sexual assault of men in the community. *Journal of Community Psychology* 25:159–166.

Kessler, R. C., A. Sonnega, E. Bromet, M. Hughes, and C. B. Nelson. 1995. Post traumatic stress disorder in the National Co-morbidity Survey, *Archives of General Psychiatry,* 52, 1048–1060.

Lehman, A., and L. Linn. 1984. Crime against discharged mental patients in board-and-care homes. *American Journal of Psychiatry* 141:271–274.

Lew, M. 1988. *Victims no longer.* New York: Harper Collins.

Link, B. G., and J. C. Phelan. 1999. Labeling and stigma. In *Handbook of the sociology of mental health*, eds. C. S. Aneshensel, and J. C. Phelan, 481–494. New York: Kluwer Academic, 1999.

Marley, J., and S. Buila. 2001. Crimes against people with mental illness: Types, perpetrators and influencing factors. *Social Work* 45(2): 115.

McCann, I. L., and L. A. Pearlman. 1990. *Psychological trauma and the adult survivor —Theory, therapy and transformation.* New York: Brunner/Mazel.

Meadows, Robert J. 2001. *Understanding violence & victimization.* Upper Saddle River, NJ: Prentice Hall.

Muram, D., K. Miller, and A. Cutler. 1992. A sexual assault of the elderly victim. *Journal of Interpersonal Violence.* March 1992 7(1): 7.

National Center for Victims of Crime website, http://www.ncvc.org.

National Center for Victims of Crime and Crime Victims Research and Treatment Center. 1992. *Rape in America: A report to the nation.* Arlington, VA: National Center for Victims of Crime.

Payne, B., and R. Civokic. 1996. Sexual assault of the elderly victim. *Journal of Interpersonal Violence* 7:70–76.

Pino, N. W., and R. F. Meier. 1999. Gender differences in rape reporting. *Sex Roles* 40: 979–990.

Rogers, P. 1997. Post traumatic stress disorder following male rape. *Journal of Mental Health* 6:5–9.

University of Tennessee website, Sexual Assault Information Page, www.utc.edu/Departments/womencenter/rapemain.php.

Teaster, P. B., and K. A. Roberto. 2003. *A response to the abuse of vulnerable adults: The 2000 survey of state adult protective services.* Washington, DC: National Center on Elder Abuse.

Whatley, M. A., and R. E. Riggio. 1993. Gender difference in attributions of blame for male rape victims. *Journal of Interpersonal Violence* 8:502–511.

Whealin, Julia M. 2005. The National Center for PTSD website, *Men and sexual trauma: A national center for PTSD fact sheet,* http://www.ncptsd.org.

## ADULT SURVIVORS OF SEXUAL ABUSE BY INCEST

Beitchman, J. H., K. J. Zucker, J. E. Hood, G. A. DaCosta, and G. Cassavia. 1992. A review of the long term effects of child sexual abuse. *Child Abuse and Neglect* 16: 101–118.

Blume, Sue. 1990. *Secret survivors: Uncovering incest and its aftereffects in women.* New York: Wiley Publishing.

Briere, J. N. 1996. *Child abuse trauma: Theory & treatment of lasting effects.* Newbury Park, CA: Sage Publications.

Briere, J., and J. Conte. 1993. Self reported amnesia for abuse in adults molested as children. *Journal of Traumatic Stress* 6:21–31.

Callahan, K., J. Price, and M. Hilsenroth. 2004. A review of interpersonal psychodynamic group psychotherapy outcomes for adult survivors of childhood sexual abuse. *International Journal of Group Psychotherapy* 54(4): 491.

Cloitre, M., and K. C. Koehen. 2001. The impact of borderline personality disorder on process group outcomes among women with PTSD related to childhood abuse. *International Journal of Group Psychotherapy* 51(3): 379–398.

Courtois, C. A. 1988. Healing the incest wound: Adult survivors in therapy. A paper presented at the American Association for Counseling and Development Conference, Cincinnati, Ohio.

de Jong, T .L., and K. M. Gorey. 1996. Short-term versus long-term group work with female survivors of childhood sexual abuse: A brief meta-analysis review. *Social Work with Groups, JP,* 19–27.

DiLillio, D. 2001. Interpersonal functioning among women reporting a history of childhood sexual abuse: Empirical findings and methodological issues. *Clinical Psychology Review* 21:553–576.

Gibson, R. L., and T. S. Hartshome. 1996. Childhood sexual abuse and adult loneliness and network orientation. *Child Abuse & Neglect* 20:1087–1093.

Gold, S. N., D. Hawes, and L. Hohnecker. 1994. Degrees of repression of sexual abuse memories. *American Psychologist* 49:441–442.

Nash, M. R., T. L. Hulsey, M. C. Sexton, T. L. Harralson, and W. Lambert. 1993. Long-term sequelae of childhood sexual abuse: Perceived family environment, psychopathology, and dissociation. *Journal of Consulting and Clinical Psychology* 61: 276–283.

National Center for Victims of Crime and Crime Victims Research and Treatment Center. 1992. *Rape in America: A report to the nation.* Arlington, VA: National Center for Victims of Crime.

National Center for Victims of Crime website, http://www.ncvc.org.

Ornduff, S. R. 2000. Childhood maltreatment and malevolence: Quantitative research findings. *Clinical Psychology Review* 20:997–1018.

Price, J. L., M. J. Hilsenroth, P. A. Petretic-Jackson, and D. Bonge. 2001. A review of individual psychotherapy outcomes for adult survivors of childhood sexual abuse. *Clinical Psychology Review* 21:1095–1121.

Saunders, E. A., and J. A. Edelson. 1999. Attachment style, traumatic bonding, and developing relational capacities in a long-term trauma group for women. *International Journal of Group Psychotherapy* 49:465–485.

Wonderlich, S. A., R. D. Crosy, J. E. Mitchell, K. Thompson, J. M. Smyth, J. Redlin, and M. Jones-Paxton. 2001. Sexual trauma and personality: Developmental vulnerabilities and addictive effects. *Journal of Personality Disorders* 15:495–504.

## Chapter 11: Homicide

Aguilera, D. C. 1990. *Crisis intervention: Theory and methodology,* Sixth ed. St Louis, MO: Mosby.

Amick-McMullan, A., D. G. Kilpatrick, and H. S. Resnick. 1991. Homicide as a risk factor for PTSD among surviving family members. *Behavior Modification* 15: 545–559.

Asaro, M. Regina. 2001. Working with adult homicide survivors, impact and sequelae of murder. *Perspective in Psychiatric Care* 37(3): 95.

Brady, K. T., T. K. Killeen, T. Brewerton, and S. Lucerini. 2000. Co-morbidity of psychiatric disorders and posttraumatic stress disorder. *Journal of Clinical Psychiatry* 61 (Suppl. 7):22–31.

Brown, Sandra L. 1991. *Counseling victims of violence,* First Ed. Alexandria, VA: American Counseling Association.

Calhoun, L. G., and R. G. Tedeschi. 1999. *Facilitating posttraumatic growth: A clinician's guide.* Mahwah, NJ: Lawrence Erlbaum Associates.

Calhoun, L. G., A. Cann, R. G. Tedeschi, and J. McMillian. 2000. Correlational test of the relationship between post traumatic growth, religion, and cognitive processing. *Journal of Traumatic Stress* 13:521–527.

McCann, I. L., and L. A. Pearlman. 1990. Psychological trauma and the adult survivor —Theory, therapy and transformation. New York: Brunner/Mazel.

Federal Bureau of Investigation. 1999. *Crime in the United States (preliminary report).* Washington, D.C.: U.S. Department of Justice.

Figley, C. R. 1985. *Trauma and its wake: The study and treatment of post-traumatic stress disorder.* New York: Brunner/Mazel.

Janoff-Bulman, R. 1985. The aftermath of victimization: Rebuilding shattered assumptions. In *Trauma and its wake: The study and treatment of posttraumatic stress disorder* (Vol 1), ed. C. R. Figley, 298–415. New York: Brunner/Mazel.

Horwitz, S. H. 1997. Treating families with traumatic loss: Transitional family therapy. In *Death and trauma: The traumatology of grieving,* eds. C. R. Figley, B. E. Bride, and N. Mazza, 211–231. Washington D.C.: Taylor & Francis.

Murphy, S. A., T. Braun, L. Tillery, K. C. Cain, L. C. Johnson, and R. D. Beaton. 1999. PTSD among bereaved parents following the violent deaths of their 12–18-year-old children: A longitudinal prospective analysis. *Journal of Traumatic Stress* 12: 273–291.

Parkes, C. M. 1993. Psychiatric problems following bereavement by murder or manslaughter. *British Journal of Psychiatry* 162:49–54.

Rando, T. A. 1993. *Treatment of complicated mourning.* Champaign, IL: Research Press.

Rando, T. A. 1997. In *Death and trauma: The traumatology of grieving,* eds. C. R. Figley, B. E. Bride, and N. Mazza, Foreword. Washington D.C.: Taylor & Francis.

Redmond, L. M. 1989. *Surviving: When someone you love was murdered.* Clearwater, FL: Psychological Consultation and Educational Services, Inc.

Rynearson, E. K., and J. M. McCreery. 1993. Bereavement after homicide: A synergism of trauma and loss. *American Journal of Psychiatry* 250:258–261.

Spungen, D. 1998. *Homicide: The hidden victims.* Thousand Oaks, CA: Sage Publications.

Tedeschi, R. G., and R. G. Calhoun. 1996. The post traumatic growth inventory: Measuring the positive legacy of trauma. *Journal of Traumatic Stress* 9:455–471.

United States Department of Justice, Office of Justice Programs, Bureau of Justice Statistics website, Homicide Trends.

## Chapter 12: Societal Trauma

American Psychological Association. 2002. *Coping with terrorism fact sheet.*

Bartholomew, R., and S. Wessley. 2002. Protean nature of mass sociogenic illness:

From possessed nuns to chemical and biological terrorism fears. *British Journal of Psychiatry* 180:300–306.

Bisson, J., P. Jenkins, J. Alexander, and C. Bannister. 1997. A randomized controlled trial of psychological debriefing for victims of acute burn trauma. *British Journal of Psychiatry* 171:78–81.

Bryant, R. A., and A. G. Harvey. 2000. *Acute stress disorder: A handbook of theory, assessment and treatment.* Washington, DC: American Psychological Association Press.

Burkle, F.M. 1996. Lessons learned and future expectations of complex emergencies. *British Medical Journal* 322:1–5.

Difede, J., W. J. Apfeldorg, M. Cloitre, L. A. Spielman, and S. W. Perry. 1997. Acute psychiatric response to the explosion at the World Trade Center: A case study. *Journal of Nervous and Mental Disorders,* 185(8): 519–522.

Kilpatrick, D. G. 2001. Psychological trauma from terrorist attacks and other mass casualty incidents. Presentation posted on Medical University of South Carolina website, http://www.musc.edu/cvc/MassDisasters.PDF.

National Center for Post-Traumatic Stress Disorder website, http://www.ncptsd.va.gov.

National Crime Victims Research and Treatment Center website, http://www.musc.edu/cvc.

NSW Institute of Psychiatry and Center for Mental Health. 2000. *Disaster mental health response handbook.* North Sydney: NSW Health.

Sprang, G. 2000. Coping strategies and traumatic stress symptomatology following the Oklahoma City bombing. *Social Work and Social Sciences Review* 8(2): 207–218.

Weir, Erica, 2005. Mass sociogenic illness. *Journal of the Canadian Medical Association* 172(1): 36.

# Index

Figures are indicated with an italicized "f" following the page number